G000036847

MANAGEMENT BUY-OUTS

MANAGEMENT BUY-OUTS

Ian Krieger
Arthur Andersen

CONTRIBUTORS

Nicolas Greenstone
Simon Olswang & Co, Solicitors
Eric Shepley
Clay & Partners, consulting actuaries
Kim Swain
Arthur Andersen

Butterworths
London and Edinburgh
1990

United Kingdom	Butterworth & Co (Publishers) Ltd, 88 Kingsway, LONDON WC2B 6AB and 4 Hill Street, EDINBURGH EH2 3JZ
Australia	Butterworths Pty Ltd, SYDNEY, MELBOURNE, BRISBANE, ADELAIDE, PERTH, CANBERRA and HOBART
Canada	Butterworths Pty Ltd, TORONTO and VANCOUVER
Ireland	Butterworth (Ireland) Ltd, DUBLIN
Malaysia	Malayan Law Journal Sdn Bhd, KUALA LUMPUR
New Zealand	Butterworths of New Zealand Ltd, WELLINGTON and AUCKLAND
Puerto Rico	Equity de Puerto Rico, Inc, HATO REY
Singapore	Malayan Law Journal Pte Ltd, SINGAPORE
USA	Butterworth Legal Publishers, AUSTIN, Texas; BOSTON, Massachusetts; CLEARWATER, Florida (D & S Publishers); ORFORD, New Hampshire (Equity Publishing); ST PAUL, Minnesota; and SEATTLE, Washington

All rights reserved. No part of this publication may be reproduced in any material form (including photocopying or storing it in any medium by electronic means and whether or not transiently or incidentally to some other use of this publication) without the written permission of the copyright owner except in accordance with the provisions of the Copyright, Designs and Patents Act 1988 or under the terms of a licence issued by the Copyright Licensing Agency Ltd, 33–34 Alfred Place, London, England WC1E 7DP. Applications for the copyright owner's written permission to reproduce any part of this publication should be addressed to the publisher.

Warning: The doing of an unauthorised act in relation to a copyright work may result in both a civil claim for damages and criminal prosecution.

© Arthur Andersen & Co. All Rights Reserved 1990

A CIP Catalogue record for this book is available from the British Library.

ISBN 0 406 51890 4

Photoset by Phoenix Photosetting, Chatham, Kent
Printed by Mackays of Chatham PLC, Chatham, Kent

Preface

The well documented problems of certain recent leveraged buy-outs have already led to bankers and investors reassessing their investment criteria. Recent experience has reinforced two basic buy-out rules. First, the business which is the subject of the buy-out must be basically sound since leverage will magnify problems as well as success. Secondly, leverage increases the risk profile of any business and high leverage will inevitably lead to some business failures. As long as these rules are followed, there is no doubt that buy-outs remain an attractive and profitable vehicle for management teams, vendors and investors alike.

The purpose of this book is to describe in detail those areas which are necessary for a comprehensive knowledge of the buy-out process. This has been achieved by major contributions to the book being made by experts in each key area of the buy-out process.

There has arisen over the years a buy-out jargon and accordingly included within the appendices is a glossary of buy-out terms.

Where relevant the law is current up to 1 December 1989.

January 1990

Acknowledgements

I would like to express my appreciation to the primary contributors to this book: Nicolas Greenstone, partner in Simon Olswang & Co (legal section); Eric Shepley, partner in Clay & Partners, consulting actuaries (pensions section); and my colleague, Kim Swain (tax section). Their commitment to the book has been outstanding. I would also like to thank Julia Palca, partner in Simon Olswang & Co, for her input on the law relating to employees and their duties, and to my partners John Ormerod and Arthur Hunking for their advice.

Acknowledgements

Contents

5 The legal aspects 87

6 Pensions – the forgotten element 156

Appendices

CHAPTER 1

Introduction

Management buy-out activity in the UK has increased phenomenally in the last decade:

	Number of buy-outs	Average value of buy-out
1979	50	£ 0.5m
1989	500	£15.0m

The decade of the 80s showed greater growth in buy-out activity than is likely to be seen again. However, most commentators believe that buy-out activity will continue at a very significant level into the future even though the number of buy-outs in 1990 is likely to fall. Many successful buy-out candidates have subsequently been floated on the Stock Exchange or sold to other companies, financially rewarding those managers who participated in the buy-out. Generally, the profitability and, as a consequence, the value of companies after the buy-out, have increased dramatically. Almost any business which is owned by one group of people and managed by another is a candidate for a buy-out. The finance is available if the deal makes economic sense.

In this book, we seek to provide a detailed insight into the process of the buy-out.

WHAT IS A MANAGEMENT BUY-OUT?

In its simplest form, a management buy-out is just what it says it is – the managers of a business become its owners or major shareholders. However, the situation is normally complicated because the managers have insufficient funds to buy the company outright and therefore need a third party to finance the deal.

This finance can sometimes take the form of bank loans or overdrafts. More often, however, the providers of finance will wish to purchase a stake in the company to give them a potential reward which takes into account their perceived risk. This creates the unusual situation of a deal involving three parties: management, vendor and providers of finance.

Each of the three parties to the negotiation has different objectives:

Objectives of members of management
i.   maximise their share of ownership of the company
ii. minimise their personal investment
iii. ensure the business has enough cash and working capital to survive and expand.

Objectives of vendor
i.   receive as high a price as possible
ii. complete negotiations quickly and smoothly
iii. give few warranties and indemnities to the purchasers
iv. fulfil moral obligations to the buy-out team and employees of the buy-out company.

Objectives of investors
i.   structure the investment so as to achieve a high rate of return in line with perceived risk
ii. receive normal warranties and indemnities from the vendor of the business
iii. ensure the management team is committed to the success of the buy-out.

A number of different types of buy-out is now talked about so it is important to clarify terms. It should be noted that there are no strict definitions and the terms are often used interchangeably.

The definitions and explanations set out below are those used throughout the book. 'Buy-out' is the generic term to cover all types of buy-out and buy-in referred to below.

i.   *Management Buy-Out (MBO)*
     This is a buy-out by management in which the management team tends to control negotiations with the vendor and controls the company following buy-out. Such buy-outs may be highly geared (leveraged) but despite this the lender is willing to take a low profile in the negotiations. MBOs are generally characterised by (i) relatively few demands by equity investors or lenders in the detailed negotiations of the purchase/sale agreement between vendor and management team and (ii) the debt being secured primarily on the assets of the business being acquired.

ii. *Leveraged Buy-Out (LBO)*
     This is a buy-out in which significant amounts of finance and, in particular, of debt are raised, and in which the providers of finance are closely involved in negotiations with the vendor. The finance providers will also ensure they have controls in place which will allow them to take action if the management team does not meet previously agreed performance targets. Management's sharehol-ding in the company after the buy-out will vary greatly but it is usual in LBOs for the managers to hold a minority stake. LBOs are characterised by (i) management's ultimate share holding depend-ing on performance by way of a ratchet and (ii) by the debt pro-viders being primarily interested in cash flow cover (they will also be interested in security but this will normally be in the value of the underlying business(es) within the buy-out company rather than in the specific assets).

iii. *Management Buy-In (MBI)*
     A buy-in is very much like a third party acquisition but by an entity created for the purpose of the acquisition where almost all the

finance is raised from outside investors. The management 'buying-in' tends to be a small team, often comprising just two or three individuals, who may all have been employed by the same company in the past or may have had different employers. As regards deal structuring, buy-ins are very similar to buy-outs (either leveraged or management) but have one very vital difference.

The benefit of an MBO or LBO is that the management team leading the acquisition has considerable knowledge of the company being acquired. As long as the management team is capable and the financing sensible the risk of failure is small. For an MBI the management team leading the acquisition would not normally have the same in-depth knowledge of the target and in this respect is in the same position as any other third party purchaser. For private company buy-ins, it is likely that the vendor will allow a level of due diligence work to be carried out, which should include an accountants' investigation, but even so it will be difficult to identify all the skeletons in the cupboard. Obviously as many safeguards as possible will be taken, such as full warranties and indemnities, but the nature of the financing of an MBI (ie the high gearing) will increase the risk of failure significantly so it is particularly important in an MBI that the management team is strong and that the members of management have an in-depth knowledge of the industry in which the company into which they are buying in operates.

As far as quoted company buy-ins are concerned these will often be hostile bids. In such situations the amount of published information is small and to reduce the risk of failure following takeover the company which is the target of the offer should be in an industry which is well understood by the buying-in management and should have reasonably predictable cash flows. Care should be taken, however, not to pay too much since once again the financing structure will add additional risk. In the USA, quoted company buy-ins are more common than in the UK although it should be noted that in the USA quoted companies publish more in-depth and regular information.

iv. *Other terms*

Reference is sometimes made to employee buy-outs (EBOs) and leveraged management buy-outs (LMBOs). EBOs are buy-outs where apart from the management team investing in shares in the buy-out company a significant number of employees also invest in shares. This arrangement carries particular tax problems which are dealt with in Chapter 4. LMBOs are leveraged buy-outs where the management team has a controlling number of shares. They would generally be called LBOs or MBOs.

IS THE DEAL LIKELY TO BE ON?

How can a potential buy-out be recognised and, once recognised, what are the signs which will indicate that a deal is likely to be on? There are no particularly relevant industries; successful buy-outs have taken place in all kinds of industries but there are certain indicators which are helpful in determining whether a buy-out is feasible. In short, the business should be an established one with predicable cash flows, existing markets, good products and a competent management team.

Loss-making companies may be suitable for buy-outs, but the management team must be able to demonstrate to prospective financial backers why a loss-making company will generate profits after the buy-out. One possible reason could be the reduction in costs which results from the buy-out company no longer having to bear a disproportionate share of head office costs.

Buy-out opportunities typically arise through three situations:

i.   disposal by parent to raise cash, often for strategic reasons, possibly as a result of a lack of 'fit' with other business activities, or because the business is not generating a sufficient return on capital employed. Fashion plays a part in strategy and if the fashion is to 'unbundle' rather than to diversify the lack of fit is more likely to be recognised by group management

ii. sale of a company by its owners (on retirement, for example), so as not to publicise that the company is for sale or because of the owners' feelings of loyalty to the people who have helped them in their business over the years

iii. sale by a receiver of, perhaps, the part of the group which was profitable or which would have been profitable if it had not been starved of finance.

There are other less common situations through which the opportunity for buy-outs arise, including the privatisation of quoted companies resulting from price earnings ratios being too low to allow the quoted company to fulfil its public ambitions. The number of such transactions is likely to be small but the size of each transaction and additional complexities involved are such that this particular type of buy-out is covered in more detail later in the book.

PRICE

The key to a successful buy-out is not to pay too much for the company; otherwise management risks not being able to service the buy-out finance. Also, the rewards to the management team must outweigh the sacrifice of the security of their existing jobs and the risk of losing the money they invest themselves.

Accordingly, even before discussions have taken place with the prospective vendor, the management team should form a view of the likely price range that will need to be paid for the business. Armed with this estimate, a 'back of an envelope calculation' should be performed to determine the likely shareholding that the management will own following a buy-out.

It should be noted that the method of calculation will have important differences depending on whether the buy-out is an MBO or an LBO and accordingly the two methodologies are dealt with separately.

Pricing an MBO

The steps for such a calculation for an MBO are as follows:

1. Estimate the likely range of prices that will need to be paid for the business and prepare two calculations, one using the highest price in the range and the other the lowest price. In practice the lowest price calculation is only performed if the highest price calculation gives an unsatisfactory result. In other words, if the highest price calculation gives the answer that the buy-out will work the chances of success are very high. If the highest price calculation shows the buy-out would not make financial sense but the lowest price calculation shows it would, the ultimate success of the buy-out will depend on the negotiations with the prospective vendors.
2. Using the balance sheet of the business to be acquired, calculate the maximum secured borrowings (or similar finance) that the balance sheet will support, assuming at this stage that profitability and cash flow are adequate to service the debt.
3. Add to the purchase prices (as determined in 1) the additional finance required for working capital and capital expenditure needs and deduct the amount of finance likely to be available from secured borrowing (as calculated in 2). This balance needs to be financed by equity.
4. Deduct from the balance representing equity the funds which the management team is willing and able to invest. This gives the amount of equity required to be raised from third parties.
5. Take into account the estimated exit route and timing of exit. For example, if it is anticipated that the company is intended to be floated or sold in three years, calculate the value of the company at that time by multiplying projected profit after tax in year 3 by the expected exit price earnings ratio.
6. Take the third party equity funding requirement and apply to it the likely internal rate of return that the third party investor will require from such an investment. This will give the required value of his investment at exit.
7. Divide the third party investor's required investment at exit (as determined by step 6) by the exit value of the company (as determined by step 5). This will give the percentage of the business required to be owned by the investor, the balance being available to the management team. The managers can then decide whether the balance which will be available to them is sufficient to outweigh the risks.

The above methodology can be illustrated by way of an example. It should be emphasised that the initial calculation is 'back of an envelope' and accordingly uses quick estimates.

Example

Buy-out company's profit after tax £2.2m. Net assets = £13m.

	£ Million
Working capital and capital expenditure requirements	3.0
Deal costs	0.1
Equity available from management team	£0.5

STEP 1

Estimate the likely range of prices and, initially, feed into the example the highest price.

In this example it is decided that the vendor is unlikely to accept less than net asset value (£13m). Also the continuing success of the business is highly dependent on the existing management team; so it is unlikely that the P/E ratio demanded by the vendors would be more than 7.

Accordingly the maximum purchase price for the purpose of this calculation is £2.2m × 7 = £15.4m (the minimum price being £13m).

The buy-out company's balance sheet is as follows:

Buy-out Company Balance Sheet

	£ Million
Fixed Assets	
Property (at value)	4
Other	3
	7
Current Assets	
Stocks and work in progress	3
Debtors	5
Cash	2
	10
Total Assets	17
Creditors and provisions	(3)
Deferred liabilities	(1)
Total Liabilities	(4)
Net Assets	13

STEP 2

What is the level of secured debt that can be raised against Buy-out Company's balance sheet?

Buy-out Company – Balance Sheet Assets and Related Borrowings

	Balance Sheet £ Million	Borrowings £ Million
Property	4	3.0 (75%)
Other fixed assets	3	1.0 (33%)
Stocks and work in progress	3	0.5 (16%)
Debtors	5	3.5 (70%)
Cash	2	2.0
	£17m	£10m

(Note: The percentages used are illustrative and will depend on the lender's view as to the break-up value of those assets. The lender may also take preferred creditors into account in the calculation; these have been ignored here).

STEP 3

Calculate the equity required

Purchase price	£15.4m
Deal costs	0.1
	15.5
Working capital requirements	3.0
	18.5
Secured debt available	10.0
Equity required	£ 8.5m

STEP 4

Calculate third party equity required

Equity required	£8.5m
Equity available from management team	(0.5)
Equity required from third parties	£8.0m

STEP 5

Consider the estimated exit route and timing. Projected profits after tax (after buy-out) are as follows:

Year 1	£1.8m
Year 2	£2.8m
Year 3	£4.0m

In this example, the decision is to float in 3 years' time and the expected P/E should be at least 10.

Therefore, the value of buy-out company at the end of year 3 is expected to be £40 million. (For the purpose of this example the valuation has been based on profit after tax. More commonly, it will be appropriate to use profit before interest and tax (PBIT) less the effective tax rate and apply the appropriate P/E ratio. The borrowings would then be deducted from the value of the company free of debt.)

STEP 6

Using the likely internal rate of return (IRR) that the third party investor will require from such an investment calculate the value of his investment at exit. In this example, the investor requires a 30% internal rate of return. In Step 4, we determined that the investor needs to inject £8 million of equity funding.

Accordingly, the required value of his investment at the end of year 3 can be calculated as follows:

	IRR	Required Value of Investment
Year 0	30%	£ 8m
Year 1	30%	£10.4m
Year 2	30%	£13.5m
Year 3	30%	£17.6m

The assumption for the purpose of this calculation is that the investor receives no yield (dividend) during the period up to exit. Accordingly, he requires his initial £8 million investment to be worth £17.6 million at the end of year 3.

STEP 7

Calculate the relative shareholdings of the third party investor and the management team. Step 5 indicates Buy-out Company will be valued at £40m. Step 6 shows the investor requires his investment to be worth at least £17.6 million. Therefore the investor will wish to own 44% of buy-out company (£17.6m divided by £40m). This leaves 56% of the equity available for the management team.

Pricing an LBO

The key difference in valuing an LBO relates only to Step 2. Whilst for an MBO the level of borrowing is dependent on the quality of security of the underlying assets of the business, in an LBO the level of borrowings is dependent, to a large extent, on the quality of security of the business itself, or preferably the businesses themselves. In other words, because the buy-out company's business or businesses could be sold to a third party purchaser, lenders will lend against that value as long as the cash flow is comfortable and interest is safely covered. The 'back of an envelope' calculation in Step 2 becomes more complicated and instead of calculating the security of the underlying assets the security of the underlying business(es) is estimated. Also greater reliance on the ability to achieve future projections is taken into account. It should be emphasised that for LBOs there are no hard and fast rules although to give some indication of how much could be borrowed in a proposed LBO the following guidelines may be useful.

i. lenders will generally lend up to between 50% and 80% of the purchase price. The greater the number of businesses which could be sold off separately and the greater the surplus assets which could quickly realise cash the greater the borrowing that can be negotiated. The experience in the United States in particular has been that the sum of the parts of a buy-out are often greater than the whole. If this is the case by borrowing, say, 60% of the value of each of the businesses, total borrowings may amount to say 80% of the total purchase price
ii. lenders will wish to see positive cash flow after servicing the buy-out debt and meeting the repayment schedule. Capital and interest holidays can help achieve positive cash flow but where there are holidays the lenders will wish to be convinced that cash flow generation will improve sufficiently in subsequent years to allow the repayment catch ups to take place
iii. interest cover should not be less than approximately 1½. In other words profit before interest and tax (PBIT) should be at least 1½ times interest cost. Once again, this is only a guideline and it has been known for significantly lower interest cover to be acceptable in the initial period. Also after taking account of mezzanine finance, which is discussed later, lower interest cover is often seen in initial periods.

Maximising management's share

While a number of assumptions has to be made in calculating the equity that will be available to the management team all the assumptions other than those relating to the buy-out purchase price are ones that have to be made by third party investors in deciding whether to invest and in structuring the finance.

It is clear from the above example that to maximise management's share of the equity in the buy-out company there are four key areas that need to be addressed.

i. how much does the management team have to pay for the business? This is dealt with in Chapter 2
ii. what is the maximum debt that can be raised? The management team's influence in this area, apart from convincing prospective lenders of management's ability and credibility, is restricted to finding those sources of finance which will maximise borrowings against the business and/or those assets carried in the balance sheet. This is dealt with in Chapter 3
iii. what will be the value of the business on exit? The value will be a function of the company's profit and ruling P/E ratios at that time. As far as P/Es are concerned, investors will take a view on this, normally assuming current market P/Es will remain unchanged. Obviously the management team has no influence here. Where management has significant influence is in convincing the investors of the level of profits to be generated by the buy-out company at the proposed date of exit

iv. what is the degree of risk inherent in the investment and therefore what rate of return will be required by the investor? The better the company's track record and the more impressive the management team the lower the perceived risk by the investor and therefore the lower the required internal rate of return.

These four key areas are all that need to be addressed in structuring finance for buy-outs.

CHAPTER 2

Purchasing the target

The first half of the buy-out equation is whether the vendor will sell and if so at what price? These two questions are not mutually exclusive. There are very few companies in the world that cannot be acquired at a price. In negotiating to buy a business there is always going to be a price at which the owner is willing to sell. The real question is whether that price is reasonable in terms of the returns the purchaser can subsequently achieve.

To attempt to assess an appropriate market price for a private company in the absence of negotiations is very difficult. The definition of market value is unhelpful since it defines the market price as what a willing purchaser is prepared to pay and what a willing seller is prepared to accept. Until the deal is struck the buyer will not know what the willing seller is prepared to accept nor the seller what the willing buyer is prepared to pay.

BUY-OUTS OF LISTED COMPANIES

The position for a listed company is very different. The market itself sets a value on the individual shares and this sets a market capitalisation for the company as a whole. Like any other take-over bid a premium is expected from a bidder in order to encourage sufficient holders of the company's stock to sell at the offered price. For a standard take-over bid the level of premium needed to win control of the target depends on a number of features, including whether the bid is recommended by the target's board of directors, the composition and relative holdings of the shareholders and whether a counter bid is likely to be in the offing.

The position is similar for a bid by management but with three additional factors having to be taken into account.

The first factor is that shareholders presume that management has a better detailed knowledge of the company than anyone else and therefore if a management team wishes to buy the company it is a sign to the 'market' that it may have misjudged the value of the company. While management does have a more detailed knowledge of the company it does not mean that shareholders are not adequately informed. It is quite possible that management is taking a more positive view of the company because it is taking a longer term view and the long term outcome will be dependent to a very great extent on the performance of management itself. There is actually a self fulfilling prophecy in this logic. The management team is likely to improve its performance significantly after a buy-out because its objectives become clear and critical: service the borrowings, repay the debt and generate significant capital rewards for the management team. If the buy-out does not proceed the company is unlikely to perform as well since management style is likely to remain one of safety and comfort. There are certain situations where the market accepts a buy-out readily and this is where the management team, which already holds a substantial equity stake, claims that short to medium term plans which are intended to create long term profitability will have adverse profit impacts until those plans come to fruition. In such situations an adequate premium will normally secure acceptance.

The second factor which is taken into account by the market when judging whether to accept a bid by a management team is the argument that public company boards have a primary responsibility to their shareholders and that this in turn means the directors should put all their efforts into maximising shareholder value and that this is not consistent with launching a buy-out. The key concept is shareholder value. The managers would argue that if they are unable to drive up the company's P/E ratio despite communicating well with investors, then regardless of the company's profitability, if a prospective purchaser, whether or not the purchaser is the management team, makes an offer significantly in excess of the market capitalisation, it should make sense for existing shareholders to sell. Management may have to accept that in making an offer for the company, the investors are likely to think their own assessment of the company is wrong and therefore demand a higher premium than in a third party bid.

The risk is that the shareholders are so suspicious of management's motives that they refuse to accept the offer at any price or demand a price which is so high as to make the buy-out impossible. It is for this reason that the target company's financial advisers have a key role to play when an offer for the company is made by a management team. This role is tied up with the issue of availability of information. The legal arguments regarding availability of information are set out in Chapter 5. However, there is also a critical practical argument. Management obviously has considerably more information (particularly regarding plans but also regarding current performance) than any other party. This, not surprisingly, is the root of shareholder suspicions. However, it would very rarely be appropriate for confidential information held by the management team to be made available to third parties because the provision of such information, if in the hands of competitors, customers or suppliers, could be damaging to the company and therefore to its shareholders. It is for this reason that the target company's financial advisers must assess all available information, take into account the possible change of management style should a buy-out proceed and recommend in clear terms to the target's shareholders whether or not the offer should be accepted. Of course the financial advisers must keep the information disclosed to them absolutely confidential. However, if the advisers believe they do not have sufficient information to make an appropriate recommendation they should consult with the target's auditors, industry experts and economic and marketing consultants. For its part the management team must make all information available to the company's advisers. In December 1989 the Panel on Take-overs and Mergers announced changes to the

City Code on Take-overs and Mergers to increase the protection for shareholders. The changes, which are set out in more detail in Chapter 5, relate principally to the importance of independent advice, and the disclosure of information to the company's independent adviser and to competitive bidders. This announcement is to be welcomed, although there must be some concern as to whether management's buy-out projection should be made available to competitive bidders. After all, these projections are based on expectations following a buy-out which may not be appropriate in other circumstances and even where buy-outs have been concluded successfully there is evidence that management's projections are not always achieved. Nevertheless, without such an announcement the public company buy-out would be a rare occurrence which would result in both shareholders and management being losers.

The third factor which shareholders also take seriously in considering whether to accept an offer from a management team is the argument that as more companies are de-listed, institutional shareholders have difficulties investing in good companies at sensible prices. The institutions wish to invest the bulk of their wealth in safe, marketable investments. A buy-out by a management team gives the investors an enhanced return on their investment portfolio but gives them the problem of where to re-invest. If the incidence of public company buy-outs were high the overall size of the stock market would be reduced significantly. The choices left to institutional investors would be (i) to invest in the remaining quoted stocks; such an action would be likely to result in an increase in share prices (the effect would not be dissimilar to that on the Japanese stock market where one of the reasons that prices are high is as a result of institutional and other surplus funds having grown at far faster rates than the underlying economy); (ii) to invest in equities overseas (the rest of Europe is yet to see this kind of takeover activity); (iii) to invest in properties or gilts (with the obvious market impact this would have) or to invest directly or indirectly (through funds) in buy-outs themselves (this may be perceived as insufficiently stable for too great a proportion of institutional funds). Generally, institutions have investment guidelines in which UK quoted equities play and will continue to play a very significant part and therefore reducing the size of the UK Stock Market is a real problem. However the problem of creating a reduced UK equity market arises when large non UK owned corporates acquire UK quoted companies as well as for listed company buy-outs. At least for quoted company buy-outs there is the possibility of a re-listing or a sale to a UK listed company at some future date.

To date, there have been very few UK buy-outs of listed companies by their management teams. There is no reason why the numbers should not increase significantly but this will only happen if existing shareholders are provided with adequate safeguards and accordingly be willing to consider offers from buy-outs teams without too much cynicism.

VALUATION METHODS FOR PRIVATE COMPANIES

While the market sets a price for a listed company there is no such market mechanism for private companies and accordingly it is necessary to consider the different valuation methods for private companies.

Although every sale and purchase negotiation will be different, depending on the circumstances, and the price will be a result of those negotiations, there are three basic valuation methods that can be used as guides.

i.   *Earnings Valuation Model*
This model is based on the premise that the company's value is the sum of its discounted future earnings stream. A discount factor would therefore be applied to projected earnings in valuing the company. The uncertainty of future earnings together with the complexity of the calculation leads to a simple method being used but which is still based on earnings. The value of the company is calculated by applying a multiple to its historic or current earnings. The benefit of using historical numbers is that the outcome is known with certainty, the disadvantage being that such figures can often be inappropriate. Current earnings, being those for the year not yet ended and therefore not known with such certainty, are likely to be a better measure of future performance.

The question of what multiple to apply is usually decided by using current market conditions as a guide. Thus one can study quoted share prices for the particular market sector containing the target company and obtain the current multiples (price earnings or P/E ratios). A quoted market P/E ratio will probably need adjusting downwards for an unquoted private company due to the lack of marketability of shares in a private company. However, since quoted P/Es are for small shareholdings a premium will normally be required if control is to be obtained.

ii. *Dividend Valuation Model*
The dividend valuation model is normally used where the purchaser is acquiring a minority stake in a company since such a purchaser has no control over how the earnings of a company are used. The dividend model computes a market value for a minority holding in a company based on its normal level of declared dividends. For the purpose of valuing a company for buy-out purposes this is not an appropriate method.

iii. *Assets Valuation Model*
The assets valuation model is based on a company being worth the value of its net assets as shown in the balance sheet. Such a model is generally only appropriate in a break-up situation and in such a situation values shown in the balance sheet are unlikely to be appropriate anyway. For example, stocks and work-in-progress do not usually realise their balance sheet value on break-up. The relevance of any asset base is the earnings stream that the asset base can generate. Nevertheless, the net asset value of the company can be used for setting a base price level and is also the price which fits comfortably from both a psychological and an accounting viewpoint, the latter since at that level the vendor realises the assets earned by the business up to the date of the sale and no accounting loss is recorded.

THE VENDOR'S OBJECTIVES

In deciding the price at which existing shareholders would be willing to sell, it is necessary to take into account their objectives.

The prospective vendor will have a number of objectives, both financial and non-financial, in deciding whether and at what price to sell the company to the management team. The balance of those objectives will vary from case to case, although price will almost always be a key objective.

In considering the vendor's objectives it is important to consider the identity of the vendor. The vendor may be a company, private or public, an individual, a number of individuals or a receiver. Sometimes the owner's objectives are driven by external forces – the need for cash, for example, as a result of pressure from bankers – and this type of pressure has to be fully understood to maximise negotiating opportunities.

The individual or family vendor

An individual or family owner may have a personal loyalty to the company and its management. The management team and the owner may have built a close relationship over the years and the owner may see the buy-out as an opportunity to reward members of management for their loyalty. In so doing he will ensure that the business continues with its employees being secure in their jobs.

The owner may be proud of the company he has created and may wish to see it continue in a similar fashion in the future. He is more likely to see this happen if he sells to the management team who have worked in the same environment. The vendor is also likely to be able to provide more safeguards to ensure there are no material changes in the business following a buy-out by keeping some of the shares or by remaining a non-executive director or non-executive chairman.

The individual may be forced to sell due to old age or ill health, in which case a sale to the management team may subject the vendor to less pressure.

There may have been a reliance on the management team without whom the company would be worth very much less. In such a situation the management may not cooperate with a sale to a third party and may demand a sale to the managers.

The parent company vendor

The target company may have been acquired as part of the purchase of a group and may not have been sought or required. The group's strategic plan may concentrate on areas of business which do not include the target company.

The parent company can usually achieve a quick, harmless and non public sale to a management team. It can be done with no real break or disruption to the ongoing business.

The parent company vendor may be keen to retain confidentiality about a possible sale. By selling to management the chance of a leak, which could be damaging to the business, is reduced.

Where there is significant trading between group companies a sale to management is more likely to lead to continuing trading relationships which could be beneficial to other group companies.

On the other hand, parent company directors sometimes do not wish to sell to management for emotional reasons; in particular they may not wish to see subsidiary management with the potential of higher rewards than they are to receive themselves. Such potential conflicts need to be treated carefully.

The public company vendor

The public company vendor is more likely to be driven by financial rather than non-financial considerations in its decision to whom to sell.

The reasons for the sale will have to be relayed to outside shareholders as being for the benefit of the ongoing business and the price received will have to be reasonable and justifiable in the circumstances. This will normally be demonstrated by showing that there will be no dilution impact on the group's earnings per share (EPS) as a result of the sale and also that no loss is made on the sale. The corollary of the EPS not being diluted is that the historic mutiple of earnings on which the business is to be sold should be greater than the group's price earnings ratio. For no loss to be made on the sale, providing the business which is the subject of the sale has been created rather than purchased, the price received has at least to equal the book value of the net assets being disposed.

Circulars
The public company vendor has a further consideration which could affect the price at which it is willing to sell. The Stock Exchange requires a circular to be issued to the existing shareholders of a listed company for, among other matters, any material acquisition or disposal by the listed company. The requirements for circulars is set out in more detail in Chapter 5.

The receiver vendor

Dealing with a company which is in receivership raises a number of additional issues. The receiver to the company is charged with obtaining as good a price as possible but within a fairly short time. To maintain the company as a going concern can be expensive and puts the receiver at personal financial risk. The receiver will also be unable to grant any of the normal warranties and so sales by receivers are normally of the business and assets rather than of shares in the company.

As management understands the business well it is likely a speedy offer and completion can be effected in a management buy-out and for this reason the receiver will often look with favour on a management purchase and not necessarily look to the management team to make the highest offer. The receiver will, however, consider the status of the management team's finances since raising third party equity can be a lengthy process.

PRACTICAL PRICING

The 'back of an envelope' calculation in Chapter 1 advises management to calculate the likely range of prices that would need to be paid for the company. In the illustration in that chapter appropriate price earnings ratios were used and the net asset base was considered. These are the usual measures of price which prospective vendors apply.

While less sophisticated vendors may be content to recover net asset value for the sale of their company, the more sophisticated vendor will want to replace the loss of earnings arising from the sale of the business with sufficient consideration to be able to invest in other assets to at least replace the lost earnings. It is for this reason that price earnings ratios are important.

Price earnings ratios

P/E ratios are defined as price divided by earnings after tax and after preference dividends (but before extraordinary items). The calculation can be performed for a company as a whole or for each share in the company.

Example

Company earns profit after tax of £500,000. It has 1,000,000 shares issued throughout the year. Applying a P/E ratio of 10 shows that Company has a value of £5m. Each of its shares has a value of £5 (£5m divided by 1 million shares).

Through the market forces of the stock market, each quoted company has a P/E ratio which determines the market capitalisation of that company at a particular time. As prices change, which can happen several times a day, so does the company's P/E since reported earnings remain unchanged. In fact it is the P/E ratio which drives the price rather than the price driving the P/E ratio as is demonstrated below. For unquoted companies there is no regular pricing mechanism and therefore no recorded P/E ratio. The absence of a pricing mechanism is only relevant if the company or some of the shares in the company are being sold or transferred.

It is worth discussing some of the fundamentals underlying P/E ratios. Why is 6 or 12 or 20 the right P/E ratio for a company and why was 8 right last week but 7 right this week? The problem with fundamentals is that P/E ratios of companies are driven by expectation of which way and to what extent other investors think the stock market as a whole will move and which way and to what extent other investors think the shares in a particular company will move. The first of these expectations is determined mostly by economic factors but not necessarily as a result of any logical or consistent analysis; the second of these expectations can be driven by the possibility of a takeover, a reassessment of the prospects of the industry in which the company operates or on a re-appraisal of the company's results for the current (uncompleted) period.

As far as fundamentals are concerned, however, and ignoring the vagaries of the market, P/E ratios can be considered by way of the following illustration. An individual with £10,000 can place his money with a bank at, say, 10% gross for a fixed period. Assuming his tax rate is 25%, his annual earnings will be £750. The P/E ratio of such an investment would be £10,000 divided by 750 = 13.3. This is the safe, no growth, all earnings distributed P/E ratio.

In this illustration 13.3 can therefore be used as the base P/E from which others can be determined. For companies the usual measure of earnings taken for P/E calculations is the historic earnings figure, ie the after tax earnings of the company for its last reported period, although prospective earnings, ie the expected earnings of the company for the current year, can also be used.

For a company, what is the appropriate P/E ignoring the vagaries of the market? The starting point for any assessment is 13.3, the safe, no growth, all earnings distributed P/E ratio. Questions then need to be answered about expectation of risk and growth and the impact of only part, if any, of the earnings being distributed. The impact of earnings not being distributed is not necessarily important, since the holder of shares in a quoted company can realise cash by selling some or all of his shares. The lack of distribution just increases the risk of the investment in that a regular dividend will provide a minimum return regardless of what happens to the share price (as long as the company continues to pay a dividend).

The analysis, then, is risk versus growth. If the company is high risk or if it is likely to see its profit performance deteriorate then the P/E ratio should be below 13.3; if it is low risk and its profits are likely to increase its P/E ratio should be above 13.3. If it is high risk and its profits are likely to increase, whether its P/E is above or below 13.3 will depend on which of the two carries more weight in the investor's view. This analysis is not inconsistent with a major price movement in the stock market, for example, as experienced in October 1987. The under-lying concern was the possible lack of profitability of the whole business sector, resulting from a decline in the world economy. However, movements both up and down are exaggerated by sentiment and by investors' expectations of what other investors are likely to do.

Earnings yield

The reciprocal of the P/E ratio is the earnings yield. For the individual placing his £10,000 in a bank his earnings yield is 7.5%.

A holding company wishes to sell one of its subsidiaries. The group is listed and has a P/E of 20; earnings yield of 5%. In other words investors are content to see earnings of just 5% on their investment (most of which will not be distributed) as opposed to 7.5% return on their bank deposit (all of which will be distributed) because of the expectation of increased profitability in the future.

Earnings per share (EPS)

While the P/E ratio (and earnings yield) for a company are determined by the market, the area which is under the control of the company is its earnings and this is best measured by earnings per share, since this is the most consistent measure of profitability.

The earnings per share multiplied by the P/E ratio gives the price per share, which when multiplied by the average number of shares in issue during the year gives the group's market capitalisation. Accordingly, if earnings per share is increased the market capitalisation should increase and if earnings per share falls the market capitalisation should reduce. More importantly, for individual investors individual share prices will react in the same way.

Accordingly, the holding company with a P/E of 20 will not wish to see its subsidiary sold at a price which will give it an earnings dilution. The group has earnings (after tax) of £1 million and 2 million shares in issue throughout the period. Accordingly its EPS is 50p. The subsidiary to be sold has earnings of £100,000. What is the minimum price the subsidiary can be sold for in order not to create earnings dilution?

At a P/E of 20 the value incorporated within the group's market capitalisation of £20 million relating to the subsidiary is £2 million (20 × £100,000). In other words it has to be sold at a price of at least £2 million which represents a P/E of at least 20.

This analysis is simplistic; if the part of the business which is sold is seen by the market to be in an unexciting sector in which the company operates, the quality of earnings following sale could be perceived to be improved and the P/E ratio marked up accordingly.

Net assets

The other important consideration for the management of the holding company is the price vis à vis the book value of the assets to be sold. The holding company may revalue the assets (particularly properties) for the purposes of negotiation but in its reporting to shareholders any consideration in excess of the book value of net assets will be shown as a profit in the year's accounts and any consideration which is less than the book value of net assets will be shown as a loss.

Where a listed company is itself the subject of a management buy-out, since the net assets of the company bear no relation to its market capitalisation, it is irrelevant from the vendor's viewpoint whether the consideration is greater or less than net assets.

NEGOTIATIONS

Having conceived the basis of pricing which the vendor is considering, the next stage is to negotiate the purchase.

Negotiating with one's employers can be one of the most difficult aspects of a management buy-out and has to be planned carefully. If the individuals selling the company are members of a family company who are happy to see the business pass into management's hands then the negotiations are likely to be friendly and the management team should attempt to keep them informal but professional. If the vendors are the holding company board, who are likely to want to resist the buy-out, it may be more appropriate for the management team to delegate the bulk of their negotiations to their advisers.

Assuming that the management team handle the negotiations themselves they enter into the most difficult yet probably most important deal of their lives. The negotiations are made more difficult since a number of the normal tactics which would be used in negotiations are ruled out because of the unusual relationship between vendors and purchasers in a buy-out.

Before entering into any negotiations the management team must determine whether there is likely to be any serious competition and at what stage the competition will be allowed to bid. It is becoming more usual in the UK in larger deals for the buy-out team to be one of a number of possible purchasers, with the management team being given no advantage over other suitors. On the other hand, there are still numerous situations where the management team is the only realistic possible purchaser.

Accordingly it is difficult to prescribe particular negotiation tactics to be used in buy-outs since all are so different but below are some which are more commonly used.

General tactics
The 'What if' tactic as a non confrontational tactic is an excellent one to use in most buy-outs particularly where relationships between vendor and management team are good. 'What if we defer payment of some of the purchase price?' If a negative response is received the management team can walk away without damage. The counter of this tactic is 'we can't' or 'we could not afford it'.

It is dangerous for the management team to lead the owners to believe the price they are willing to pay is higher than they are ready, willing and able to pay. On the other hand, sometimes it is necessary to generate interest to sell from the owners and in such situations a useful tactic is to talk about a purchase price which would depend on certain assumptions which are probably optimistic. Based on the correct assumptions the purchase price is likely to be significantly lower but the opening may have generated an enthusiasm to sell which can create a momentum of its own. It should be emphasised that this approach should only be used where the existing owner is unlikely to be interested in selling in normal circumstances.

The third general tactic to be considered is the piecemeal approach. Take a big issue and slice it into a number of smaller issues and negotiate the smaller ones until the big issue is won. For example, the starting point for a management buy-out may be raising the issue of how the management team will continue to be motivated without an equity stake.

Tactics related to concessions
During the planning for the negotiations, determine the bargaining range and the limits to that range. Fall back positions should be developed and the range of concessions from minor to major which the buy-out team is willing to make should be established. The cost of each concession should be calculated in advance, but no concession should be made until all the demands are known. Any concessions which are made should not be made lightly. The other side should know the sacrifice that is being made. A record of concessions made should be kept and none should be made without getting something in return.

In most buy-outs, the price should not be discussed too early in the negotiation. It is important to communicate the benefits of selling to management rather than to a third party first.

The flinch and the feint are two other useful tactics. Flinching when the other side makes a request is likely to make them feel uncomfortable. The feinting technique is to ask for something which will almost certainly be refused, followed by a request for the important concession that could be granted. People often are embarrassed by saying 'no' repeatedly, particularly to people they know well.

The key to most successful buy-outs is goodwill on both sides and therefore none of the negotiation tactics adopted should be confrontational.

CHAPTER 3

Can the finance be raised?

INTRODUCTION

Chapter 2 covered the first half of the buy-out equation – acquiring the target from the vendor. This chapter covers how the finance is to be raised to fund the acquisition.

In broad terms there are three requirements which are needed if outside providers of finance are to invest in a buy-out.

First, the management team needs to demonstrate that it is both committed and competent. Commitment would include showing positive reasons for wanting to buy the company, rather than defensive reasons such as job protection. It is usual for the managers to show their commitment by investing their own money. Outside investors normally take the view that the amount invested by managers should be great enough to demonstrate commitment, but not so high that the individuals (and their families) spend all their time worrying what will happen if the company fails. Nevertheless, managers will normally need to liquidate personal assets or re-mortgage their homes to raise the necessary finance.

Competence is even more important and investors and bankers will be looking for a balanced management team that has the skills needed to run the business as an independent company following the buy-out.

Secondly, the investors will wish to see an adequate return from their investment, normally in the form of an annual dividend (or yield) together with appreciation in the value of any shareholding. Until there is a market for the shares, the only increase in value will be a paper gain and while this will be acceptable to investors in the short term, management will need to plan an 'exit route' to allow the investors ultimately to realise their gains.

Exit routes include:

i. obtaining a quotation for the company's shares, either on the Stock Exchange or the Unlisted Securities Market
ii. selling out to a larger company
iii. buying back the investors' shares at an appropriate price. This is the exit route to be pursued if management wishes the company to remain private. This possibility is more feasible following changes in company law, introduced in 1980, and changes in the tax rules in 1982.

Thirdly, bankers who provide the debt finance wish to see that their lending is secure and that the company is able to service and repay its borrowings.

TYPES OF FINANCE

Broadly there are just two types of finance – equity and debt.

Equity

Equity is essentially ownership. It is normally permanent and it is the highest risk finance. The equity shareholder has a right to income after all other providers of finance have taken their return, and a right to whatever assets of the business remain after other providers of finance have been repaid.

Since equity finance carries the greatest risk and the greatest potential return, the management team, in an MBO, invest in equity. The incentive is for managers to make the business such a success that they do not merely provide the other investors with their required returns but that sufficient income and assets are created to give them a reasonable income and/or a significant capital gain.

The permutations of equity finance are enormous. The basic ordinary share is the pure form of equity finance. It ranks for dividend and repayment of capital behind absolutely every other type of finance. However, if the business is successful, due to its residual nature, there is the potential for ordinary shareholders to make the largest gains. Ordinary shareholders are the true and eventual owners of the business.

Ranking ahead of the ordinary share is the preference share. Preference shares normally carry a fixed dividend, the dividend often being cumulative, ie if there are insufficient profits to distribute in any one period the right to the dividend is carried forward until the company does have sufficient distributable profits. The preference shareholders' rights rank behind providers of debt and creditors but before ordinary shareholders. Preference shares may be convertible into ordinary shares. They may also be redeemable, either at a particular time or when certain events have taken place. The advantage to the ordinary shareholder of having preference shareholders in place is that extra finance is provided from a source of funds, which is classified as equity in the reserves section of the company's balance sheet, the holders of which cannot normally take action against the company if the company has insufficient distributable reserves with which to pay its preference dividends. The distinction between ordinary and preference shares is not always clear and actual rights of different classes of shares are embodied in the Articles of Association of the company. It is not unusual to see a class of shares with a number of characteristics of both ordinary shares as well as of preference shares. For example, the preferred participating ordinary share is preferred to ordinary shares in the event of a winding up and participates in that it receives a dividend, all or part of which varies with the underlying profits of the business. In addition to this it also has the same voting rights as the ordinary shareholders. The rights and obligations of each share can be drawn up specifically to meet the objectives of the investor and investee and there is enormous flexibility. Some of the other commonly used shares are described later.

Debt

Unlike the equity holder who is a member of the company the provider of debt finance is a creditor of the business in the same way as is a supplier of raw materials. There are, however, some notable differences. Apart from the delayed period over which a debt provider is repaid, the other major difference is that the provider of debt finance normally wishes to take security to protect his lending. Accordingly, before agreeing to make the finance available, the lender will want to know whether security is available and how the debt will be serviced and repaid.

Hence the lender will examine the strength of the balance sheet and cashflow of the business to ensure:

i.   that the business is capable of earning the level of profits to cover the required interest payments
ii. that the business is capable of producing positive cashflow to meet the interest and capital repayments
iii. that the business maintains assets over which security is available and which will have value if the business gets into difficulties; or that the business itself has inherent value which could be realised if the company becomes unable to service its debt.

The secured lender will safeguard his position by the imposition of numerous conditions and covenants. Examples of covenants may include ratios such as, borrowings must not be greater than 50% of stocks plus 70% of debtors under 90 days or that interest cover must always be at least 1.5. Any breach of covenant normally allows the lender to demand immediate repayment or to renegotiate terms. While a simple breach is unlikely to lead to such an outcome failing to meet covenants regularly is likely to lead back to the negotiating table very quickly.

Types of debt

We have considered, in broad terms, the requirements of the debt provider. However, there are two categories of debt finance the providers of which have slightly different objectives; the first category is known as secured or senior debt. Security is paramount to a lender of such debt. The second is known as junior or subordinated. For the lender of this type of finance profits and cashflows have to be sufficient to service borrowings but there does not necessarily need to be security available. Mezzanine finance, which is explained below, often takes the form of junior debt.

Types of senior debt.　Term Loans are normally repayable over 5 to 7 years. It is not unusual to see an interest moratorium for the first one or two years. As far as capital repayments are concerned, most lenders like to see repayments starting in year 1 but this is often not feasible and a bullet repayment (ie all the capital being repaid at the end of the loan) is quite common, particularly when the lender expects to be repaid from exit proceeds.

Evergreen facilities are those where, for as long as the facility is available, no capital is repayable and the balance can be repaid and drawn down at will. This is a particularly valuable facility in a buy-out where maximum flexibility gives the buy-out its greatest chance of success.

For fluctuating working capital needs either overdraft facilities or revolving lines of credit are required. While overdrafts are repayable on demand, revolving lines of credit are available at the option of the borrower for a defined period at which time they are normally renewed. Larger borrowers would normally be offered revolving lines of credit facilities rather than overdraft facilities.

Additionally, banks will consider themselves as much at risk with bonding facilities as they will with loans so any financing has to take this into account. Bonding facilities will include VAT, Custom & Excise, performance bonds and letters of credits.

Mezzanine finance

Providers of mezzanine finance take a greater risk than secured lenders and accordingly require a higher return. Often this takes the form of debt which carries a higher than average rate of interest. The disadvantage of high interest debt is that the risk to the company of not being able to service and repay its debt is compounded. An alternative way of providing a return to the mezzanine finance provider commensurate with the extra risk, but without saddling the buy-out company with very high interest costs, is through the provision of some right to share in the profits or share capital of the company in addition to providing normal interest rates on the debt.

Mezzanine finance can take a variety of forms. As noted above it can comprise high interest debt; it can also comprise debt with a lower rate of interest but with options or warrants to subscribe for equity (often known as an equity kicker).

The mezzanine finance provider's favoured form of finance is interest bearing debt at say 2% above primary lenders' rates, the debt being secured but subordinated to that of the primary lender. It should be noted that under English law if a debt is to be called subordinated it must be subordinated to all creditors, for this reason so-called subordinated debt is secured so as to rank above all unsecured creditors but is subordinated to the senior debt by way of an inter creditor agreement in which the senior and junior lenders agree their relative rights and rankings. An equity kicker would provide the mezzanine finance provider with his required internal rate of return (IRR) normally between 20% and 30%. This form of finance is popular with certain investors since the interest provides a healthy return on the cost of funds, there is some security (albeit ranking behind the primary lenders) and there is an equity upside. The management team's choice of mezzanine finance is normally for a low yield preference share, which converts into equity to give the mezzanine finance provider his required IRR at exit since this minimises the business's negative cash flow. It also provides a safeguard in that if the dividend cannot be paid equity holders can take little action (non-payment may give them the right to vote) whereas if debt is not serviced there is a default under the loan with the resulting consequences. A further benefit is that dividends are shown 'below the line' (ie after profit after tax) in the profit and loss account and that the preference shares are disclosed in the equity and reserves section of the balance sheet as opposed to debt which is shown as a liability.

It should be noted that whatever the precise form of mezzanine finance the demands for covenants and conditions will normally be far less strenuous than for senior lenders.

INTEREST RATES

The amount of interest payable by buy-out companies can be critical to their success or failure. It is therefore important to consider how interest rates are set.

While mezzanine debt will sometimes be charged at an absolute interest rate most borrowings will be charged at a margin over either LIBOR or over the bank's base rate. LIBOR, which stands for 'London Inter Bank Offered Rate', represents the rates of interest at which banks lend to and borrow from each other. LIBOR is consistently changing to reflect the market and is quoted for 1 month, 3 months, 6 months and 1 year. By using 12 month LIBOR this effectively fixed the borrower's interest rate for a period of a year, thus protecting it from interest increases but conversely not allowing the borrower to benefit from interest rate reductions over that period. Generally in buy-outs a significant part of the borrowing tends to be for periods in excess of 1 year but by linking to LIBOR, 12 months is the maximum period for which interest rates can be fixed. One vehicle for overcoming this limitation is the swap which effectively allows the borrower to fix its borrowing for a period of up to 5 years. The mechanics of swaps are explained below.

Base rates are set by individual banks to provide stability to their borrowers and ease of administration to themselves. They are varied only when the bankers take the view that there has been a more permanent change in market interest rates. Base rates therefore tend.to lag behind the market so when interest rates are increasing base rates will tend to be below LIBOR; when interest rates are falling base rates tend to be above LIBOR. Because the banks' marginal borrowing costs are based on LIBOR they will only wish to lend based on their base rate for smaller buy-outs.

The profit for the lending banks is earned through the margin (over LIBOR or base) that they charge their customers. Accordingly when considering borrowing costs in a buy-out, account has to be taken of both the relevant LIBOR/base rate and also the margin. The margin on senior debt in the UK is generally between 1½% and 2½% but this will depend critically on the risk inherent in the lending.

For larger buy-outs, and certainly for LBOs, some form of interest protection will be a condition of the provision of finance. Such protection can either be through the use of a swap as referred to above or through other instruments. These interest rate hedges are explained in more detail below.

Interest rate hedges

Interest rate swaps
An interest rate swap is an agreement by two parties usually through an intermediary financial institution in which the parties exchange interest rate payments over a period of time, there being no exchange of capital amounts. The beauty of the swap transaction is that all parties meet their objectives.

The phenomenon of an all win situation is made possible by the fact that fixed rate and floating rate funds are available to different borrowers at different rates depending on their perceived credit-worthiness. A company with a higher credit rating will have a relative advantage over a lower rated company in the borrowing of fixed rate debt as against the borrowing of floating rate debt. The effect of a swap is best illustrated by way of an example.

Example

Let us assume two companies with credit ratings as follows wish to enter into a swap agreement and credit is available to these companies at the following rates:

Company	Credit Rating	Fixed Rate	Floating Rate
A Ltd	AA	13%	LIBOR + 1%
B Ltd	BB	15%	LIBOR + 2%

These two companies enter into a swap of their interest expense streams as detailed in this diagram.

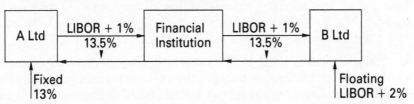

A borrows fixed at 13%; B borrows floating at LIBOR + 2%. However, A does not wish its borrowing to carry a fixed rate of interest, while B, which is the buy-out company, does. Accordingly, A agrees with B that it will pay LIBOR + 1% to the swap, while it is agreed that B will pay 13½% to the swap.

The gains for both companies are demonstrated in the following table:

	A Ltd	B Ltd
Interest payable on facility drawn	13.0%	LIBOR + 2%
Receipt from swap	(13.5)%	(LIBOR + 1%)
Payment to swap	LIBOR + 1%	13.5%
Net payment	LIBOR + .5%	14.5%
Payment had A Ltd taken out floating rate funds and B Ltd borrowing fixed rate funds	(LIBOR + 1%)	(15.0%)
NET GAIN	0.5%	0.5%

The swap has therefore enabled both A Ltd and B Ltd to obtain funds more cheaply than they could have done had they borrowed directly from financial institutions. The institution arranging the swap will charge a one-off fee for the arrangement.

It should be stressed that the swap of interest rate payments does not mean that the parties have exchanged the principal loan amount at any time, and in fact, both companies will be responsible for their own debt to the end of its life.

The market for swaps is a well developed market which is generally suited to larger transactions and should therefore be considered for LBOs. However options, caps and collars, which are described below, can be widely used to hedge interest rate risk on even the smaller transactions thus providing an effective hedge against interest rate movements on all types and sizes of transactions.

Interest rate options
An option is a contract that confers the right (to the purchaser of the option) to buy or sell a particular financial transaction at a particular price on or before a future fixed date.

The purchaser (holder) of an option can either buy a 'put' option or a 'call' option. A put option enables the option holder to sell the transaction struck in the option and a call enables the holder to buy the transaction. It should be emphasised that an option may or may not be exercised by the holder since there is no obligation for him to do so.

An option cost is basically made up of three elements:

i.   intrinsic value. This is the value inherent in the option and is basically the difference between the exercise price of the option and the current value of the item to be transacted. For example, if a call option on a share is set at a strike price of 15p, and the market value of the share is 20p, the intrinsic value of the option is 5p. In other words, this option is said to be 'in the money' by 5p.

An option cannot have a negative intrinsic value because as soon as the strike price is above the market price, the option will not be exercised and therefore the intrinsic value will be nil

ii. time value. This is the value attributed to the option for being able to exercise the option at some future date. This time value is based on the possibility that at some future date the option may be 'in the money' even though at present it may be 'out of the money'. Therefore, generally, the longer the life of the option, the greater its time value

iii. the premium payable to the seller of the option which is based on the risk the market perceives in the interest rate market. The lower the perceived risk and volatility of interest rates, the lower the premium payable on the option.

Interest rate options are widely traded on the world's financial markets. The principle behind the interest rate option is that when interest rates rise, there is a corresponding change downwards in the price of fixed interest government bonds. The option bought and sold therefore is one that allows for the purchase and sale of these bonds.

A buy-out team facing the servicing of acquisition debt of say £10 million could buy an 'out of the money' put option to sell government bonds. When the interest rate rises the price of the bonds will fall thereby taking the option into the money. The buy-out team can then sell the bonds at the strike price which will be higher than the current purchase price. The profit so generated is then used to meet the extra interest cost.

To ensure effective hedging a procedure known as 'delta hedging' is normally used. Delta hedging is the process of buying options at various strike prices and then selling them at appropriate times so as to maintain an effective hedge at all times. Owing to the high transaction costs involved such tactics are better suited to the larger buy-outs.

Interest Rate Caps
An interest rate cap is an arrangement between a borrower and a financial institution where the institution effectively provides insurance that the interest rate relating to specified debt will not rise above a certain rate. This rate is called the cap rate.

A fee based on the time for which the cap is effective, on the difference between the cap rate and the current rate (generally the greater this difference, the lower the cost of the cap) and on expected future interest rates movements will be payable to the institution for the cap.

An interest rate cap can be purchased from an institution other than the one from which the senior debt is drawn. A cap may also be sold in the market if the debt of the company drops to such a level that the cap is no longer required. To achieve optimum capping levels it may be appropriate to purchase a number of caps, each for, say, a fifth of the total sum to be capped, and then dispose of each cap as the capital sum is repaid.

A cap will take the form of a payment to the company by the institution should the interest rate rise above the cap rate. Accordingly, the cap can be seen as an insurance policy except that the insurer will pay out even if the company taking out the policy has repaid its debt and therefore no longer needs the insurance.

The obvious advantage of a cap is that the risk of future higher interest rates is hedged but all the benefits of future lower rates will be available to the borrower.

The cap, however, does have the disadvantage of cost. Also, and perhaps more importantly, the cost of the cap (the premium) is to be paid upfront at a time when the buy-out company can least afford to pay it.

Example

Senior debt = £10,000,000
Current interest rate = 10% pa
Cap rate = 12% pa
Cost of cap = £200,000 (say)

SCENARIO A

Interest rates rise to 15% pa for one year.

$$\text{Savings due to cap} = £10,000,000 \times (15\%-12\%) - £200,000$$
$$= £300,000 - £200,000 = £100,000.$$

In this example, interest rates would have to rise more than 2% above the cap rate and would have to remain at that level for at least one year to make the cap worthwhile.

SCENARIO B

Interest rates do not rise above 12% pa.

In such a situation the loss is the cost of the cap of £200,000.

However, while the cost of a cap can be factored into the total buy-out cost a significant increase in interest costs where they are unprotected may be critical.

Interest Rate Collars
A collar is a variation on a cap in that, unlike a cap, a collar also sets a lower limit on interest rates below which the benefit of low interest rates will not be derived by the company. The main advantage of a collar is to reduce the cost of the cap.

Cost of collars are usually 25–35% lower than the cost of caps, on the basis that the upper and lower limits are equidistant from the current interest rate.

Example

Extending the example used to illustrate the interest rate cap, the details are as follows:

Senior debt = £10,000,000
Current interest rate = 10% pa
Collar rates = Below 8% pa
　　　　　　　Above 12% pa
Cost of Collar = £150,000

SCENARIO A

Interest rates rise to 15% pa.

Savings due to collar = £10,000,000 × (15%–12%) – £150,000
　　　　　　　　　　　　= £150,000

This saving is £50,000 greater than the saving with the cap.

SCENARIO B

Interest rates stay between 8%–12% pa.

The loss in this situation is limited to the cost of the collar of £150,000 which is lower than the loss incurred had a cap been purchased.

SCENARIO C
Interest rate falls to 7%.

If interest rates actually dipped this far, the company would lose the benefit of the fall in interest rates below the collar floor. The effective cost of the collar therefore becomes £10,000,000 × (8%–7%) + £150,000 = £250,000.

The more sensitive period of the buy-out with respect to profitability and cash flow is usually the first and second years following the buy-out. Whilst a fall in interest rates will reduce the burden on the company, a rise in rates above a certain level can work towards destroying the buy-out company altogether. Therefore the collar gives the buy-out team a hedge against interest rate rises that could potentially destroy the buy-out at a price that is substantially lower than that which would be paid for a cap. On the other hand the downside of the collar (Scenario C above) may not be so critical since although the full benefit of lower interest rates may not be gained there should be no damage to the buy-out as a result.

REQUIREMENTS OF BANKERS AND INVESTORS

Apart from wanting to be convinced that management is capable and committed and that the business is viable, secured debt lenders will want to know that the cashflow projections show, by a comfortable margin, that the debt will be serviced and repaid. In case the projections are not achieved and the company is unable to meet its financial obligations, they will also want to be sure that there is adequate security in place.

Investors will be looking for a return commensurate with their risk. Unless the management team is able to buy the business at a very competitive price (which includes being able to repay a significant proportion of the purchase price out of short term cash flow) it is likely management will need to improve the profitability of the company to generate the required returns. Often the target company has been under the control of its parent company and the managers will have to be able to demonstrate that they can be entrepreneurs as well as managers. For example the investors will want to ensure the management team can anticipate and respond to opportunities, take measured risks and change tack should the need arise. The managers need to be motivated by profit gains and the achievement of ever improving results.

Even with the most able and committed management team investors and bankers need to be convinced that the buy-out company is viable.

For a business to be viable after buy-out it must generally achieve the following:

i.   it must be capable of developing cash balances not only for servicing debt but also for financing working capital and its capital expenditure requirements
ii. it must be able to generate increasing profits. The investors will be looking for significant growth in their investment and the target company has to be operating in a market and have a potential demand curve capable of sustaining the necessary level of growth
iii. it must be able to foresee an exit route. This could be by sale to a third party or by flotation within, say 3 to 5 years, on the stock market. The business therefore has to be or become attractive to future acquirors or investors.

In summary the potential investors will be looking for the following features in a possible buy-out:

i.   proven management team
ii. existing and expanding products and markets
iii. the ability to borrow either against the balance sheet or the business
iv. the ability to generate cash quickly.

Management's view that the target company is suitable for a buy-out has to be communicated to potential investors. For the largest buy-outs potential investors will be willing to invest their time in considering whether a buy-out is viable. For smaller buy-outs investors have to be convinced a deal is viable without spending too much time. To achieve this it is essential that at an early stage a business plan is prepared.

The business plan

At the beginning of this chapter mention was made of providers of finance needing to be convinced of management's competence and commitment and of investors requiring an acceptable return. Set out below are some of the more detailed requirements the providers of finance are seeking. These are generally set out in a document called the business plan.

If the 'back of envelope' calculations set out in Chapter 1 indicate a buy-out is possible a business plan should be prepared. The initial purpose of the business plan is as a selling document to prospective financiers and it therefore has to be written professionally. It will often be used as the base for an accountants' background report which will be commissioned by an interested investor. However, if the plan is not well thought through it may never capture the interest of prospective investors and the buy-out may never get past the first hurdle. The business plan sets out management's idea of how the target company will develop and be run under the management team's control. The business plan, both in terms of quality and content, will communicate a lot to the investor about the management team itself; whether they are clear and commercial thinkers, whether they know enough about the business and its markets to be in control, whether they are entrepreneurial and whether they are able to communicate effectively with third parties.

There are certain key areas that need to be covered in the business plan but that is only the beginning. Once the business plan has done its job as an initial selling document it is up to the management team to convince, through discussions, prospective bankers and investors to back the buy-out on favourable terms. The areas in which bankers and investors will be particularly interested can be divided under financial and commercial headings.

Financial aspects

i. *Profitability*
    The business plan should detail the past results and future projected results for the target company. The past trading record may need adjustment to show the company's 'real' performance. For example, excess expenditure which took place as a result of the previous ownership structure of the company should be stripped out and shown as a non-recurring item. Once this is done significant items or trends will need to be explained. The major objective is to convince the prospective investor why he should believe the future projections. The projections should take into account all additional costs required to reorganise or restructure the target company following the buy-out but these should be identified separately since they will not have an ongoing impact on future profitability.

ii. *Sensitivities*
    The projections will be based on a stated set of management

assumptions, which will be challenged by the reader of the business plan. The impact on the profit and cash flow projections of different assumptions should be shown although only sensible sensitivities should be tested. The number of sensitivities shown should be limited although the model on which the projections are based should be designed in such a way to allow the extraction of further meaningful sensitivity analysis, should this subsequently be deemed necessary.

iii. *Cashflow*

The projected profit and loss accounts will not be reviewed in isolation. The business plan needs to contain details of past cashflow movements but more importantly cashflow projections which will be compiled using the projected profit and loss accounts as a base. Cashflow is at least as important as profitability following a buy-out and cash flow projections must be completed with great care since it is even more difficult to predict cashflows than it is to predict profits. The projections should include, where possible, reductions in borrowing requirements resulting from planned disposals of surplus assets.

iv. *Assets*

The size and quality of assets to be acquired with the business together with an idea of their replacement and realisable value should be disclosed.

Prospective lenders will be looking for high quality assets over which to secure debt financing but will also be concerned to see that the business has the necessary capital base to generate future profits at its projected levels. Otherwise, significant investment in fixed assets may be required.

v. *Research and development*

Where a company requires significant research and development expenditure to maintain its competitive advantage it is important to consider the likely time lag between investment and return on that investment or indeed whether there is a risk of no return at all. Since R and D expenditure does not provide security or positive cashflow to a lender, companies whose operations require significant expenditure in this area find it more difficult to arrange buy-outs. On the other hand the value of past research and development expenditure which is now generating cashflow and from which the company has gained competitive advantage should not be forgotten.

Commercial aspects

i. *Management*

The skills and commitment of the management team need to be demonstrated. The team should be shown to be well balanced. Past experience of the key team members, giving actual achievement as well as titles held, both within the buy-out company and in previous employment should be provided. Commitment should also be demonstrated; in particular the personal financial resources the individual members are willing to invest.

ii.   *Market share*
The target company's market and its place in that market needs to be identified and explained in detail, in terms of past, current and anticipated future market share.

iii. *Threats, risks and weaknesses*
The business plan should be a balanced document and should include threats, risks and weaknesses as well as competitive advantages. It should also explain how the impact of such un-favourable aspects are to be mitigated. For example, if the company relies heavily on very few customers or suppliers or if the company is likely to be particularly badly affected by a down turn in the national economy, such items should be addressed. Although over reliance on customers or suppliers can be a risk this can often be mitigated by the drawing up of formal supply or purchase agreements which would safeguard the company's position. Often, if there are no such mitigating factors available, management needs to think seriously about diversifying its product base or taking some other more radical action to reduce the risks to the business.

iv.   *Product quality*
This is an area where credibility is enhanced by the inclusion of third party reviews, analyses or press comment. The question is not one of quality alone but of perceived quality in the market place and of value for money.

v.   *New products*
The nature of the company's business or the need for continuing growth may require the introduction of new products. The investors must be satisfied that, to the extent necessary, such new products are already developed, capable of development or can be acquired at a cost that makes economic sense. Management will also have to demonstrate that appropriate quality controls for the new products exist and that market research has been undertaken, if necessary, to ensure the new product is acceptable in the market place.
    If the business involves high or new technology these require-ments will be of even greater importance.

vi.   *Technological change*
Where technological change is important either in production or in design terms, skill in these areas needs to be demonstrated. Costs of development also need to be projected and management will have to demonstrate that it can finance these costs in the buy-out company.

vii. *Volatility*
In a market that is prone to volatility risk of not being able to service debt is heightened and the terms of the buy-out must take

this into account either by having a lower gearing or by the debt provided being more flexible in terms of servicing and repayment. In addition, management should consider looking for ways to diversify into new products and explore compensating markets.

viii. *Headcount*

Buy-outs often lead to a reassessment of the numbers and responsibilities of personnel and provide the opportunity for a reduction in headcount. Any plan for such a reduction and its cost should be included in the business plan.

Alternatively, the planned growth may lead to a need for more personnel and management will need to show from where the additional employees are to be recruited as well as how the management team intends to motivate and manage the increased numbers, if the increase is significant.

ix. *Government legislation*

There is a whole raft of current and potential legislation that can affect a business directly or indirectly. Management must demonstrate that they are aware of how current legislation may impact their business.

STRUCTURING THE DEAL

Having reviewed the type of finance available and what the providers of that finance are looking for, the key issue is how to structure the deal.

While most MBOs are financed with just senior debt and equity most LBOs are financed through a combination of senior debt, equity and mezzanine. The order in which each of these types of finance should be put in place is as follows:

i.   senior debt
ii. mezzanine
iii. equity

There are two alternative ways of going about this; the horizontal slice or the vertical slice approach. The idea of the horizontal slice is that the company finds three different providers or sets of providers of finance, one for senior debt, one for mezzanine and one for equity. The vertical slice approach cuts the financing up differently and insists that each investor takes a proportion of equity of secured debt and of mezzanine. In this way the less attractive part of the package is put together with the rest of the package, making that part easier to raise. Both approaches are used but with development capital arms of the clearing banks working closely with their lending colleagues and with investors generally becoming more flexible the use of the vertical slice approach has a number of advocates in the MBO area. For LBOs a partial vertical slice approach has often been adopted. A limited number of LBO providers will invest in all types of finance but generally the debt providers are not interested in equity and the equity providers are not interested in debt. Until recently there were few organisations in the UK which were particularly interested in financing the mezzanine layer. Accordingly, both equity and debt finance providers would provide some mezzanine finance if they wanted a share of the LBO. This practice is likely to reduce with the increasing number of specialist mezzanine finance providers in the UK market.

The balance between equity and debt

There is a direct relationship between risk and return. However well the management team knows the target company and its business, the level of debt in most buy-outs is bound to increase the risk for the company after buy-out. The managers will want to ensure that their own investment generates the maximum possible return for the minimum capital outlay. The aim is therefore to have a small equity base that gives the management team a significant share of the company for a relatively small investment, the corollary of which is for the structure to carry a comparatively high level of debt finance. The business must therefore be capable of producing the profits and cash required to meet the servicing and repayment schedule for the debt finance.

Optimising the capital structure

As explained above, the effects of financial leverage are to increase both the risks and the potential rewards to investors.

The starting point for optimising the capital structure is consideration of the maximum debt capacity of the company. This is calculated by dividing the operating profit (ie profit before interest and tax) by the interest rate. To illustrate this by way of an example: if the effective interest rate is 15% and operating profits £6m, maximum debt capacity is

$$\frac{£6m}{0.15} = £40m$$

In other words profit after interest at a debt level of £40m would be nil. If operating profits were to fall below £6m a loss after interest would be sustained.

Interest cover is a ratio which measures the level of safety of the company's debt, and is calculated as

$$\frac{\text{operating profit}}{\text{interest cost}}$$

In the above example, operating profit is £6m and interest is £6m (£40m × 15%). Accordingly the interest cover is 1. The higher the interest cover, the safer the capital structure; the lower the interest cover the riskier the capital structure. If interest cover falls below 1, it means the company is sustaining losses after interest.

The rewards of high gearing to the investors can be seen by extending the same example. If the company borrows £20 million, its profit after interest will be £3m (£6m minus £20m × 15%). If its operating profit increased by 100% to £12m, profit after tax would increase from £3m to £9m (£12m minus £20m × 15%). In other words, while operating profits double, profits after interest (ie those profits attributed to share-holders) increase three fold.

The value of management's share in a company is maximised through finding the lowest weighted average cost of capital, which, given the returns demanded by equity investors, means maximising leverage.

WHAT IS THE MAXIMUM DEBT FINANCE THAT CAN BE RAISED?

In order to maximise debt finance it is necessary to consider the different types of debt finance provider.

The clearing bank

Clearing bank finance is normally the best source of borrowing for MBOs. Talk to a more progressive clearing bank manager, particularly one who spends all his time on corporate business, and if the cash flow projections make sense he will be willing to stretch his lending far beyond traditional gearing levels. A few years ago such lending would have been refused on grounds that the gearing was far too high and accordingly lending would be imprudent. The competitive environment and a changing view on gearing has led to clearing bankers being amongst the leading players in providing buy-out finance, certainly on all but the largest finance packages.

To understand the clearing banks' change in approach it is worth considering current perceptions of gearing. The traditional gearing ratio calculation is debt divided by equity. For this purpose debt generally includes all bank borrowings (including overdrafts) and other finance lines, including hire purchase and lease finance. Equity comprises share capital and reserves; or looking from the other side of the balance sheet, net assets.

Historically, gearing of one to one was considered acceptable; two to one was considered racey. Buy-out gearing ratios of ten to one would have been totally out of the question. This is no longer the case. One of the reasons for the change is that corporate lending bank managers now understand their customers' businesses better and instead of applying the traditional gearing as one of the critical measurements in deter-mining the risk attached to the proposed lending they now use a combination of understanding the business, assessing that adequate security is in place and calculating the interest gearing ratio. The interest gearing ratio measures the number of times interest is covered by profit before interest and tax (PBIT). If PBIT is twice the interest charge immediately after buy-out clearing banks will generally be interested in providing finance as long as other criteria such as quality of business and management are apparent and the ability to service and repay capital can be shown.

Having made a case for the clearing banks to be high on the list for potential providers of debt finance, maximising borrowings is of such importance if management is to achieve the greatest possible share of equity, that other sources of debt finance should be considered.

Other providers of debt

Factors
Debt factors have been fighting hard to change their image as lenders of last resort – the organisations to approach when your company is really in difficulties. This image prevails despite its not being deserved. Accordingly the possible stigma which attaches should it be known that a factoring service is being used can be reason enough for not using a standard non recourse factoring service. There is however a service provided by factors which provides the benefits of cash flow without the disadvantage of customers knowing a factor is being used. This service is often known as confidential invoice discounting. This is where the company 'sells' to the factor, with recourse, debts due from its customers. This is normally done by the company providing copy sales invoices to the factor on a regular basis. As far as the customer is concerned he continues to pay his supplier and is chased for payment by the supplier. He has no knowledge that sales invoices issued to him are being factored.

The percentage advanced against invoices is negotiable and depends on the type of business as well as the financial standing of the company. Receipts from customers are paid into a separate bank account from where they are transferred to reduce the balance owing to the factor. If a debt has not been collected after 90 days the factor generally will no longer finance it and an adjustment to the funding for that period will be made. Interest is normally charged on the outstanding balance at interest rates which are close to if not the same as comparable overdraft rates. There is an additional cost of using a factor and this represents the monitoring fee which the factor charges to ensure the systems and controls necessary to maintain an accurate sales ledger are in place at the company. It is not unusual to achieve advances of 80% of debtor balances under 90 days through this route which is generally significantly more than a clearing bank will lend against debtor cover. From a practical view point, facilities from debt factors have the added advantage of not having upper limits on the size of the facility which increases as the volume of the company's business increases.

Fixed assets finance
A marketable property, particularly freehold offices or all purpose factories, may be a very attractive investment to a pension fund or insurance company. The main objective of such an institution is to see

capital growth while benefiting from a regular yield. Accordingly, the quality of the rental covenant is important. Immediately after buy-out, buy-out companies' balance sheets are highly geared and therefore do not always provide a first class rental covenant. However, if other tenants could easily be found should the buy-out company fail to pay its rent, pension funds and insurance companies would not be deterred from entering into a sale and lease back by a buy-out company.

A common problem for the buy-out company entering into a sale and lease back is the creation of a tax liability arising from the gain on the sale. Arrangements have been devised in which properties are sold to a company which is still for tax purposes part of the buy-out company group (with any tax liability being rolled over) but with some of the benefits of capital appreciation being available to the third party financier. Alternatively a mortgage secured against the property can be arranged with insurance companies, pension funds or banks. Seventy per cent of the value is the normal amount which will be advanced although it is often possible to negotiate a higher percentage. Subject to the tax impact, the benefits of sale and leaseback are clear. The additional 25% to 30% raised through selling the property can often result in a straight reduction of equity. An alternative route used to raise 100% finance on a property is through the use of an indemnity policy from an insurance company. If the commercial lender is willing to advance 70% of the property's value, an indemnity policy for the balance of 30% will often allow the lender to advance 100% of the value. The premium for such a policy is normally between 4% and 10% of the amount insured. Commercial mortgagers provide money for terms of up to ten years and will price their lending very competitively. The interest rate on a floating basis is generally between 0.75% and 1.75% over LIBOR. Various interest rate management instruments, which have been discussed earlier, will eliminate or reduce the risk of increasing interest rates over the period of the mortgage.

A sale and leaseback transaction will leave the buy-out company with an operating lease. For new buildings the lease period is normally 25 years with rent reviews at five year intervals to open market rental values and full repairing and insuring liabilities being the responsibility of the tenant. One of the possible pitfalls in such a transaction is the restrictions over change of use of the property and the buy-out company management should take care when entering into such a transaction.

Motor vehicles
Motor vehicles are perfect candidates for hire purchase or lease finance arrangements, even those which have already been purchased outright and are one to two years old. For second hand vehicles finance can normally be raised up to 75% of current value. For new vehicles lease finance arrangements create less immediate cash requirements than hire purchase but carry the disadvantage that for expensive cars there are tax disadvantages in entering into lease agreements rather than hire purchase contracts.

Machinery and equipment

Machinery and equipment is less attractive as security to providers of finance. The lease or hire purchase company will be aware of the lack of marketability of such items and will be more concerned about the viability of the company, often in terms of balance sheet ratios, which as mentioned above tend not to look too healthy immediately following buy-out.

STRUCTURING THE EQUITY

The mechanics

Having maximised the debt finance (both senior and mezzanine) the balance will comprise equity. The exact form will depend to a large extent on the house style of the lead equity investor but generally the equity will comprise ordinary shares, for which the management team will also subscribe, and preference or preferred ordinary shares, the precise terms of which will vary depending on the deal, but which will always rank ahead of the ordinary shares. The concept is that the ordinary share capital is sufficiently small to allow the managers with their limited resources to subscribe for that number of ordinary shares which will give them the agreed percentage of the ordinary share capital of the company.

Example

The buy-out purchase price (including costs) is £10 million. Debt is £7 million leaving a balance from equity investors and management of £3 million. The managers agree to invest £200,000 of their own money with the balance of £2.8 million being invested by the equity investors. To achieve their required IRR the equity investors are to subscribe for 60% of the ordinary shares.

Accordingly, the managers' investment of £200,000 will purchase 40% of the ordinary share capital. In other words the issued ordinary share capital will be £500,000 (£200,000 divided by 40%) and the equity investors will subscribe £300,000 for their 60% stake in the company. The balance of their investment, being £2.5 million, will be invested through subscribing for preference shares. The preference shares will provide a yield which will have been taken into account in arriving at the equity investors' required IRR.

Terms of the equity investment

Equity investors' primary consideration is the internal rate of return (IRR) that the investment will produce evaluated against the risk of investment. A number of investors will also be interested in receiving a running yield since this will cover or partly cover their cost of money and will also limit the risk of the investment since some return will be received in the early years following the buy-out.

In most buy-outs the equity investors will expect to generate the bulk of their return at the time the company exits (eg flotation or sale). As such the expected value at the date of exit is key to determining management's share of the ordinary share capital of the company being bought out.

What will be the value of the business on exit?
Value on exit will be a function of ruling P/E ratios and earnings at that time. Investors will almost invariably assume exit will be by way of flotation, even though early sale is becoming an increasingly popular route. The main reason for investors taking this view is that in most situations it is impossible to assess, with any degree of accuracy, sales prices at the time of exit or the appetite of the market to acquire the company at that time. Even in terms of flotation future price earnings ratios are for the crystal ball gazers. But if the buy-out team is unable to influence the investors' view of future PE ratios it is able to influence the investors' view of future earnings. This influence can probably be seen in terms of the following key factors:

i.   historic performance: How much does the business need to grow to generate its projected profits and has it grown at that rate in the past?
ii. how good is the management team?
iii. what is the potential for the company's product in the market place?
iv. how good has the company's budgeting been in the past?
v.   will the company have financial constraints on its growth as a result of financing the buy-out?

The first four factors have been covered earlier in this book and in large part are qualitative. Key factor number five is quantitive. If one starts with the premise that there is a maximum amount of debt that can be raised to finance the buy-out the management team has a decision to make regarding the balance of third party equity and the level of funds available for expansion. What this means is that generally as much debt as possible is raised to meet the purchase price with the result that most cash generated over the first few years following the buy-out is used to service and repay the debt. The company's ability to borrow further will also be limited until significant repayments of the buy-out debt are made. Since any additional funding is likely to be largely in the form of equity, the financial decision to be answered by the buy-out company management is whether the return that is expected to be generated on the additional equity funding which would need to be raised to fund additional growth will be greater than the internal rate of return required on that equity finance.

At likely IRRs of between say 30% and 45% the buy-out company will have to perform exceptionally well to achieve a marginal return on capital employed in excess of those levels. Despite this, investors will wish to see growth and the balancing of growth against capital will be one of the most difficult problems for the management team to deal with. Where the growth is to be fuelled by capital expenditure it may be possible to raise a separate capital expenditure loan in addition to the buy-out facilities but this is only likely to be acceptable if the additional cash flow resulting from the capital expenditure can finance the additional loan facility.

In negotiations with the providers of buy-out finance the question as to how and when the lenders will be repaid and the equity investors realise their investment needs to be addressed. In particular, the amount of debt that is left in the company on exit will determine the exit value as well as the future growth potential of the company.

Obviously the buy-out company's profits in the period after buy-out will be adversely affected by the heavy debt servicing costs. To the extent the debt has not been repaid prior to sale or flotation, should the debt be repaid on exit or left outstanding? As far as sale is concerned it should make no difference.

As far as flotation is concerned the answer will appear to depend primarily on what the funds being raised are to be used for. Are the funds being raised on flotation to be used for growth or for repayment of debt? In other words will the management team want to use the funds being raised to repay debt or to retain in the company for growth? This question is important since it will determine whether the sponsor to the flotation will apply the appropriate P/E ratio to the company's earnings after interest charges or before interest charges. If the additional funds are to be used for repaying debt, it is appropriate to take earnings before interest; if the funds are for growth, it is more appropriate to take earnings after interest. Which of the two gives a greater valuation of the company is dependent on whether the appropriate P/E ratio is greater or less than the P/E inherent in the interest charge. This can be illustrated by an example showing the two ways of calculating the value of a company being floated.

METHOD 1

Profit before interest and tax	£2.0m
Interest on acquisition debt of £5m	0.5
Profit before tax	£1.5
Taxation (33%)	0.5
Profit after tax	£1.0m
A price earnings ratio of 12 would value the company at	£12.0m

METHOD 2

Profit before tax	£2.0m
Taxation (33%)	0.67
Profit after tax	£1.33m

A price earnings ratio of 12 would value the company at	£16.0
Less repayment of debt	5.0
	£11.0m

Method 2, which is appropriate where the new funds being raised by the company are to repay the acquisition debt, gives a lower value for the company. The reason for this is that the price earnings ratio inherent in the interest rate is greater than that for the company. In the above example the interest rate is 10%. After deducting tax at 33% the interest rate after tax is $6\frac{2}{3}\%$. To calculate the inherent price earnings ratio the reciprocal of $6\frac{2}{3}\%$ is taken, ie 15, which is greater than the P/E ratio being applied to the business of 12.

Looked at from an earnings yield viewpoint the company's earnings yield on a P/E of 12 is $8\frac{1}{2}\%$ compared to an after tax interest rate of $6\frac{2}{3}\%$, which shows that as long as investors' perceptions are correct the company will get a better return if it invests its funds in growth than if it repays its borrowings.

This illustration demonstrates that in negotiations with prospective investors it is important to consider and plan for what is likely to happen after exit.

What is the degree of risk inherent in the investment?
There are numerous qualitative factors which need to be considered in determining the degree of risk inherent in the investment. Most of these have been covered elsewhere in the book and include whether the buy-out is highly leveraged or whether the purchase is a buy-in where the management team know less about the vehicle into which they are buying. It is one of management's tasks to convince its backers of the lack of risk inherent in the investment.

Investors will normally require at least a 30% to 40% internal rate of return on their pure equity investments. There is not a great deal of science in this but history has shown that investors earn a reasonable profit after taking successes and failures into account if they demand that level of return.

Typically, investors will assess the buy-out company's prospects in detail, often commissioning an accountants' report to review the projected profit and loss account and cash flows, and also employing marketing experts to provide a view as to the market in which the company operates and of its position in that market.

Having carried out their due diligence the investors will prepare a base case on which they will compute their expected IRR. The base case is normally set at 5% to 10% below management's expectations and it is therefore important for the management to convince the investors of the achievability of the projections.

Ratchets

The investors' base case is likely to be more prudent than management's projections. Since the percentage of equity the investor requires depends on this assessment a mechanism called a ratchet is often used to allow the exact split of share holdings to be determined only after future results are known. Investors will not allow the ratchet mechanism to limit totally their upside potential if the buy-out performs better than they expect but they will share that upside with the management team. Even if investors' and managers' views of the future do not differ, since projections cannot be known with certainty, where the managers perform better than projected it may be reasonable for them to receive a larger share of the company.

Example

Company X is projected by management to generate profits after tax of £3m in three years' time. It is currently generating £1m (on a comparable basis). The company is subject to an MBO and the investor believes it is likely that profits will be £2m in three years time. The investor requires 30% of the equity to achieve his required internal rate of return based on £2m after tax profits at the end of three years. If he believed the company would make £3m profit after tax he would only require 20% of the equity.

A ratchet is agreed. Management receives 70% of the equity now. The ratchet agreement provides that in year 3 for every £100,000 profit after tax in excess of £2m and up to £3m management will receive an extra ½ per cent of the equity. Accordingly if they meet their target of £3m they will end up owning 75% of the company. If management had managed to negotiate an extra 1% of the equity for every £100,000 of profits above £2m, they would have ended up owning 80% of the company. In this example there is an upside limit to management's share of the company. This is normally but not always the case.

Ratchets can be both upward and downward. In the example above the ratchet was upward; the managers had the opportunity to increase their stake. They could have been given 75% and had their holding reduced to 70% if they had not achieved their projected profit. Most investors and management teams like ratchets to be upward but the main reason for this is one of psychology.

Ratchet mechanisms can take various forms and depend on the financing structure. One which has become quite common is the convertible redeemable preference share. These shares are held by the investors and all or part are redeemed if projections are achieved or partially achieved but converted into ordinary shares if results fall short of projections thus diluting management's holding in the ordinary shares.

Apart from the tax consequences to the management team, which have to be considered carefully, the other problem with ratchets is that they often result in disputes. Arguments over the accounting treatment of unusual items or over a change in strategy which is responsible for short term costs in return for long term profits are typical of disputes which arise. Even where the problem is foreseen and attempts made to renegotiate the ratchet, difficulties often arise and for this reason ratchets are not always used.

It is usual, however, for LBOs to incorporate ratchet mechanisms and these are often based on value at exit (normally flotation) as opposed to being based on profits. The benefits of ratcheting in this way are that both management and investors have the very clear objective of finding a suitable exit in the shortest possible time at the highest possible price.

Example

An example of such a ratchet might be:

Investor IRR	Management Share
0–35%	5%
40%	15%
60% upwards	40%

Management's share at market capitalisations between the ratchet points would be determined on a straight line basis using investor IRR at the base measure. In other words at investor IRR of 37½% management share will increase to 10% (halfway between 5% and 15%) and at investor IRR of 50% management share is 27½%.

The ratchet may be structured as follows:

Purchase price (including costs)	£100.2 million
Management equity injection agreed at	£0.2 million
Senior debt	£50 million
Mezzanine debt (providers of this debt receive an equity kicker by subscribing for 5% of the ordinary share capital)	£20 million
Third party equity investors	£30 million

Management subscribes for 40% of the ordinary share capital for £200,000, the mezzanine lender subscribes £25,000 for 5% and the equity investors subscribe £275,000 for the remaining 55%. Of their remaining £29.725 million investment, £3.5 million is invested in convertible redeemable preferred ordinary shares ('convertibles') with the balance of £26.225 million invested in redeemable preference shares.

The convertibles then act as the ratchet mechanism. If Newco achieves its upper target all of the £3.5 million convertibles are redeemed, leaving management with 40% of the ordinary share capital of Newco. If the ratchet operates such that management are to hold, say, 10% of the ordinary share capital of the company (because at this level the IRR to the equity investors is 37.5%), then the equity investors will redeem 2 million of the convertibles and convert the balance of £1.5 million into ordinary shares in Newco. The conversion leads to an increase in ordinary share capital from £0.5 million to £2.0 million, thus diluting management's stake to 10%. If management's entitlement is restricted to 5% (ie an IRR to the equity investors of 35% or less) then all of the £3.5 million convertibles will convert into ordinary shares, increasing the ordinary share capital to £4 million.

No account has been taken of the mezzanine lender's dilution resulting from the increase in ordinary share capital. In practice the mezzanine lender's equity participation would be protected, wholly or partially, in the ratchet formula either by the mezzanine lender subscribing for convertibles or through some form of warrant or option mechanism.

It can be seen that in this example management never gets less than 5% nor more than 40%. While it makes sense to ensure management has a stake, however low, to keep management motivated regardless of the buy-out company's performance there is, in principle, no reason why the ratchet should not allow management an infinitely high share of the company as long as the investor IRR targets are achieved. Ratchets are one of the key areas of negotiation in any LBO.

MEZZANINE FINANCE

The role of mezzanine finance in deal structuring is difficult to define precisely. In the US non-securitised bonds ('junk bonds') play a prominent role in LBO financings. In the UK mezzanine finance has only come to the fore in the last two to three years. Initially, and still predominantly, the mezzanine finance that is available is closer to debt than to equity. In other words, it is likely to take the form of junior debt on which interest cover is adequate but security thin; it will demand a high interest rate (say, 2% over senior lender's rates) and an equity kicker taking the IRR up to say 25%. The equity kicker will normally be in the form of share options or detachable warrants.

A newer but growing type of mezzanine finance is also available. This can be classified as equity related mezzanine since the yield is far lower and the equity kicker a far more important part of the finance. The IRR is in fact sometimes related directly to the IRR earned by the equity investors.

In order to minimise the amount invested by the pure equity investors, the amount of debt finance should be maximised and the amount of mezzanine also. It should be noted however that to the extent that mezzanine is raised it should reduce the amount of equity funding not the debt funding.

THE VENDOR

It is sometimes overlooked in a buy-out that the price to be paid for the business can be less important than the timing of payment of the purchase price. The argument that there is a finite amount of finance available from providers of debt for any buy-out and that the equity providers who provide the balance will want to extract a far greater return commensurate with the risk their investment carries is correct as far as it goes. But if the providers of debt finance have different objectives to a commercial lender (whose primary objectives are a reasonable return and low risk on monies lent) such a lender may be willing to provide reasonably cheap finance without the commensurate security. Apart from family and friends (who should not be discounted in very small MBOs) the other party which sometimes falls into this category is the vendor.

The reason that the vendor may take such a view is normally to facilitate the sale. Where the vendor is, for example, the family that owns the business deferral of some of the consideration is just one of the factors that the owners will take into account in deciding whether or not to sell to the buy-out team. Deferring part of the purchase price can also be attractive to a listed company vendor. The reason for this is that generally in such a situation the most important single criterion for the vendor is achieving an acceptable price. If the parent sells too cheaply the consolidated accounts of the holding company will record a loss which the holding company directors are likely to want to avoid. Therefore, a possible way around this problem is for the buy-out team to pay an acceptable price but to defer some of the consideration.

It should be noted that if the deferred consideration is payable in the future and does not carry interest it may be appropriate for the vendor to discount the amount receivable to its present value and this needs to be taken into account in the calculation. An example of how deferred consideration may assist both the holding company directors and the management team is set out below:

Example

Net book value of assets of buy-out company is £10m.

Purchase price for buy-out which can be financed and which is supported by current profitability is £8m.

ALTERNATIVE 1

The sale goes ahead at £8m all of which is payable on completion.

1. £2 million loss is recorded in holding company consolidated accounts.
2. Management team buys for £8 million and raises £5 million by way of debt (being the level of debt the balance sheet will support). The management team is able to invest £0.2m and the third party equity providers invest £2.8m. For their £2.8m the

outside investors require 45% of the company taking into account their view of the company's value at exit and their own required IRR.

ALTERNATIVE 2

The sale goes ahead at £10m, with £5m paid on completion and £5m deferred. The deferred consideration is payable at £1m per annum and the outstanding balance carries interest at a commercial rate. The deferred consideration is either unsecured or is secured with the security subordinated to that of the bank which provides the £5m debt finance.

1. No loss is recorded in the holding company consolidated accounts.
2. Management team raises £5m by way of debt and pays the deferred consideration out of the buy-out company's future cash flows. Accordingly no outside equity is needed and management retains 100% of the company.

Obviously by extending unsecured or inadequately secured credit the holding company is taking a risk, although this is mitigated to some extent by the holding company board's knowledge of the strengths and weaknesses of the buy-out company's management and business. Often in such situations the vendor will take some equity kicker in the buy-out vehicle to balance reward against the additional risk being taken.

The other disadvantage to the vendor is lost cash flow. If the generation of cash is the primary reason for the sale by the parent, it is unlikely to be willing to accept deferred terms. A further risk to the vendor is that the buy-out company may refuse to pay the deferred payments when they become due claiming they should be offset against warranty claims.

As far as the management team is concerned, the risk is the increased commitment of debt repayment and servicing which could lead to financial difficulties if the buy-out company underperforms.

LBO BASED LENDERS

For LBOs there is a number of banks (principally subsidiaries of US banks but also Japanese, French, Canadian and UK banks as well as a number of others) which combine the attributes of the more progressive corporate lending clearing bankers with that of providing substantial resources to finance buy-outs. Through gaining a close understanding of providing the business, the real value of its security (normally the underlying value of the business or businesses rather than of the assets) and predicted cash flows, such lenders will raise very substantial levels of debt. These lenders are key players in the large buy-out deals and have specialist departments set up for this purpose. Some of these banks are able to lend upwards of £100m on their own account to support a transaction although they will wish to place a significant proportion of the debt with other lenders shortly after the buy-out has been completed.

CHAPTER 4

Tax considerations

OVERVIEW

A buy-out is, theoretically at least, a 'simple' transaction involving only
the sale of certain assets by one group of persons to another. However,
the multitude of different ways in which this 'simple' transaction could
be, and is, structured, the often conflicting objectives of the parties
involved and the complexity of the tax legislation combine to ensure
that a buy-out is not such a simple process and thorough tax planning
becomes an essential ingredient to its success. As will be seen, the
potential tax pitfalls are many and varied.

The overall objectives of tax planning in respect of a management-led
buy-out are, generally, to reduce the incidence of taxation on the
buy-out transaction so as to minimise the cost to the buy-out team (and
external investors, if any) while maximising the sale proceeds to the
vendor. (There will be occasions, however, when these objectives prove
to be mutually exclusive and may be resolved only by negotiation). In
addition, the structure determined should lead to the lowest possible
taxation on an on-going basis so as to maximise the returns to the
buy-out team and external investors. Objectives may be slightly
different where the buy-out is not management-led particularly as such
a buy-out might result in only a very small minority of the shares being
held by management.

It is appropriate at this stage, whilst considering the objectives of tax
planning, to review the current fiscal environment and determine the
attitude of the Inland Revenue and the courts to such planning. The
present Conservative Government has, since 1979, advocated a policy
of reduction in direct taxation in favour of indirect taxation together
with incentives for investment in (small) business. It is clear that
reductions in direct taxation have been achieved although recent levels
of trade deficit and inflationary pressures eliminated the Chancellor's
ability to further reduce direct tax rates in his 1989 Budget.

However, the elimination of first year capital allowances has, despite
a reduction in corporation tax rates, mainly seen a shift in the tax
burden to the manufacturing sector from the service sector. In addition, the Business Expansion Scheme and its predecessor, the Business
Start-up Scheme, have, in general, not been available to the management team while the continued existence of the close company
apportionment provisions until 31 March 1989, despite the effective

equalisation of income tax and capital gains tax rates, exacerbated the already difficult task of financing the deal.

The judicial approach to tax avoidance is also worth considering. In *W T Ramsay Ltd v IRC* [1982] AC 300, [1981] STC 174 it was established that a circular series of pre-ordained transactions having no commercial purpose other than tax avoidance could be considered as one transaction by the Revenue with the resultant tax implications. This principle was extended in *Furniss v Dawson* [1987] AC 474, [1984] STC 153 to include a linear series of pre-ordained transactions where one or more of those transactions had no commercial purpose and was inserted in order to avoid tax.

Over the years since *Ramsay*, the Revenue has attempted to interpret this new approach widely. However, the principle has been limited, but not overturned, in the consolidated appeals to the House of Lords known collectively as *Craven v White* [1989] AC 398, [1988] STC 476. Following the decision in these appeals, it remains clear that the Inland Revenue can look through transactions where there is a pre-ordained scheme or arrangement where artificial steps having no business *purpose* (as opposed to no business *effect*) are inserted solely with the object of avoiding tax. However, it must be certain at the outset of the scheme that all pre-ordained steps were designed and expected to occur and that the overall result could not be achieved by the particular scheme without giving effect to all the steps.

Consequently, where the taxpayer arranges his affairs so that the tax liability arising from a particular transaction would be reduced if an unknown, speculative or contingent event should occur, the Revenue should be unable to set aside any of the steps. Strategic tax planning which is not part of a scheme for the avoidance of tax therefore lives on and the principle laid down in *IRC v Duke of Westminster* [1936] AC 1, (1936) 19 TC 490, that a taxpayer is entitled to arrange his affairs so that the tax under the appropriate Acts is less than it otherwise would be, remains basically undisturbed.

In a bona fide strategic tax planning exercise or in an arm's length commercial negotiation for the buy-out of shares in a company or its trade, steps taken to avoid or reduce a charge to taxation would fall almost certainly within the *Westminster* principle rather than the *Furniss* principle. However, care must be taken that all steps in a series of transactions do have a commercial purpose and can be justified if challenged.

OBJECTIVES

The overall objectives outlined above are simply stated and it is useful to put into context the main objectives of each of the parties involved.

Vendors

The reasons for the desire for, or agreement to, a buy-out by management will clearly be individual to the vendors – it may be a desire to realise the value of their investment in order to invest in more worthwhile investments or simply to raise cash; a large group of companies might take a strategic investment decision simply to cease trading in one particular sector or, as is often the case in family buy-outs or successions, the vendors wish simply to retire from the business and realise the value of their investment.

All the above cases simply amount to a divestment of assets and, accordingly, the vendors' straightforward objective is to realise the proceeds in the most advantageous and tax efficient manner.

Management team

The management team's reasons for a buy-out will normally be either offensive – where the team believes it can do a better job of running the enterprise if it were allowed to do so unfettered by the constraints of the present owners and/or can see the opportunity for significant gains – or defensive, where the desire is to avoid, for instance, a closure or sale to an unwelcome third party.

It is normally the case that the team will need to borrow, possibly substantially, in order to fund their equity investment. Consequently, a principal objective is to obtain tax relief on such borrowing. In addition, the team will wish to reduce their individual tax liabilities on gains arising on the ultimate disposal of the shares and ensure tax relief is available should there be any loss arising on the disposal.

External investors

If the buy-out is not insubstantial, it will require additional financing which can come from a variety of sources but is likely to be institutional (including banks). The final structure of the mix of types of finance will be determined by a combination of the institution's priorities for income return, capital growth, security and, particularly in a leveraged buy-out, management incentivisation. The tax objective is, therefore, to optimise the financing mix and incidence of tax in order to produce the best overall combination of these factors.

METHODS OF STRUCTURING THE BUY-OUT

The reasons for selection of a particular buy-out structure will clearly depend upon the requirements, both immediate and future, of all parties to the transaction. This inherent conflict of interest between the parties leads to the need to consider each party at every stage of the transaction but sometimes will come down simply to negotiation between them.

Notwithstanding the variety of ways of structuring the buy-out, there are only two ways to buy a business – first, to buy the business directly from the company carrying it on and, secondly, to buy the company itself. In the vast majority of cases, the buy-out will entail the creation of a company (inevitably known as 'Newco'), initially controlled by the management team, which will act as a vehicle to receive equity and other finance from the team, and almost certainly from external investors, in order to purchase the shares of the target company (also inevitably known as 'Target').

Other methods of structuring the buy-out will generally follow one of the following routes:

i. the purchase by Newco of the trade, assets and liabilities of Target
ii. the hive-down of certain or all of the trading activities and assets into a subsidiary company of the vendor, Target, and the subsequent purchase of Target by Newco or the management team
iii. the outright purchase of the trade, assets and liabilities of Target by the management team in partnership
iv. the repurchase by Target of its own shares so as to leave the management team with a controlling interest
v. demerger.

Each of the above methods will be considered in turn.

PURCHASE OF TARGET BY NEWCO

Other than a sale of shares by the vendors directly to the individual members of the management team, which is generally precluded by lack of funds, this route is, in essence, the most straightforward. The vendors will receive the proceeds of the sale directly and this will fix their tax liability as a capital gain. However, there are disadvantages for the purchasers.

When the company is purchased, its history and contingent liabilities go with it rather than with the vendors. The purchasers will inevitably desire comprehensive warranties and indemnities from the vendors, particularly in respect of tax liabilities. Determining the number and extent of warranties and indemnities to be given generally consumes a sizeable part of negotiation and professional time; this issue is covered in more detail in Chapter 5.

Newco will receive no immediate tax deduction for the cost of acquisition of Target's shares and, indeed, no deduction except on a subsequent disposal.

The normal sequence of events, both parties having agreed to the terms of the buy-out, is as follows:

i. the incorporation of Newco (or more normally the purchase of an 'off-the-shelf' company) and investment in its equity by the management team in whatever proportions are agreed between them
ii. the investment in Newco by external (institutional) investors and/or the obtaining of bank finance
iii. the purchase of the shares in Target by Newco.

At a later date, as discussed below, the trade, assets and liabilities of Target may be transferred to Newco followed, if appropriate, by the liquidation of Target.

Having identified the above stages, it is appropriate to describe the tax considerations of each separately.

(i) Incorporation/purchase of Newco

The main problems associated with the acquisition of shares by the managers were substantially reduced by the Finance Act 1988 with effect from 26 October 1987 by amendments to the share incentive scheme provisions (which could tax increases in the value of shares as income) and by the equalisation of the rates of tax on capital gains with those on income for tax years 1988/89 onwards. However, given the availability of the indexation allowance and annual capital gains exemptions separate from personal income tax allowances (additionally available to husband and wife individually from 6 April 1990), it is likely that it will remain beneficial to the managers for any increase in value of their shares to be taxed as capital gains rather than as income and particularly if this can be effected only on an actual disposal. Additionally, as discussed below, deferral or avoidance of a charge to capital gains tax may be possible. Of course, certain shelters exist against income but, in general, these entail investing further sums on which tax relief is available and this might not be attractive or possible.

The amended share incentive scheme (also now known as un-approved employee share schemes) provisions, which are somewhat difficult to follow, apply where a person, or a person connected with him, acquires shares, or an interest in shares, in a company in pur-suance of a right conferred on him, or an opportunity offered to him, by reason of his office as a director of, or his employment by, that or any other company (s 77(1) FA 1988).

The first line of defence from falling within these provisions is that which was used to attempt to avoid the old provisions of s 79 FA 1972 et seq ie that the shares are 'founder' shares. It is argued that if the managers obtain shares in Newco in their capacity as shareholders in the company and not as directors or employees, the shares are not acquired in circumstances to which s 77(1) would apply. This line of argument is open to challenge by the Revenue which could argue that the acquisition arose from an opportunity offered by reason of an office or employment with Target. Also, given that there must be at least two officers of a company, these two members of the management team could well have replaced the initial director and secretary of the off-the-shelf company in order to effect the issue of shares to themselves and their fellow managers. In addition, other managers might already have implied contracts of employment with Newco at the time of the share issue notwithstanding there had been no formal engagement. Con-sequently, it is an objective that the structure is such that no income tax charge may arise even if it has to be conceded that the managers' share acquisitions are prima facie within s 77(1).

If it is the case that the managers fall within the ambit of s 77(1), and have not ceased to have beneficial interest in the shares, a charge to tax under Schedule E will arise in two circumstances:

i. on the occurrence of a chargeable event in relation to the shares (s 78(1) FA 1988), or
ii. on the receipt of a 'special benefit' by virtue of ownership of or interest in the shares (s 80(1) FA 1988).

A chargeable event in relation to shares in a company is any of the following events if it increases, or but for the occurrence of some other event would increase, the value of the shares:

i.   the removal or variation of a restriction to which the shares are subject
ii. the creation or variation of a right relating to the shares
iii. the imposition of a restriction on other shares in the company or the variation of a restriction to which such other shares are subject, or
iv. the removal or variation of a right relating to other shares in the company (s 78(2) FA 1988).

An event is not a chargeable event in relation to shares in a company unless the person who acquired the shares or interest has been a director or employee of the company or an associated company or of the company in which the shares or interest are acquired (if different), at some time within a period of seven years before the date on which the event occurs (s 78(4) FA 1988).

An event is also not a chargeable event in relation to shares in a company where the removal, variation etc applies to all shares of a class and, at the time of the event, either

i.   the majority of the relevant class of shares is held other than for the benefit of directors or employees of the company, an associated company or directors or employees of such an associated company, or
ii. the company is employee-controlled by virtue of holdings of shares of that class, or
iii. the company is a subsidiary which is not a dependent subsidiary (see below) and its shares are of a single class (s 78(5)–(6) FA 1988).

A benefit, received by virtue of ownership or interest in the shares, is a 'special benefit' unless it is excepted under similar provisions to the exceptions from the definition of a chargeable event ie the benefit must be received in respect of all shares of the same class as those acquired and either (i) or (ii) or (iii) above applies (s 80(2)–(3) FA 1988).

In this context, 'benefit' has no specific definition and therefore must be construed widely. No charge will arise under this head, however, if the benefit is chargeable to income tax by any other part of the legislation (s 80(6) FA 1988).

These provisions must be examined very carefully because it may be too easily assumed that, if there is only one class of share with the same rights or restrictions on the formation of Newco, no chargeable event will arise because of the exemptions of s 78(5)–(6) FA 1988 outlined above provided the rights or restrictions are applied to all the shares. However, the emphasis of s 78 has changed from that of s 79 FA 1972 – the prior provisions had to be considered immediately after the relevant shares were acquired; s 78 is considered at the time of the occurrence of the event.

The extension of the founders' share argument under the old provisions of s 79 FA 1972 was, as outlined above, that the similar exception criteria to (i), (ii) and (iii) above were applied immediately after the shares in Newco were acquired. Consequently, if the managers established Newco with their own capital and controlled it before the institutional investment, the argument was that the shares were excepted from charge. Since the exceptions contained in s 78 FA 1988 are considered at the time of the event, exception (ii) above is now less likely to be utilised compared with exception (i) in buy-outs with institutional equity holdings. Given that the event (if there is one) will probably occur after the issue of equity to the institutional investors, the exceptions must be looked at most carefully and planning is essential to ensure that the managers do not fall into this potential trap.

The previous legislation contained in s 79 FA 1972 et seq would, if applied, tax as income the full increase in value of the shares over the relevant period. If a Schedule E charge arises under the current legislation, it will be for the year of assessment in which the chargeable event occurs or the benefit is received and it is meant to catch only artificial increases in value arising from the removal or variation of rights etc or any actual special benefit received. However, any actual increase in value will be caught if not excepted. It was therefore possible for s 79 FA 1972 to apply where a manager had borrowed money to purchase his equity in Newco and had secured the loan on the shares. The removal of this restriction would be unlikely to cause an increase in value of itself but a charge could well have arisen under s 79 FA 1972. A charge is now unlikely under s 78, although still possible if there is any increase in value. It is not considered likely, however, that the Revenue would take the point in this case.

The manner of charge of old s 79 FA 1972 is retained by s 79 FA 1988 where the shares are in a company which is a 'dependent subsidiary' at the time of the acquisition or becomes one before the person making the acquisition ceases to have any beneficial interest in the shares. In other words, a charge to Schedule E on any increase in value of the shares since acquisition will arise under s 79 FA 1988 on the earlier of seven years from the date of acquisition of the shares and the time when the taxpayer ceases to have beneficial interest in the shares. There are onerous annual compliance responsibilities in order to prove that a subsidiary is not a dependent subsidiary (which it is assumed to be unless proven otherwise). These responsibilities and the definition of dependent subsidiary are contained in s 86 FA 1988. Consequently, it is most important that shares in a subsidiary company are not issued to the management team (or any individual) as part of the buy-out arrangements unless the company can be held not to be a dependent subsidiary or if the exemptions in s 86(1) apply.

Since most investments by institutions generally entail the issue of shares of different classes and types, each class must be considered separately. Given the nature of the exemptions contained in s 78(5)–(6), it is unlikely that they will apply to the managers' shares (if they are within the ambit of s 77(1) in the first place) because, being of a different class to the institution's equity, neither will the majority of shares of the class acquired by the managers be held other than by them nor will the company be employee-controlled by virtue of holdings of shares in that class (unless institutional equity financing is small). Reliance must therefore be placed on a chargeable event not occurring.

A common feature of buy-outs is the desire of management to increase its proportion of the equity when the company is performing well and the requirement of the institutions to take greater control if the performance is poor in order to safeguard their investment. This is typically achieved by the 'equity ratchet' which generally means that management's share of equity is increased if a certain profit target is met and is reduced (or the opportunity to increase lapses) if the target is not met. The ratchet can also take the form of any variation in dividend rights, voting rights, share of assets on a winding-up etc.

It may be difficult to use the founders' share argument here ie that there is no creation or variation of a right by the event of meeting the target but simply the operation of an inherent right to the shares which existed from the time the shares were issued. This will be because it would appear difficult to issue founders' shares, with the appropriate rights, before the deal for the buy-out is struck and the external financing is negotiated.

A better argument is that the value of the shares will increase as the target is reached such that on reaching it, even if this is an event, any increase in value is minimal. This argument applies equally well to the more usual situation where the external investors' preference equity or debt is either converted into ordinary equity or not, or certain equity or debt becomes redeemable or not, based on the meeting of the target.

It may not be necessary to construct arguments on the above grounds, however, as the Inland Revenue's Press Release of 14 April 1988 indicated its agreement that such performance-related ratchets would not normally give rise to a charge on meeting the predetermined performance level, provided the ratchet was in place from the outset. However, the Press Release points out, the Revenue still needs to ensure that the price paid for the shares reflects the true value, including the effect of any ratchet, for normal Schedule E purposes.

A charge to Schedule E can arise where shares are acquired by directors or higher-paid employees in pursuance of a right or opportunity available by reason of their employment at an under-value (s 162 TA 1988). In these circumstances, the director or employee is treated as receiving a beneficial loan until the shares are disposed of (or treated as disposed) and will be liable to tax on an amount equal to interest at the official rate on the deemed beneficial loan. The charge continues each year until either the employee dies, he pays up the under-value to the company or any obligation to pay up is waived. Any such waiver or shortfall gives rise to tax under Schedule E on an equal amount in that year. It should be noted that the beneficial loan treatment only applies to so much of the under-value as is not chargeable to tax as an emolument (s 162(3) TA 1988 and see *Weight v Salmon* (1935) 19 TC 174).

Where share options are granted to a director or employee, s 135 TA 1988 must be considered as a charge to Schedule E could arise on any gain realised by the exercise, assignment or release of the option. This point must be watched carefully if share options form any part of the equity ratchet.

Both these charges would need to be considered where the price paid for shares (or options) by the managers is less than that paid by the institutional investors. In a case where a substantial premium is to be paid by the external investors, the problem should not arise in relation to the initial investment in Newco by the managers provided it is done before the external investment. It is therefore important that the initial shareholdings are agreed to and effected by the managers before the institutions invest.

(ii) *Investment in Newco by institutional investors*
As described in Chapter 3, there are many different forms of loan and equity finance and combinations thereof which can be used to effect the investment. Certain aspects of financing are discussed below. The other principal matter to be aware of is the effect on the close status of the company, particularly in respect of interest relief for the management team – see below.

(iii) *Purchase of shares of Target by Newco*
In the majority of cases, the consideration given by Newco to the vendor for the shares of Target is simply cash. This may or may not be a good thing for the vendor. If the vendor has brought forward or current capital losses and/or a high capital gains tax basis in the shares at 31 March 1982 together with indexation allowance, the capital gain resulting from the disposal of shares might be reduced significantly, or even eliminated. However, if there are no losses and the 31 March 1982 valuation is low, considerable capital gains tax (now at up to 40%) would become payable. In order to mitigate, or at least to defer, this tax cost, the vendor might be persuaded to exchange the shares in Target for a mixture of cash, loan stock and even equity of Newco including redeemable preference shares. The exchange for paper would allow the vendor to utilise the reorganisation provisions of s 78 CGTA 1979 et seq to defer part or all of any capital gain until a subsequent disposal of the replacement paper.

This share or security exchange could also have substantial benefits for the management team since Newco would need lower immediate funding from external sources. However, the vendor will be taking additional risk in accepting paper in Newco.

The vendors could defer gains by retaining an interest in Target, perhaps by converting part of their equity to redeemable preference shares. This route poses particular problems. The purchase price of the Target shares will by definition, if there are gains, exceed the nominal value of the shares. In order to safeguard the retained interest, the vendors will wish to receive the redeemable preference shares at a par value equal to the agreed value of their ordinary shares exchanged or at least ensure that an adequate premium is paid on redemption to equate to the agreed value. This is a reorganisation within s 78 CGTA 1979 but will constitute a distribution by virtue of s 209(2)(c) TA 1988 on the excess of the par value of the preference shares (plus any redemption premium) over the par value of the ordinary shares exchanged which, in these circumstances, is the amount of the new consideration mentioned in that sub-section.

Not only is the issue of redeemable share capital or securities a distribution, it is also a non-qualifying distribution by virtue of s 14(2)(a) TA 1988. Consequently, no ACT is required to be paid by the company but no tax credit will be available to the vendor and a charge to tax at up to 40% will arise.

Where the exchange is for redeemable shares in Newco, s 209(2)(c) will not bite; firstly, because the shares would not be issued in respect of shares in the company (Newco) – they would be issued in respect of shares in Target – and, secondly, as the shares would be issued in exchange for shares in Target, they would be issued wholly for new consideration. It is advisable that clearance for the exchange be obtained under s 88 CGTA 1979.

A possible solution to the problem of s 209(2)(c) mentioned above is firstly to exchange the ordinary shares in Target for another class of share giving rights equivalent to those of preference shares and then to grant the vendors a put option requiring the shares to be repurchased by the company at an agreed price on a future date. It would be argued, subject to careful wording of the option, that this did not result in beneficial interest in the shares being lost by the vendors at the time of the grant of the option so that this would in any way constitute a disposal of the shares at that time.

If the managers already have a shareholding in Target, these shares could also be exchanged for shares in Newco under the same reorganisation provisions mentioned above and a potential capital gain deferred. Again, it is advisable that clearance under s 88 CGTA 1979 be obtained.

It should be noted that the securities received will probably be qualifying corporate bonds so that the gain on ultimate disposal is limited to that which would have arisen had the shares been disposed of and not exchanged (para 10 Sch 13 FA 1984).

In all the above transactions, the need for a clearance application under s 707 TA 1988 should be considered.

Purchase by Newco of shares in Target (member of a group)

The tax implications of the purchase of shares for Newco and Target, where Newco is owned directly by the vendors, are as discussed above. However, where Target is a member of a tax group, certain tax problems could arise to the vendor group and the structure of the buy-out transaction might need to be amended in order to assist with the resolution of these problems.

The vendor company ('Vendor') will wish to reduce as far as possible any capital gain arising on the disposal of shares in Target. In particular, if Target contains substantial cash, Newco will effectively have to pay cash to buy cash with the attendant uplift in the proceeds to Vendor. In order to reduce this potential gain, a dividend may be taken out before the sale to Newco which will reduce the proceeds received for Target and, hence, reduce the gain. This dividend will be group income in Vendor and will, therefore not be taxable.

Provided the above dividend is paid out of post-combination profits, the dividend should not be treated by s 281 TA 1970 as a depreciatory transaction under s 280 TA 1970 (ICAEW TR 588, 25 September 1987). If the dividend is out of pre-combination profits, however, the transaction will be depreciatory and any capital loss created on the shares would be subject to adjustment.

It must be borne in mind that only realised distributable profits, as defined by the Companies Act 1985, may be paid up by way of dividend and unrealised revaluation surpluses cannot be utilised. It is understood that the Revenue does not consider such a dividend strip to be within the ambit of *Furniss v Dawson* nor, indeed, the transfer of assets within the group in order to utilise capital losses of other group companies (ICAEW TR 588, 25 September 1987).

The Finance Act 1989 has made the value shifting provisions of s 26 CGTA 1979 et seq much more complicated. However, provided the distribution is attributable to past or current income profits and not to intra group disposals at an undervalue, the provisions should not apply with the resultant adjustment to the capital gain or loss.

It must be ensured that Vendor has beneficial ownership of Target immediately before the dividend is paid in order that the election under s 247 TA 1988 for payment of the dividend without accounting for ACT will be valid (ss 838(1) & (3) TA 1988). Consequently, the existence of any heads of agreement or other potentially binding arrangements could negate the s 247 election and such arrangements must be closely scrutinised. If there could be any doubt, the dividend should be paid before any such arrangements are entered into. Following the Finance Act 1989, apportionment of group income of a close company is no longer an issue.

If the above distribution is substantial, it may reduce the net assets of Target to such a level that the managers do not need to form Newco to finance the acquisition but are able to purchase the shares in Target for a small sum. The working capital requirements of Target can be refinanced in Target after the buy-out or, if the dividend has been declared but remains effectively unpaid (or equivalently on loan account), the loan can be refinanced in Target after the buy-out and the loan repaid.

Section 77 FA 1988 must be considered by the managers on any direct purchase of the shares in Target as must their general Schedule E position including s 135 TA 1988 and s 162 TA 1988 especially if an equity stake is taken by external investors at a price representing a premium over the price paid by the managers.

As Target is leaving the vendor group, a capital gain could arise under s 278 TA 1970 where assets have been transferred into Target at no gain/no loss under the group provisions of s 273 TA 1970 at any time within the previous six years. In these circumstances, Target would be deemed to have disposed of those assets at their market value at the date of acquisition and the base cost would be the original cost to the group (as adjusted by any available indexation allowance).

Where a charge arises under s 278, no roll-over relief is available to Target. Roll-over relief would be available if the relevant assets were transferred from Target to another company within the vendor group and then sold separately although, of course, the rolled-over gain would remain in the vendor group after the sale. This problem would probably be dealt with between the parties simply by an adjustment to the purchase consideration.

However, the most likely source of a s 278 charge, other than free-hold property, is goodwill attaching to a trade which was transferred into Target under the provisions of s 343 TA 1988. Although certain intangible assets such as trade marks, patent rights etc can be specifically identified, there remains a 'rump' of goodwill which attaches to the trade. It is not possible to divorce this goodwill from the trade and transfer it to another group company and, supposedly, leave the trade, without goodwill, in Target.

Arguments have been put forward that, in certain cases, the goodwill is a group asset owned by the ultimate parent. This argument has not been tested in the courts (although some assistance is given by *Kirby (Inspector of Taxes) v EMI plc* [1986] STC 200) and could well prove litigious if attempted. It is probable that the only potential area of success would be in relation to trade names or other registerable intangibles.

Whether the disposal of the shares in Target yields a capital gain or a loss, consideration should be given to the capital gains position of other members of the group. If necessary, Target can be transferred within the group at no-gain/no-loss under s 273 TA 1970 in order to crystallise the capital gain or loss in the appropriate company in order to obtain the best utilisation of capital losses. As already noted, it is understood that the Revenue would not seek to apply the *Ramsay* principle to such a transfer of assets prior to disposal where the purpose is to offset capital gains and losses within the group. However, it is important to ensure that beneficial ownership of Target is retained at the time of the transfer so that s 273 would not be precluded from applying.

In circumstances where Target has not been successful, and in particular if the vendor group is considering closure rather than a sale, the buy-out purchase price may reflect a considerable discount on book value of the assets. The Schedule E impact on the managers must be considered but it is likely that, in these circumstances, the purchase price can be justified as the market value or realisable value of the assets of Target given the alternative of a break-up and consequent closure and redundancy costs.

In this situation, it is likely that there will be substantial sums owed by Target to Vendor which will not be fully repaid. Normally, in such cases, the shares in Target are sold at a nominal value, the inter-company indebtedness is repaid to an agreed extent out of the new finance obtained and the balance of the loan is either waived or is assigned by Vendor to the managers for a nominal sum.

If the loan is waived, a charge to tax could arise in Target under s 94 TA 1988 to the extent that the loan is a trading loan and has given rise to a deduction against taxable profits in Target.

If the balance of the loan is transferred to the managers, any subsequent repayment by the company would give rise to a capital gains liability on the managers rather than an income tax liability. Although the benefit of this is now somewhat reduced given the equalisation of tax rates on income and capital gains, a separate capital gains tax annual exemption would be available.

If the inter-company indebtedness arose on trading account, Vendor may argue successfully that any write-off constituted a genuine bad debt but resistance could be expected from the Revenue. If the indebtedness arose on capital account, no relief will likely be available to Vendor in respect of the amount written off unless the debt constituted a debt on a security. Although following s 139(2) FA 1989, any non-group indebtedness which has been structured as a debt on security will now be likely to be a qualifying corporate bond within s 64 FA 1984 and exempt from capital gains tax, s 64(6) FA 1984 excludes such indebtedness within a 75% group from being a qualifying corporate bond. Consequently, any loss arising could generate an allowable capital loss by virtue of s 134 CGTA 1979. However, indexation allowance would be denied by Sch 11 FA 1988.

Consideration must be given to the availability of group relief with Target in respect of its final period in the Vendor group. Section 410 TA 1988 operates to deny group relief for the whole of any accounting period during which any 'arrangements' exist for Target to leave the group. The ambit of s 410 is potentially very wide although the Revenue has given some guidance of its interpretation in its Statement of Practice SP 5/80.

Generally, negotiations for the disposal of Target will not be considered as 'arrangements' until such time as the members of the company have given their consent to the disposal or when the directors are in a position to be certain that such consent will be given, if earlier. This latter interpretation of the inception of arrangements could well prove a difficult matter of fact to prove should the Revenue ask the question. Consideration can be given to shortening the period of account of Target to a date immediately prior to the date that formal consent is given so that there is a corresponding, shorter tax accounting period. This device, however, might fall within the Ramsay principle rather than under the Westminster principle.

It should be noted that it is a reasonable interpretation of s 409 TA 1988 that group relief would be available for the part of the accounting period of Target falling before the date of the arrangements and that group relief is not denied for the whole of the accounting period.

OUTRIGHT PURCHASE OF ASSETS BY NEWCO

Although this is perhaps the simplest method of all, it is one which is likely to cause most problems during the sale negotiations because of directly conflicting tax effects to the purchaser and the vendor.

The purchaser will, in general, desire as great a part of the purchase consideration to be allocated to those items which will provide tax relief – capital allowances, stocks and work-in-progress etc – and as little to those items on which no relief is available such as goodwill. However, the vendor will generally want the opposite in order to reduce any balancing charges on assets qualifying for capital allowances, stock profits etc. In addition, indexation allowance and rebasing to 31 March 1982 would be available on any goodwill.

Such conflicting requirements are soluble only by negotiation of the parties. If the vendor has the upper hand in the negotiations, it is likely that one of the previously discussed alternative buy-out methods would be insisted upon.

Generally, the main reason for not selling the assets directly out of Target is the potential 'double' capital gain which could arise. If there are no brought forward or current tax losses in Target, some part of the proceeds, particularly in respect of goodwill, is likely to be taxable at corporate rates up to 35%. On a subsequent disposal of the shares on a liquidation, capital gains tax would likely arise on the vendors. However, provided there is ACT capacity in the company (which there should be because of the disposal gains) and assuming sufficient distributable profits, the after tax profits can be paid out as a dividend which will reduce the overall rate of tax because of the associated tax credit but not necessarily below the shareholder's marginal rate of tax on a share disposal. Indeed, the necessary calculations must be performed as, through rebasing of capital gains to 1982 and indexation, the effective capital gains tax rate on a share disposal could be significantly lower.

A further factor in the calculation is that the capital gain on a liquidation should actually, through indexation and rebasing, be a loss. s 574 TA 1988 can then be examined to determine if that loss may be set off against the dividend income (if no other capital gains are available for offset) – see below.

PURCHASE OF TRADE OF VENDOR THROUGH HIVE-DOWN INTO TARGET

Sometimes only part of a trade or an operating division is the subject of a buy-out. Alternatively, the buy-out may arise out of the receivership of all or part of the vendor group. In these circumstances, the relevant assets and liabilities will often be transferred into a subsidiary, Target, on loan account – the 'hive-down'. The shares are then sold to Newco or the managers directly and the loan account with the former parent is settled after Target has been refinanced. The intention is that this combines the advantages to the vendor of a share sale with those to the purchaser of an asset purchase.

There are certain matters to consider other than have already been discussed.

The object of the transfer is for any tax losses and capital allowance tax written down values to be transferred into Target by s 343 TA 1988 although the amount of losses transferred could be restricted by the operation of s 343(4) TA 1988 where Target has a deficiency of assets over liabilities. For the transfer to be successful, what is transferred must constitute a trade and must be carried on in Target before the buy-out. In addition, Target must be beneficially owned by its parent at the time the trade is transferred (*Wood Preservation Ltd v Prior* (1968) 45 TC 112 and *JH&S Timber Ltd v Quirk* (1973) 48 TC 595).

If there is the likelihood that there will be a major change in the nature of the trade hived into Target so as to put at risk the carry forward of trading losses by s 768 TA 1988, it could be beneficial instead to transfer the trade, assets and liabilities of Target directly to Newco rather than sell the shares. In this case, any balancing charges etc could be offset by the losses brought forward together with, if necessary, a disclaimer of capital allowances in prior years. Newco would therefore receive a higher capital allowances base cost instead of vulnerable losses. Stocks and work-in-progress could also be sold at market value, instead of being transferred at cost on a sale of shares, thus utilising losses and passing on a higher base cost.

PURCHASE OF TARGET'S ASSETS BY MANAGEMENT TEAM IN PARTNERSHIP

Partnerships can offer certain advantages as a medium in carrying on a trade rather than through a company

i.   no PAYE on drawings; tax paid in two instalments
ii. lower NIC (but lower state benefits)
iii. no audit requirements
iv. greater flexibility to make loans to partners or allowing drawings in excess of earnings
v.   no winding-up procedure to be followed

vi.   narrower (ie Sch D disallowances) benefit-in-kind provisions
vii.   no potential double capital gain on retained earnings
viii.   opening year rules when profits are rising
ix.   potential s 381 TA 1988 relief on early year losses.

However, the principal disadvantage of operating through a partnership is joint and several unlimited liability. However, limited partnerships are possible and although there must be at least one 'general' partner with unlimited liability, this liability can effectively be limited by the general partner being a limited company (probably with the other partners as members).

If there are plans for flotation of the entity, it is likely that the external investors will be seeking to make a capital gain on their investment at that time. Since there are no shares in the partnership, this can prove a difficulty. It could be possible to make the institutional investor a limited partner and adjust profit sharing ratios but this is probably too great a complication for too little reward from taking the partnership route.

Thus, from a tax standpoint, there could be advantages in operating through the vehicle of a partnership. The principal problem, however, is likely to be persuading the institutional investors to invest into this arrangement and it is unlikely that this route will be taken in practice.

REPURCHASE OF SHARES

This method assumes that the management team already holds shares in Target and that the company repurchases the shares of the existing shareholders leaving the management team as the only shareholders of the company and therefore in control. If the managers held only a small part of the equity before such a repurchase, it is likely that almost all of Target's asset value would need to be paid out on the repurchase. Consequently, the company would almost certainly need to be re-financed by external institutional investors.

The Companies Act 1985 envisages that such a repurchase should either be out of distributable reserves or be funded by the proceeds of a fresh issue of shares. It is possible for the company, if private, to repurchase the shares out of capital but there are strict procedures which must be followed.

Notwithstanding the company's power under the Companies Act 1985 to repurchase its shares, any payment by the company in excess of nominal value would be treated as a distribution by s 209 TA 1988 unless exempted under the provisions of s 219 TA 1988 et seq. The conditions of which, relevant to a buy-out, are in summary as follows:

i.   the company must be an unquoted trading company or the unquoted holding company of a trading group and the repurchase must be made wholly or mainly for the purpose of benefiting the trade of the company (or any of its 75% subsidiaries) and must not form part of a scheme or arrangement the main purpose (or one of the main purposes) of which is to enable the owner of the shares to participate in the profits of the company without receiving a dividend, or the avoidance of tax (s 219 TA 1988)

ii. the vendor of the shares must be both resident and ordinarily resident in the UK at the time the shares are purchased and must have owned them for five years. In addition, the vendor's shareholding must be substantially reduced by the purchase which is taken as at least a 25% reduction in the original shareholding (ss 220–221 TA 1988).

Advance clearance is possible under s 225 TA 1988 and contemporaneous application for clearance under s 707 TA 1988 is advisable.

The principal matter to be overcome if it is sought to fall within the exemptions of s 219 is to ensure that the transaction can be seen as benefiting the trade. In the case of the buy-out of a company which has not been successful and it is envisaged that new management/owners will improve the situation, the benefit would appear plain. However, the benefit to the trade is less obvious in the case of minority shareholders who are not directors (the repurchase must be considered for each outgoing shareholder individually although, if part of an arrangement for the repurchase of many individuals' shares, overall objectives would be relevant). To this end, the Revenue has issued some guidelines which outline certain types of situation which will normally be regarded as being of benefit to the trade.

However, it is now often beneficial for the vendors if s 219 does not apply. The section was a relieving provision when income tax was at up to 60% and capital gains tax was 30%. However, now that the rates are equal and capital gains are rebased to 31 March 1982, a dividend can be more attractive. Provided the company has ACT capacity, the deemed dividend route would produce an overall maximum tax rate of 20%.

In addition, if a capital loss can be generated and utilised under s 574 TA 1988, the tax rate can be reduced to nil or even negative. The rationale is as follows:

Firstly, clearance should be sought that s 219 does *not* apply. It may be possible to use the grounds that the choice of the repurchase is not for the benefit of the trade but simply for the personal benefit of the vendors. Alternatively, it may be necessary, for example, to transfer to a non-UK resident nominee (see s 220(1)). Clearance has the added virtue that if it were simply assumed that s 219 did not apply and ACT was paid over, this would be unlikely to be recoverable if it should be held that s 219 *did* apply.

After the shares have been repurchased, a claim is made under s 574 TA 1988 for the loss to be offset against income. A loss should result as, since the excess of the proceeds over nominal value is taxed as income, s 31 CGTA 1979 will apply such that the capital gains tax proceeds are limited to nominal value. A claim under s 96(5) FA 1988 for assets to be rebased to 31 March 1982 will be necessary. If this is a large value, a loss, augmented by indexation allowance, should result. Two further points are, firstly, it must be demonstrated that the condition of s 575(1)(a) TA 1988 is met and the disposal is by way of a bargain at arm's length for full consideration and, secondly, s 62 CGTA 1979 should not apply as, although there is a disposal by the vendors (who are connected with the company), there is no acquisition by the company but simply a cancellation of the shares.

If the above conditions can be met, the matter will reduce to agreeing a 31 March 1982 valuation with Shares Valuation Division. By way of example:

Example

Assume 10,000 ordinary £1 shares subscribed for, at par, in 1975 and repurchased at £50 each in June 1989. Market value of the shares at 5 April 1982 was £25 each.

Proceeds	£ 500,000
Less: Par value	(10,000)
Distribution	490,000
Associated tax credit (ACT paid by company)	163,333
Gross dividend	653,333
Section 574 claim (below)	(353,250)
Taxable income	£ 300,083
Tax at 40%	£ 120,033
Tax credit	(163,333)
Tax repayable	£ (43,300)
Total proceeds (£500,000 & £43,300)	£ 543,300
Effective tax rate	− 8.66%

Associated capital gain/loss

Proceeds		£ 500,000
Less: Taxed as income (above)		(490,000)
		10,000
Less: Market value at 5 April 1982	250,000	
Indexation allowance thereon (45.3%)	113,250	
		(363,250)
Capital loss claimed under s 574		£(353,250)

This contrasts with a capital gains tax only treatment (assuming an unused annual exemption):

Proceeds		500,000
Less: Market value at 5 April 1982	250,000	
Indexation allowance (as above)	113,250	
		(363,250)
		136,750
Annual exemption		(5,000)
Taxable gain		£ 131,750

Tax at 40%	£ 52,700
Effective tax rate	+ 10.54%

In this example, the difference in net cash available is £96,000.

The provisions of s 574 TA 1988 are considered in more detail below. However, the provisions of s 231(3A) TA 1988 (as inserted by s 106 FA 1989) must be examined carefully if the company is a close investment-holding company as defined (s 13A TA 1988). If it is, and there is more than one class of shares in the company, s 231(3A) could apply to deny a repayment of the tax credit. If the benefit of the distribution treatment simply reduces an overall charge to tax by offset of the tax credit, s 231(3A) should not apply.

ESOPs

An alternative to the repurchase by the company of its shares is for the company to establish an employee share ownership trust (commonly known as an ESOP) and for the ESOP to purchase the shares from the out-going management. Although s 67 FA 1989 has formalised the relief and charge to tax on a qualifying ESOP, non-qualifying ESOPs have been in existence for some time.

The perceived advantages of an ESOP are that relief may be obtained against profits of the company for payments made into the ESOP and that shares may be distributed to employees on a basis which provides incentive or, alternatively, on a basis of the directors' discretion. However, some of these benefits are more perceived than real.

Relief must be obtained for the payments. If the trust meets the conditions contained in paras 2–11 Sch 5 FA 1989 and s 67 FA 1989, it will be a qualifying ESOP and a deduction will be received. If the trust does not qualify under these conditions, assistance is required from case law to obtain a deduction (*Heather v P-E Consulting Group Ltd* (1972) 48 TC 293, *Jeffs v Ringtons Ltd* [1986] 1 All ER 144, [1985] STC 809, *E Bott Ltd v Price* [1987] STC 100). However, if the trust is not established with care, it is possible to fail to qualify for relief – see, for example, *Rutter v Charles Sharpe & Co Ltd* [1979] STC 711.

The cost to the company can be less than the share repurchase/ distribution route to provide the same after tax proceeds to the individuals. Consequently, the tax relief obtained by the company can be passed on to the individuals by way of a larger payment to the ESOP and, hence, a higher purchase price by the ESOP.

The payment to the ESOP will be out of profits and will, therefore, reduce the profits for the financial year as reported in the company's accounts. A share repurchase, although made out of distributable reserves, would be a balance sheet movement and would not reduce the current year profits as disclosed.

There are numerous safeguarding provisions contained in Sch 5 FA 1989 which are designed to protect the members of the ESOP. These, in particular, disqualify directors and those with a material interest in the company from being trustees and also restrict the discretion of the trustees in the basis of their distribution to members. A non-qualifying ESOP may be used to circumvent these restrictions but there is no guaranteed deductibility in respect of the payments by the company to the ESOP.

Overall, the benefits of ESOPs lie in the field of incentivisation for companies with large numbers of employees. Although, in a particular case, the ESOP might produce the right result, it is unlikely to be used frequently in buy-outs.

DEMERGERS

Where the managers are already shareholders, it may be possible to utilise the demerger provisions of ss 213–218 TA 1988 or a non-statutory liquidation demerger under the terms of s 110 Insolvency Act 1986 and using the provisions of s 267 TA 1970.

Although both methods can achieve the same end result, ie one or more parts of an original company being owned by different groups of shareholders, they are different in approach, complexity and claw-back provisions.

One of the main disadvantages of either method is the necessity to create the correct share structure immediately before the demerger. Since the basis of the demerger is that one group of shareholders obtains part of the company, leaving the other shareholders with the balance, the remaining shareholders will want to ensure they receive a fair value for the business disposed of. It may therefore be necessary to subscribe for additional share capital of Target or to issue shares to a Newco owned by the managers but leveraged by external borrowing.

Sections 213–218 TA 1988 were originally introduced in the Finance Act 1980 'for facilitating certain transactions whereby trading activities carried on by a single company or group are divided so as to be carried on by two or more companies not belonging to the same group or by two or more independent groups' (s 213(1) TA 1988). Generally, the relief is given by excluding for tax purposes as a distribution any 'exempt' distribution. Consequently, no ACT would be payable on the distribution and no income tax liability would arise on the recipients. There are two classes of distribution which can qualify as an exempt distribution:

i.   a distribution consisting of the transfer to all or any of its members by a company ('the distributing company') of shares in one or more companies which are its 75% subsidiaries, and

ii. a distribution consisting of the transfer by a company ('the distributing company') to one or more other companies of
    a. a trade or trades; or

b. shares in one or more companies which are its 75% subsidiaries,

and the issue of shares by the transferee company or companies to all or any of the members of the distributing company.

In addition, numerous conditions contained in ss 213(4)–(12) must be satisfied which, in summary, are:

i. each relevant company must be resident in the UK at the time of the distribution

ii. the distributing company must be either a trading company or a member of a trading group and each relevant subsidiary must be a 75% subsidiary

iii. after the distribution, the distributing company must be either a trading company or a member of a trading group and, where a trade or shares in one or more subsidiaries is distributed, shares are issued in a new company to the members of the distributing company, the only or main activity of the transferee company must be either the carrying on of the trade or the holding of the shares transferred to it

iv. where shares in a subsidiary are distributed, these shares must not be redeemable and must constitute the whole or substantially the whole of the ordinary share capital and voting rights of the subsidiary

v. where a trade is distributed, the distributing company must not retain more than a 'minor' interest in the trade

vi. the distribution must be made wholly or mainly for the purpose of benefiting some or all of the trading activities which were carried on by the former company or group and are now carried on by the new companies or groups

vii. the distribution must not form part of a scheme or arrangement, the main purpose or one of the main purposes of which is the avoidance of tax (including stamp duty). In addition, it must not be made with a view to the cessation of a trade, the sale of a trade or the acquisition of control of a relevant company by persons other than members of the distributing company.

There is an exemption to (3) above where the transfer relates to two or more 75% subsidiaries and the distributing company is then wound up without there being any remaining assets available for distribution.

Definitions of the above terms are contained in s 218 TA 1988.

Where the conditions are met, it being advisable to obtain advance clearance under s 215 TA 1988, the distribution will be an exempt distribution so that no ACT will be required to be paid over by the distributing company and there will be no income in the hands of the transferee members.

Where the distribution falls within (a) above, there will be no capital distribution for purposes of capital gains tax under s 72 CGTA 1979. In addition, the reorganisation provisions of ss 77–81 CGTA 1979 would apply to equate the new holding of shares with the old shares (para 9 Sch 18 FA 1980).

However, where the distribution falls within (b) above, there is no automatic capital gains tax exemption. Consequently, unless the demerger qualifies as a reconstruction within s 86 CGTA 1979, a capital gains tax charge will arise on the members.

Paragraph 10 Sch 18 FA 1980 provides exemption from s 278 and s 279 TA 1970 where a company leaves the group by reason of an exempt distribution. However, this is the only exemption available to the distributing company. Unless the conditions of s 267 TA 1970 can be met, corporation tax on capital gains will arise on the disposals made by the company of shares or trading assets.

In addition to the above, a charge to tax under s 214 TA 1988 can arise where a 'chargeable payment' is received by a member within five years of the exempt distribution. Unless excepted, a chargeable payment is any payment made by a company concerned in an exempt distribution in connection with the shares of that or any such company to a member of that, or any other, company concerned in the distribution, which is not made for bona fide commercial reasons or is made for the purposes of avoiding tax. Income distributions, exempt distributions or payments made to other group companies are excepted.

Where s 214 TA 1988 applies, the chargeable payment is assessable under Case VI of Schedule D, is not deductible for corporation tax purposes and, if not in money's worth, is subject to deduction of income tax at source.

It is clear from the above that this 'statutory' method of demerger poses significant problems and is unlikely to feature in many buy-outs.

However, a non-statutory demerger offers better possibilities. Although the administration is complicated and involves a liquidation, the taxation is more straightforward. This form of demerger is customarily referred to as a non-statutory demerger following the Inland Revenue Statement of Practice 5/85.

The steps to the demerger, in outline, are as follows:

i.   the demerger utilises a voluntary liquidation under s 110 Insolvency Act 1986. Consequently, the relevant trade, assets, etc must be transferred into the appropriate vehicle ('A' Ltd) if they are not already there. Thus, in a group of companies, where only one company or a sub-group is being sold, this would be at the 'bottom' of the group corporate tree. Where the whole group was being sold, the appropriate company is the ultimate holding company

ii. the share structure in A Ltd is reorganised. Essentially, the idea is for each group of shareholders to hold separate classes of shares where the relevant separate parts of the undertaking are allocated to the different classes. Depending on the circumstances, the separate parts of the undertaking can be separate trades or separate holdings of shares in subsidiaries.

It will inevitably be the case that the value of the existing shares of each group of shareholders will not match the respective parts of the undertaking to which they are allocated. Consequently, the existing share structure before reorganisation may need to be amended by further share subscriptions and/or share repurchases

iii. the separate groups of shareholders of A Ltd – for this example groups B and C – form B Ltd and C Ltd under their own control in the proportions agreed between them

iv. the members of A Ltd pass a resolution to enter voluntary liquidation

v. the liquidator transfers to B Ltd the undertaking or assets allocated to it and B Ltd issues the consideration shares directly to the B shareholders. The same procedure is followed in respect of the C group and C Ltd

vi. A Ltd is wound up.

The end result is that groups B and C now only have shares in companies B Ltd and C Ltd respectively, these companies owning the appropriate parts of the original undertaking.

The distributions by the liquidator are not distributions for tax purposes by virtue of the exclusion in s 209(1) TA 1988 relating to distributions made on a winding-up. Provided the provisions of s 267 TA 1970 are complied with, given the relaxation provided by SP 5/85, no chargeable gain will arise on the transfer of trades. However, s 278 must be considered if any of the assets of A Ltd are shares in subsidiaries. On the transfer of those assets under v. above a charge could arise.

The reconstruction provisions of s 86 CGTA 1979 will apply and no capital gain will arise to the members of A Ltd.

Unless one of the groups of A Ltd shareholders owns 75% or more of that company, s 343 TA 1988 will not apply to the transfer. Relief from any balancing charges on assets qualifying for capital allowances can be sought through a claim under para 13 Sch 8 FA 1971 provided the transfer takes place between connected persons within the meaning of para 13(3) Sch 8 FA 1971 and s 839 TA 1988.

FINANCE

Interest payments by Newco

Assuming Newco remains a holding company and Target remains the trading company, Newco must obtain sufficient funds to service the interest on and repay the capital element of its borrowings.

As apportionment has been abolished by the Finance Act 1989, the simplest method is simply to pay up dividends under a group income election.

Alternatively, a straightforward method of funding the interest payments, provided that Target has sufficient taxable profits, is for the excess charges of Newco to be surrendered to Target by way of group relief under ss 402–412 TA 1988 and for Target to pay for the losses surrendered pound for pound. By virtue of s 402(6) TA 1988, such a payment is not taken into account in computing profits or losses of either company for corporation tax purposes to the extent that the payment does not exceed the gross value of the losses surrendered.

As Newco is not trading, it must meet the definition of an investment company under s 130 TA 1988 in order to obtain relief for its expenses of management under s 75 TA 1988 and its charges on income under s 338 TA 1988.

If Target has insufficient taxable profits to utilise the tax relief on Newco's interest payments, the surplus will be carried forward in Newco as excess management charges and can be set off against future income of Newco. However, it should be noted that no account is taken of such brought forward charges in determining current year excess charges available for surrender by way of group relief which is at variance with the treatment of trading losses brought forward under s 393(1) TA 1988 in a trading company.

By way of example, if Newco has income of £50,000, excess charges brought forward of £60,000 and interest paid of £40,000, no group relief surrender is possible as the interest paid does not exceed the income and there are no excess charges, as defined (s 403(4) TA 1988). The assessment is £nil and £10,000 of the brought forward excess is utilised, after relieving the charges, reducing the carry forward to £50,000. If Newco had been a trading company, the excess charges would have become s 393(1) TA 1988 losses brought forward and would have been set off against the income of £50,000. The charges paid would be excess and would be available for surrender by way of group relief.

Should Newco commence to trade (for instance by acquiring the trade of Target – see below), any excess management charges unutilised would be lost.

Other alternative methods of funding are management charges and loans although, assuming Newco is not trading, s 770 TA 1988 effectively limits the profits which may be paid up to an arm's length profit on provision by Newco of the services on which the management fees are paid.

A problem theoretically arises in respect of loans in the form of s 419 TA 1988. The Revenue has argued that where part or all of the sale consideration paid to the vendors is loaned to Newco by Target, s 419(5) TA 1988 applies to treat the loan as if it were a loan to a participator. Consequently, a sum equivalent to ACT on a dividend of an amount equal to the loan must be deposited with the Revenue.

It must be remembered that this is not 'real' ACT and cannot be utilised against corporation tax liabilities but it is assumed that s 419(4) TA 1988 would apply when the loan is repaid to allow the ACT equivalent to be repaid to the company.

The 1982 representations by the CCAB on anomalies in the UK tax system raised the question of whether this interpretation (of then s 286(7) TA 1970) was one generally to be taken by the Revenue. No satisfactory response was given although, in specific cases, it is known that the Revenue has been persuaded to confirm that it would not take the point. However, it must not be assumed that this will be the case and, if possible, such loans should be avoided.

A loan by Target to Newco to fund its bank interest payments should not fall within the above provisions as only participators who are individuals are considered for purposes of s 419 TA 1988.

It must always be borne in mind that such intra-group loans could be prohibited as financial assistance under s 151 CA 1985 unless Newco is a private company and the procedures of s 155 CA 1985 are followed. This is covered in more detail in Chapter 5.

Deep discount securities

Securities defined under the provisions of Sch 4 TA 1988 as deep discount securities can offer certain tax advantages. Essentially, a deep discount security means any redeemable security issued by a company where the issue price is less than the amount payable on redemption and the discount is:

i. more than 15% of the amount payable on redemption, or
ii. less than 15% but more than ½% of the redemption price for each complete year between the issue date and the redemption date.

The general rules are that the lender is taxed only on the redemption or sale of the security but the borrower can obtain relief for the discount as it accrues. It is normally suggested, therefore, that financing by deep discount securities is advantageous to a company where cash is limited. This is certainly so but, of course, the lender receives nothing from his investment until redemption other than any coupon which is likely to be nominal. Consequently, the borrower would require the level of discount to be such as to reflect the time value of the interest or dividends foregone through this financing method. In net present value terms, the positions of both lender and borrower are likely to be similar to their positions with more traditional financing methods.

If this route is considered attractive, certain conditions in Sch 4 TA 1988 must be met in order that the 'income element' of the discount is available for relief as a charge on income to the borrower. The income element is that part of the discount which is allocated to each income period, such period being the period for which any actual interest is payable or, if there is no interest, annual periods from the date of issue.

The main rules are contained in para 5(4) Sch 4 TA 1988 which specifies that one of the following conditions in respect of the company must be satisfied:

i. it must exist wholly or mainly for the purpose of carrying on a trade, or
ii. the deep discount security must have been issued wholly and

exclusively to raise money for purposes of a trade carried on by the company, or

iii. it must be an investment company.

In addition, the discount must be borne by the company and must not otherwise be deductible for corporation tax purposes (para 5(3)), the lender must not be a participator in the company, an associate of a participator, or a company under control of a participator (para 10(1)), must not be an associated company (within the meaning of s 416 TA 1988) or a member of the same group of companies (para 9(1)) and there must be no scheme or arrangements made such that the sole or main benefit of issuing the securities is the obtaining of a reduction in tax liability by relief for an income element (para 5(6)).

By way of example, assume the following:

Example

Issue price £50,000 with redemption in five years time at par of £100,000. Annual coupon rate is 0.125% on the par.

The calculated yield to maturity is 15.06% and the income elements are as follows:

Year 1	7,531.53
2	8,647.17
3	9,930.87
4	11,407.94
5	13,107.49
	£50,000.00

Relief to the borrower for a charge on income will comprise the above income elements plus £125 actual interest paid in each year. Assuming the lender holds the security to redemption, he will be taxed under Case III of Schedule D only on the actual interest of £125 per annum in years 1–4 and £50,125 in year 5.

If the security is disposed of before redemption, the total of all the income elements from the date of acquisition to disposal, including the appropriate proportion in any short period ending with the disposal date, will be chargeable under Schedule D Case III.

With effect from 14 March 1989, s 139(2) FA 1989 removes from the definition of a qualifying corporate bond the requirement that, from the time of its issue, the bond has been quoted on the UK Stock Exchange or dealt in on the Unlisted Securities Market, or was issued by a UK company or other body with shares or securities quoted on the UK Stock Exchange or dealt in on the Unlisted Securities Market. Consequently, non intra-group deep discount securities are likely to be qualifying corporate bonds under s 64 FA 1984 and will be exempt from capital gains tax and corporation tax on capital gains.

Convertible preference shares

As discussed in Chapter 3 this type of share is often used in buy-outs since one of the characteristics of preference shares is that they carry a dividend which is not taxable in the hands of a UK resident company as it is franked investment income. This is not necessarily as advantageous as might be expected because the paying company receives no deduction for the dividend payments, unlike interest, and the dividend rate will, therefore, reflect this. In addition, the requirement of the paying company to account for ACT will cause it some cash flow disadvantage. Often, the shares are convertible into ordinary shares for purposes of the 'ratchet' if the company's performance does not meet a pre-defined target. The conversion will be covered by the reorganisation provisions of ss 78–81 CGTA 1979 and no tax charge will arise at that time.

Notwithstanding that all share capital is now redeemable, preference shares are often explicitly redeemable. Any premium payable on the redemption will constitute a distribution by virtue of s 209 (2)(b) TA 1988 and the paying company must account for ACT.

Corporate bonds

A bond is a certificate of the intention to pay the holder a specified sum on a specified date and, generally, means loan stock or debenture stock.

The only tax matter for the borrower is to comply with the provisions of s 349 TA 1988 to deduct income tax at source and to obtain a deduction for the interest.

If the bonds are 'qualifying' bonds by virtue of s 64 FA 1984, they will be exempt from capital gains tax. Section 139 FA 1989 has removed the quoted requirements and, consequently, most non intra-group loan and debenture stock will be exempt from capital gains tax – which may or may not be advantageous to the lender. If, because of the particular circumstances of the lender, it is considered that capital gains tax treatment is favourable, the bonds should be issued so as to fail to meet one of the conditions contained in s 64(2)(b)–(c) FA 1984 ie not represent a normal commercial loan or be expressed in a currency other than sterling. The accrued income scheme rules of s 713 TA 1988 et seq would apply if the bonds were traded before redemption.

Just as preference shares can be issued on terms that they are convertible into ordinary shares, so can corporate bonds be convertible. Special rules contained in Sch 13 FA 1984 replace ss 78–81 CGTA 1979 in these circumstances. Essentially, this results in a step-up (or down) in the capital gains tax basis in the ordinary shares to the market value of the bonds at the date of conversion.

Business expansion scheme

As has been indicated, relief under this scheme is not available to the management team because, as employees of the company, they are connected with it by virtue of s 291(2) TA 1988 and fail to qualify under s 291(1) TA 1988.

Relief will be available, however, to other qualifying individuals ie external individual investors provided the company meets all the other necessary conditions. Individuals would not, except for the smallest buy-outs, provide sufficient funds for the buy-out given the annual maximum amount of £40,000 available for relief. Consequently, the team could look to a BES fund as a source of finance. This route could be attractive to the team as, given the clawback provisions of s 300 TA 1988, it is unlikely that any of the investment would be required to be repaid for at least five years. However, since 15 March 1988, the maximum investment available for relief in a company is £500,000 per annum unless the company undertakes certain specific activities. Consequently, this form of finance is likely to be of limited use.

TRANSFER OF TARGET'S TRADE TO NEWCO

Although the problems which could arise to a close investment company in attempting to finance the repayment of its debt have been substantially removed by the repeal of apportionment, there are other disadvantages of a structure comprising a close non-trading holding company with one or more trading subsidiaries. Often, therefore, the trade, assets and liabilities of Target are transferred to Newco – the so-called 'hive-up' – and Newco then becomes a trading company.

The transfer of Target's assets and liabilities would generally be made at net book value and the consideration would be held on interest-free loan account. There would be no requirement for the transfer to be made at market value (if this was different from net book value) since s 273 TA 1970 would apply to treat the transfer as producing no gain/no loss for capital gains tax purposes.

Target's tax losses and written down values for capital allowances purposes would be transferred automatically to Newco under s 343 TA 1988. If there should be a major change in the nature of the trade carried on firstly by Target and now by Newco within three years of the date of the buy-out, s 768 TA 1988 would apply and any trading losses transferred to Newco would be lost. If it appears that such a major change is possible, consideration should be given for Target to disclaim capital allowances in earlier periods so as to convert carried forward losses into higher tax written down values for capital allowances purposes.

Similar provisions as s 768 TA 1988 also apply under s 245 TA 1988 to any surplus ACT of Target.

After the transfer, the only asset of Target will be the amount due from Newco. If Target should be liquidated, a capital gain could arise in Newco's hands if the purchase price of the shares in Target reflected a discount on asset values or if the transfer was undertaken some time after the buy-out and Target had grown in value. However, provided Target has distributable reserves, the capital gain can be easily eliminated by the payment of a dividend without ACT providing the group income election has been validly made.

As noted above, any unrelieved interest charges carried forward in Newco will be lost when it changes its status from investment company to trading company. In addition, any future excess charges arising from interest payments could not, technically, be carried forward as they would not have been incurred for purposes of the trade but to acquire Target (s 393(9) TA 1988). However, the Revenue has confirmed that interest on a loan to acquire Target's shares can be regarded as incurred for purposes of the trade where the trade is transferred to Newco before any interest payment is made.

Reducing the number of companies in a group should, generally, be beneficial with respect to the small companies rate of corporation tax. However, given sufficient flexibility to fragment profits between companies, the very nature of the anti-fragmentation provisions ensures the total tax bill of a wholly UK group of companies can be the same regardless of the number of companies. Where such fragmentation is not possible, or where there are overseas companies in the group, there can be a permanent annual increase in the total tax bill of the group by having additional companies in the group.

It should also be noted that a company is associated for purposes of the reduction in the small companies rate thresholds if it is so associated at any time during the relevant accounting period. Dormant companies are not counted although if a company is simply in receipt of interest or group income, it is considered by the Revenue to be active. It is also understood that the Revenue will not count as an associated company any institution which is not itself close and which controls Newco through a holding of fixed rate preference shares provided it holds the shares in the ordinary course of its business and is not involved in the management of the company's business.

Schedule 30 TA 1988 applies to phase in the reduction of long payment dates for corporation tax to a standard nine months. A transfer of Target's trade would automatically lead to a nine month payment period for Newco.

There are certain other types of loss relief etc which cannot be transferred to Newco including surplus ACT, Schedule A and D Case VI losses.

TAX RELIEF FOR MANAGERS

Interest paid on loans

It is inevitably the case that the managers will have had to raise a reasonable amount of cash to inject as equity into Newco if only to evidence their commitment to the institutional investors. It is also likely that the managers will not have been able to subscribe for their share of Newco's equity directly from their own resources and will have borrowed the necessary money. Interest paid on overdrafts is never deductible for income tax purposes and relief for loan interest paid will depend on satisfying the conditions of s 360 TA 1988 (Loan to buy an interest in a close company) or s 361 TA 1988 (Loan to buy an interest in an employee-controlled company).

(i) *Close company*
    The following conditions laid down by s 360 TA 1988 must be met:

The loan must have been applied to acquire ordinary share capital in a close company complying with s 13A(2) TA 1988, no capital has been recovered from the company other than any reducing the eligible loan by virtue of s 363(1) TA 1988 and, when the interest is paid, the company continues to comply with s 13A(2) and either the individual has a "material interest" in the company or works for the greater part of his time in the actual management or conduct of the company.

A material interest is defined in s 360A TA 1988 and essentially means beneficial ownership, directly or indirectly, of 5% or more of the ordinary share capital or entitlement to more than 5% of assets on a winding up. Holdings through associates or trusts are considered but not an interest of the trustees of an approved profit sharing scheme where the shares have not been appropriated to the individual nor, interests through trustees of employee benefit trusts in certain circumstances.

A company ('the relevant company') complies with s 13A(2) TA 1988 in any accounting period if throughout that period it exists wholly or mainly for one or more of the following purposes:

(a) the purpose of carrying on a trade on a commercial basis or for the purpose of such a trade carried on by one or more qualifying companies or by a company which controls the relevant company,
(b) the purpose of making investments in property provided the property is not let to persons connected with the relevant company,
(c) the holding of shares or securities in, or making loans to, one or more qualifying companies,
(d) the purpose of co-ordinating the administration of two or more qualifying companies, and
(e) the purpose of making, by one or more qualifying companies or by a company which has control of the relevant company, of investments as defined in (b) above.

A 'qualifying company' is a company under the control of or controlling the relevant company and which exists wholly or mainly for either or both of the purposes in (a) or (b) above. 'Control' has the meaning ascribed by s 416 TA 1988.

A person (or two or more persons together) controls a company if he exercises, or is able to exercise or is entitled to acquire, direct or indirect control over the company's affairs and, in particular, if he possesses or is entitled to acquire:

(a) the majority of the share capital (issued or not) or voting power in the company; or
(b) such part of the issued share capital as would, if the whole of the company's income was distributed among participators, entitle him to receive the majority of the amount distributed; or
(c) such rights on a winding up of the company to receive the majority of the assets available for distribution among the participators.

For purposes of this definition, a person is treated as entitled to acquire anything which he is entitled to acquire at a future date, or will at a future date be entitled to acquire.

The requirement to work in the actual management or conduct of the company is interpreted narrowly by the Revenue and, although directors would certainly fall within the interpretation, employees will do so only if they are properly involved in the running of the business.

Section 360 does not stipulate that the company must continue to be close at the time the interest is paid, only that it was close at the time of acquisition of the shares as confirmed by Statement of Practice SP 3/78.

The definition of a qualifying company is now linked with s 13A(2) which defines companies which are not to be treated as close investment holding companies. However, the s 13A(2) definition has the requirement of compliance throughout an accounting period. Consequently, if the managers invest in Newco, an off-the-shelf company, obtain external finance and then acquire the trade of Newco or shares therein, Newco cannot comply with s 13A(2) from the date of incorporation until the end of its first accounting period and relief is not available. Although it is believed this is an unintended result of the drafting, a further step is require until clarification is forthcoming from the Revenue.

Newco can comply with (a)–(e) above as soon as the intention to carry on those activities is formed ie by appropriate amendment of the Memorandum and Articles of Association. However, the commencement of an accounting period is required before the principal investment in Newco is made so that compliance throughout the accounting period is possible.

This could be done by opening a bank deposit account with a small amount of funds on initial subscription creating a source of income so that s 12(2)(a) TA 1988 would apply. The main subscription can then take place but relief would be denied in respect of the initial subscription.

(ii) *Employee-controlled company*
Interest is eligible for relief if it is interest on a loan obtained to

acquire any part of the ordinary share capital of an employee-controlled company and the following conditions are satisfied:

(a) the company must, throughout the period from acquisition of the shares to the date on which the interest is paid, be unquoted, UK resident and a trading company or the holding company of a trading group,

(b) the shares must have been acquired within 12 months of the date on which the company first became employee-controlled,

(c) in the year of assessment in which the interest is paid, the company must have either become employee-controlled or be so controlled for a period of at least 9 months,

(d) the person paying the interest or his spouse must be a full-time employee from the date on which the loan proceeds are applied to the date on which the interest is paid or to within 12 months before the interest is paid.

A company is employee controlled when more than 50% of both the issued ordinary share capital and the voting power in the company is beneficially owned by persons (or their spouses) who are full-time employees of the company.

There is no provision for continued relief for interest paid in a period longer than 12 months after the company ceases to be employee-controlled, something which may be completely outside any employee's control. Consequently, although there may be significant reasons why the company should wish to avoid being close, it is generally better for the manager to qualify for interest relief under the provisions of s 360 rather than s 361.

Losses on shares

Clearly one of the main objectives of a buy-out is for the managers to obtain the possibility of increasing the value of their shares in Newco by dint of their efforts. However, not all buy-outs are successful in this respect and losses can be made.

As has been detailed above, if the conditions of s 576 TA 1988 are met, an individual may claim under s 574 TA 1988 that a capital loss on shares in an unquoted trading company (or the holding company of a trading group) be deducted against income. Certain companies are excluded if their trade consists of dealing in shares, land, commodity futures, etc. As has also been noted, s 574 relief can be used in circumstances where the only capital loss is that arising from indexation.

Termination payments

Where director shareholders are selling their shares to the new management and retiring from the business, the opportunity to make termination payments arises.

Where it can be clearly demonstrated that such payments are gratuitous and not in respect of past services, the first £30,000 should be free of tax by virtue of s 188 TA 1988. However, it is likely that the paying company will receive no relief for the payment as it will be considered capital, forming part of the arrangements for the sale of the company or its trade – see *Snook (James) & Co Ltd v Blasdale* (1952) 33 TC 244.

A further point of caution is in respect of clearance applications under s 225 TA 1988 in respect of share repurchases. It is the Revenue's practice to enquire as to all payments made or to be made to persons whose shares are to be repurchased. Clearance may only be given if termination payments are treated as part of the repurchase consideration. Thus, whether clearance is given that s 219 TA 1988 does apply so that the termination payments are treated as capital gains tax disposal proceeds or, if clearance is given that s 219 TA 1988 does not apply so that the termination payments are treated as distributions, they will not be termination payments to which s 188 TA 1988 will apply and no relief will be given to the recipient.

OTHER TAX CONSIDERATIONS

Planning for post buy-out gains

Ultimately, the managers will wish to divest themselves of some or all of their shares in Newco when the opportunity to do so at a gain presents itself. Whether this occurs on a flotation of the company's shares onto the market or by way of a trade sale or a further buy-out, the result will generally be the same – a capital gains tax disposal.

If it is simply the case that a small number of shareholders wish to 'cash in' on the value of their shares, particularly if they are leaving the employment of the company, it would be better for them to persuade the company to arrange to repurchase their shares. As mentioned above, this can result in a significantly lower tax burden on the individuals if the repurchase is treated as a distribution. However, the professional costs of the exercise must be considered as it might prove uneconomical for the company, particularly if the repurchase is small, without a contribution by the outgoing shareholders.

The most effective tax planning is always that which is put in place in anticipation of an event rather than after it has occurred. The majority of tax planning in this area is with the use of trusts and the greatest advantages arise where these are created before, or contemporaneously with, the buy-out. Even greater advantages are available to non-UK domiciled individuals but this discussion will be limited to the majority of the management team who are likely to be UK resident, ordinarily resident and domiciled.

It must be determined what advantage is sought – is it to transfer the benefit of the shares to others in a tax efficient manner or is it the avoidance of taxation, if possible, which would otherwise fall on the individual? The general purpose of establishing a trust is, of course, not to save tax: it is to provide a means for the transfer of property from one person for the benefit of others. Since a trust is considered a separate entity under UK law from the settlor, trustees and beneficiaries, the legal transfer of property is fairly straightforward. However, simply because of this separation, much anti-avoidance legislation has arisen to counter what could be simple avoidance devices.

Consequently, there are no particular income tax saving features of trusts whether UK resident or not, assuming the income is UK source ie dividend income from Newco:

i.   if the settlor retains an interest in the trust, all trust income not distributed to other beneficiaries is treated as his own and taxed accordingly

ii. if the settlor does not retain an interest but the beneficiaries include his unmarried minor child, the child's income from the trust is treated as the settlor's

iii. if the settlor does not retain an interest, the income will not be treated as his and the liability will fall on the trustees and ultimately the beneficiaries. There may then be a saving of tax if the beneficiaries' marginal tax rate is less than the settlor's and this will therefore be a more efficient means of passing the income to the beneficiary rather than the settlor receiving it and gifting it.

The main advantage of creating the trust at the time of the buy-out is, effectively, to pass the future potential gains to the beneficiaries at a time when they are nil so that there can be no capital gains tax or inheritance tax on the disposal by the settlor to the trustees.

A capital gains tax advantage can arise where the settlor does not retain an interest in the trust. In this case, the trustees will be liable to capital gains tax at their marginal rate (25% or 35%). Assuming these net gains are distributed to the beneficiaries immediately as cash, no further gains will arise and the beneficiaries may have the benefit of a lower marginal tax rate ie from 40% to 25% or 35%.

There is a potential and more substantial advantage, however, in establishing a non-UK resident trust ie where the majority of trustees is not resident or ordinarily resident in the UK. As a non-resident, the trust is not liable to capital gains tax (assuming it does not carry on a trade in the UK through a branch or agency). However, by virtue of s 80 FA 1981, the capital gains of the trust will be treated as chargeable gains assessable on the beneficiaries to the extent that they receive a capital payment which can be attributed to the gain. A capital payment is any payment not chargeable to income tax on the beneficiary.

Consequently, if the shares in Newco are held by an overseas trust, the gains will only be subject to capital gains tax if they are distributed. This leads to two main benefits. Firstly, the proceeds are retained in the trust gross and may be invested or utilised gross (subject to any caution the trustees may have in speculating with potential tax payments) including on the UK stock market, thus realising further capital gains. Secondly, there is the possibility of avoiding tax completely on these gains. If a beneficiary is not resident and not ordinarily resident in the UK at the time he receives the capital payment, he will not be subject to capital gains tax. Two matters arise from this. Firstly, if he is to be neither resident nor ordinarily resident, his foreign residence position must be determined and exposure to foreign tax determined. Secondly, there is always the risk of legislation to counter this route. The Revenue Consultative Document on Residence indicated its intention to propose legislation that would require a considerable physical absence from the UK for the route to be successful. No actual legislation has been enacted but the possibility remains.

It must be remembered, however, that interest relief will be lost on any borrowings taken out to acquire shares which are then disposed of to a trust. This loss of interest relief must be weighed against any potential capital gains tax advantages before a decision is made to proceed.

VAT

VAT planning, particularly in respect of groups, is not within the scope of this book. However, a number of matters warrant mention.

Where the buy-out is effected by the purchase of shares of Target, there will be no transfer of the trade as a going concern. However, a sale of shares is an exempt supply of services where the purchaser belongs in the EEC. Consequently, input VAT attributable to the sale of shares would be irrecoverable. The input VAT at risk will principally relate to professional fees which will be in respect of all services provided to the company on the buy-out. Customs & Excise accept, however, that only services relating to a share disposal provided after the decision was taken by the directors to sell will be subject to a disallowance as attributable to an exempt supply. It is understood that the time of the decision is that of the passing of the appropriate formal resolution to sell the shares at a Board meeting and not, simply, the time when the directors resolve to proceed with the disposal of the company by way of a sale of shares. Consequently, the amount of input VAT on legal and professional services which must be attributed to the sale of shares itself other than on all other aspects of the buy-out can be very small. However, it is advisable to obtain separate VAT invoices from the professionals for the respective parts of their services.

Recently Customs & Excise have been taking a hard-line approach in respect of the recoverability of input tax by holding companies in respect of costs on acquisitions. A distinction was sought to be drawn between the active management of its investments and the passive holding of the investments. Customs' view was that the latter did not relate to the making of any taxable supply and, accordingly, attributable input VAT would be disallowed. However, following discussions with the European Commission and other Member States, Customs has accepted that this approach was too narrow. Consequently, input VAT in relation to acquisitions will be deductible in the normal fashion. Thus, where it is not possible directly to attribute the input VAT to taxable or exempt supplies, it will be considered as related to a general overhead and be recovered according to the taxable or partially exempt status of the company.

Where the business of Target is acquired then, provided the relevant conditions of Article 12 VAT (Special Provisions) Order 1981 are met, no VAT will be chargeable on the transfer of the business as a going concern. Generally, this will pose no particular problems; however it should be noted that if VAT is erroneously charged on such a transfer, it will not be recoverable by the purchaser. Also, by virtue of s 29(A) VATA 1983, if the acquiring company is, or becomes within the tax year, a member of an exempt or partially exempt VAT group, the transfer of assets will be treated as a supply by and to the company at market value and any associated disallowed input tax will be collectable from it. It should be noted, however, that assets acquired by the transferor more than three years before the transfer are ignored for the purposes of s 29(A) as also is any goodwill.

One potential anomaly relates to land and buildings forming part of the business assets transferred as a going concern. If this property was subject to an option to tax by virtue of an election under para 2 Sch 6A VATA 1983 (as inserted by Sch 3 FA 1989), it would appear that no VAT is chargeable on the supply but the requirement to standard rate supplies out of that property lapses but may be revived by an election by the new owner. It is known, however, that Customs & Excise intend to introduce anti-avoidance provisions in relation to groups and it must be viewed as likely that this anomaly will be rectified.

CHAPTER 5

The legal aspects

INTRODUCTION

For the lawyers involved in them, buy-outs can be amongst the most complex transactions. The component parts of a typical buy-out, the acquisition of shares or assets, the raising of debt and equity finance, the creation of management and control mechanisms in the target company, the incentivisation of managers and employees, are familiar to company lawyers. It is the simultaneous fusion of these parts, usually under great pressure, which is the major complicating factor. Moreover, buy-outs have their own legal problems, such as conflict of interest, duties of confidentiality and disclosure and the provision and timing of financial assistance to secure debt finance. Against this legal back drop will be acted out a drama with a large cast of characters, some of whom will not be reading from the same script. The lawyers will have to possess not only acute legal skills but the ability to handle multi dimensional transactional and emotive issues.

The characteristics of a transaction, whether it is a management buy-out of a private company, the privatisation of a listed company, or a leveraged buy-out, will set the legal scene for the lawyers involved. They will have to analyse the particular features of the transaction and, if they are acting for the buy-out team, rehearse them together.

The distinctions between various types of transaction have no impact on the legal analysis of a buy-out and will therefore be ignored for the purposes of this chapter.

Although the buy-out of a public or quoted company shares many of the characteristics of a buy-out of a private company, public and quoted company buy-outs present their own particular problems. They will therefore be treated separately.

One other category of transaction requires comment. This is the management buy-in, whose distinguishing feature is that the management team is on the outside trying to buy in rather than on the inside attempting to buy out. In the legal analysis, the buy-in differs little from the classic private company acquisition or take-over bid for a quoted company.

It is in the area of disclosure of information and confidentiality that particular problems arise for the public company buy-out or buy-in team. These problems will be highlighted.

THE LEGAL POSITION OF THE MEMBERS OF THE BUY-OUT TEAM

Conflict of interest and fiduciary duties

Before making or entertaining any approach to or from a third party regarding a possible buy-out, each proposed member of the buy-out team must analyse his legal position in relation to the companies of which he is a director or employee and their shareholders. This analysis must be carried out as the first stage to forestall allegations of breach of statutory duty, unfair prejudice and breach of contract.

The buy-out team must carefully consider:

i.   directors' and employees' fiduciary duties
ii.   service agreements and any other contractual arrangements between the individual and the companies concerned, including restrictive covenants and inducement of breach of contract
iii. common law duty of confidentiality
iv.   statutory constraints and obligations
v.   regulatory constraints and obligations imposed by the rules of The Stock Exchange and the City Code on Take-overs and Mergers.

Fiduciary duties

In the United States, leveraged buy-outs of listed companies are commonplace. Despite their frequency, the fairness of the buy-out for the public shareholders has attracted much criticism, focused on the separation of the fiduciary duties of the members of the buy-out team to selling shareholders from their position as buyers. Because the management team has access to inside information, it has the ability to affect the share price of the target company and consequently its valuation. The director members of the buy-out team and their colleagues must therefore be mindful of their obligations, if the target company or its parent is quoted, to avoid the creation of a false market in its shares.

The resultant opportunity for manipulation has created a fundamental concern that the management team may be benefiting from an opportunity which properly belongs to the company and its shareholders. These concerns about conflicting interests, inside advantages and misappropriation of corporate opportunities impose a much higher standard of fiduciary duty than will be required in an arm's-length transaction.

The doctrine of shareholder protection, both as regards fiduciary duties owed and the misappropriation of corporate opportunity, does not deal satisfactorily with the issues. The established rules in the United Kingdom are that directors only owe a fiduciary duty to the company (*Percival v Wright* [1902] 2 Ch 421; *Bell v Lever Bros Ltd* [1932] AC 161, 228 (HL); *Pergamon Press Ltd v Maxwell* [1970] 2 All ER 809, [1970] 1 WLR 1167) and that the primary fiduciary duty is to act honestly and in good faith in the exercise of their powers (*Re Smith*

& Fawcett Ltd [1942] Ch 304; *Gething v Kilner* [1972] 1 WLR 337). Directorial powers are to be exercised by directors bona fide in the best interest of the company, as they determine (*Re Smith & Fawcett Ltd*).

Section 309(1) Companies Act 1985 added a statutory duty which requires the directors to have regard to the interest of the company's employees in the performance of their functions. Sub-section (2) makes it clear that this duty is owed by the directors to the company alone and is enforceable in the same way as any other fiduciary duty owed to the company by its directors. There is scope for conflict if the management buy-out team consists of employees but it is considered unlikely that the obligation is enforceable, even by an employee who is also a shareholder.

Despite the provisions of section 309 and apart from the exceptional circumstances of a liquidation, the accepted view is that the criterion for measuring the standard by which directors should exercise their fiduciary duties is 'the interests of the company as a commercial entity, to be judged in most cases by a reference to the interests of present and future shareholders alone' (*Gore-Brown on Companies*)

In *Dawson International plc v Coates Patons plc* [1989] BCLC 233, ((1988) Times, 25 March), Lord Cullen said that whereas 'it was well recognised that the directors owed fiduciary duties to the company, [there was] no good reason why it should be supposed that the directors were, in general, under a fiduciary duty to shareholders and in particular current shareholders with respect to disposal of their shares'.

If the buy-out team member is a director only of the target company and not of its parent company, the conflict between the fiduciary duties of a director on the one hand and proposed purchaser of shares in the company on the other hand will be easily resolvable if the initiative for the buy-out comes from the parent company. If the initiative comes from management and is accepted by the parent, the economic and commercial advantages of the buy-out for the company and its existing shareholders must be capable of clear demonstration to the parent.

The issue of conflict of interest was addressed in the case of *Re Posgate & Denby (Agencies) Ltd* [1987] BCLC 8. Hoffmann J heard a motion in a petition under section 459 Companies Act 1985 for an injunction to restrain a company and its directors from disposing of a substantial part of its business until the transaction had been approved by the holders of a majority of a class of shares which, according to the articles of association of the company, carried no right to vote on such an issue.

In the absence of outside offers for various businesses which the directors had put on the market as going concerns, the directors proposed a series of management buy-outs. These buy-outs gave rise to a conflict of interest since eight out of the eleven members of the board of the vendor company were interested or proposed to acquire interests in one or other of the purchasing companies. The directors of the vendor company, however, complied fully with the provisions of the articles of association of the company dealing with conflicts of interest and section

320 Companies Act 1985 under which shareholder approval is required for the disposal of non-cash assets to directors.

In his judgment, Hoffmann J referred to the dictum of Lord Wilberforce in *Ebrahimi v Westbourne Galleries Ltd* [1973] AC 360, [1972] 2 All ER 492 that in most cases the basis of the association among members of the company would be adequately and exhaustedly laid down in the articles of association and that therefore the 'superimposition of equitable considerations' requires something more. Hoffmann J said that, in his judgment, it is equally necessary for a shareholder who claims that it is 'unfair' within the meaning of section 459 for the board to exercise powers conferred by the articles to demonstrate some special circumstances which create a legitimate exception that the board would not do so. It was plain from the articles that the holders of the equity shares had no right to prevent the directors from exercising the power of the company to sell its assets. In the absence of breach of fiduciary duty, which was not alleged in the case, it was decided that there was no arguable basis for establishing that the petitioner would be unfairly prejudiced.

From the decisions in *County Pallatine Loan and Discount Co, Cartmell's* (1874) 9 Ch App 691 (directors should apply an objective test to determine what is in the best interests of a company), *Hirsche v Simms* [1894] AC 654 (directors are not guilty of breach of trust merely because in promoting the interest of the company they were also promoting their own interests), and *Bell v Lever Bros* [1932] AC 161 and *Pergamon Press Limited v Maxwell* [1970] 1 WLR 1167 (fiduciary duties are not owed by directors to other companies or bodies corporate, such as holding companies), it is clear that directors are under no legal incapacity when they are on both sides of a bargaining table in a management buy-out provided that they observe due process.

The issue becomes more acute in the context of a hostile management-led buy-out of a listed company where there are competing offers. If the buy-out team is offering a significant premium over the price offered by a third party, the shareholders may question whether the management is privy to information which should be available to shareholders generally. If the premium is small or non-existent, the same question arises.

In these circumstances, the role of independent and non-executive directors on the board of the target company and the advisers to those directors will be paramount. The Panel on Take-overs and Mergers has recognised this by adopting, in December 1989, a new note to rule 3.1 of the City Code on Take-overs and Mergers, which obliges the board of the target company to obtain competent independent advice on the bid and to furnish that advice to shareholders. This note, headed 'Management buy-outs and offers by controlling shareholders', states:

'The requirement for competent independent advice is of particular importance in cases where the offer is a management buy-out or similar transaction or is being made by the existing controlling shareholder or group of shareholders. In such cases, it is particularly important that the independence of the adviser is beyond question. Furthermore, the responsibility borne by the adviser is considerable and, for this reason, the board of the offeree company or potential offeree company should appoint an independent adviser as soon as possible after it becomes aware of the possibility that an offer may be made.'

If there are directors independent of the members of the buy-out team and these directors are fully and competently advised by an independent third party who makes known that advice to the shareholders of the target company, the conflict of interest between the members of the buy-out team as buyers and their position of directors should be settled. In the absence of independent directors, the responsibility will fall on the merchant bank or other financial adviser.

In the case of a Class 4 transaction, an independent expert will be required to opine on the fairness and reasonableness of the transaction so far as the shareholders of the target company are concerned.

The case law and statutory provisions do not combine to produce a clear set of guidelines for the buy-out team. The following principles emerge, however:

i.   the industrial and commercial logic should be capable of clear demonstration
ii. the director members of the buy-out team must be able to convince shareholders that the price offered is better than fair and that the buy-out team is not arrogating to itself an opportunity which should be made available to all shareholders
iii. the position of the director members of the buy-out team on the board of the parent company and the target should be clearly and publicly defined
iv. any directors who are not members of the buy-out team should form a separate committee of the board charged with ensuring that standards of honesty and good faith are maintained
v.   the buy-out team and the independent directors should obtain separate independent financial advice at the earliest possible stage
vi. due process must be rigorously observed at all times. The provisions of relevant statutes and the articles of association must be strictly followed and supporting documentation, whether board minutes or notes of meetings between buyer and seller, must be properly kept and accurate.

Service agreements and contractual arrangements

A director's fiduciary duties will be supplemented in his service agreement, which will underline the director's duty to act bona fide in the interests of the company and to act for proper purposes. It will also establish the relationship of employer/employee between the company and the director. In the absence of any service agreement, the fiduciary duties of a director are still implied into the director's contract.

Unless their contracts of employment specifically impose fiduciary duties on them, senior managers who are not directors are under less onerous obligations to their employers. Nevertheless, these obligations, which also apply to directors, include restrictions upon the employee not to compete with his employer at any time during his spare time. This duty extends to preparations made by the employee during his employment with a view to competing with his employer following the termination of his contract of employment (*Thomas Marshall (Exporters) Ltd v Guinle* [1979] Ch 227, [1978] 3 All ER 193).

If an employer learns of any breach by a director or employee of the duties implied into the contract, it can obtain an injunction from the High Court restraining the employee from committing further breaches. The employer can also, in the longer term, obtain damages from the employee if it can show that it has suffered financial loss as a result of the breaches.

A company can waive, either expressly or impliedly, its right to require compliance by the employee. If the director/employee keeps the company informed of his proposed course of action before taking it and the company consents to this action, the company will not be able to argue subsequently that the director/employee was in breach of his duties to the company.

The members of the buy-out team must bear in mind the effect of the failure of the buy-out on their employment. Even if the buy-out is amicable and there have been no breaches of contracts of employment, the strains generated by the negotiations among the members of the buy-out team, the target company and its parent, may well change and could prove fatal to the relationship between the management and the target. In that event, the buy-out team members may be facing loss of their jobs as well as the collapse of the deal.

The target company may attempt to justify the dismissal of members of the buy-out team by establishing breaches of the fiduciary and other duties owed to the company. If breaches are established, the courts will normally uphold dismissals as justified and, provided that a reasonable procedure is followed, fair. If the target company cannot establish that breaches have taken place, members of the buy-out team may be entitled to damages for unfair and/or wrongful dismissal.

If the target company or its parent does not dismiss a member of the buy-out team but obliges him to resign by demolishing the relationship of trust and confidence between them, he may be entitled to claim damages against the target company for his constructive dismissal, provided that he has not himself committed breaches of contract.

Confidentiality

Service contracts will normally contain an express provision requiring the director/employee not to disclose or use confidential information belonging to the employer company either during the contract of employment or after its termination. This restriction gives the members of the buy-out team a 'Catch 22' problem. Meaningful discussions with the putative vendor will be difficult without a firm proposal from the buy-out team on the table. Yet the formulation of a serious proposal will almost certainly require input from outside advisers.

In the absence of any express contractual duties, a director/employee will be under an implied duty not to use or disclose certain information confidential to the employer during the course of his employment and trade secrets following the termination of the employment.

In the leading case of *Fowler v Faccenda Chicken Ltd* [1987] Ch 117, [1986] 1 All ER 617, the Court of Appeal determined that information of a highly confidential nature, such as details of a secret process, could never be divulged by an employee either during his employment or after its termination. The Court then identified, as a second category, information which an employee should treat as confidential either because he has been expressly told that it is confidential or because, from its character, it is obviously confidential. An employer can always prevent an employee from using or disclosing this class of information during the course of his employment but can only stop the employee using or divulging such information after the termination of the contract if it is specifically entitled to do so by virtue of express provisions in the employment contract.

Previously unpublished details of a company's business plans, accounts, finances and other information which a buy-out team might wish to use in determining its buy-out strategy will undoubtedly be classed as confidential. A company will therefore be able to restrain its directors and employees from making use of this information during the course of their contracts of employment, whether or not there is an express contractual stipulation regarding confidential information.

A company can only act to protect information so long as its nature remains confidential. As soon as the information is in the public domain, no action for breach of confidence can be brought. Further, if the information is already in the possession of several other people, even if not available to the general public, it may nevertheless cease to be described as confidential. In *Coco v AN Clark (Engineers) Ltd* [1969] RPC 41, the relevant company had made available to 43% of its shareholders certain information regarding a take-over proposal. It had also entered into confidential discussions with another shareholder, disclosing similar information with a view to persuading that shareholder to mount a rival take-over bid. Megarry VC decided that, in the circumstances, the company was no longer able to argue that the information was sufficiently confidential to prevent third parties, including its employees, from making use of it.

If a company is able to establish that certain categories of information are confidential and can be protected, it can only seek to restrain a director/employee from using that information provided it can show that unauthorised use has caused or will cause the company some detriment (*Coco v AN Clark (Engineers) Ltd* above). Since discussions with a professional adviser for the purpose only of obtaining general advice are strictly confidential and the adviser has an absolute obligation not to make use of or reveal the contents of such discussions unless ordered by a Court so to do, it is strongly arguable that a director who seeks initial advice from such an adviser will not have acted in such a way as to entitle the target company to bring an action against him. As soon as the director commences discussions with potential financiers or other third parties and divulges information confidential to the target company, he is likely to be in breach not only of his general fiduciary duties to the company but also of his duty of confidentiality.

Therefore, any director who makes use of information confidential to the company during the course of preparations for a buy-out will be at risk unless he has first obtained the consent of the parent and target company to discuss the information for the purposes of mounting the buy-out.

The position of the members of the buy-out team and the target company and its parent can best be safeguarded if a confidentiality agreement is concluded between the company providing the information and the company to which it is provided. The buy-out team will be protected by the acquiescence of the donor and the donor by a legally enforceable undertaking given by the donee.

In the case of a hostile buy-out, the director or employee will not wish to disclose his plans to the target company before they reach a certain stage of maturity. The consequence is that the members of the buy-out team will almost certainly have been in breach of their duty of confidence to the employer during the course of formulating the buy-out plans. If the target company learns of them, it is probable that it will be able to restrain the buy-out team from further disclosing confidential information. If no injunction is brought before buy-out discussions begin in earnest and the buy-out is successful, proceedings for damages for breach of confidence are unlikely to be instituted.

If the buy-out is unsuccessful, members of the buy-out team may be sued for damages for breach of confidence but may be able to argue that, even if there has been a breach, the company has not suffered any loss which would entitle it to anything other than nominal damages.

If a hostile take-over bid does not succeed, the target company will have sufficient reason to dismiss the team members if they have disclosed confidential information during the course of their employment.

Members of the board of directors of the target company or its parent who are also professionals, such as solicitors or accountants, should also pay particular attention to the rules of confidentiality imposed upon them by their respective professional organisations. It will be a clear breach of these rules if information obtained by a person in his capacity as a director is then used in a different capacity as adviser.

Clearly, the director/employee member of the management team must tread warily around the obstacles raised by his employment contract and his duty of confidentiality. He must weigh carefully the risk of his employer's hostile reaction which might lead, at the very least, to damage to his career prospects or, at worst, to termination of his employment for breach of fiduciary duty as well as an action for damages for breach of the duty of confidentiality.

Wherever circumstances permit, the ground should be prepared well in advance and the flow of information should be two way between buyer and seller, employer and employee. Approval for the divulging of confidential information must be unequivocally documented. The buy-out team should persuade the target company of the merits of separate confidentiality agreements between the target company, its parent, if required, and those to whom the information is to be provided.

If the buy-out is hostile, the director/employee participating in it must take care to ensure that any confidential information which is divulged to third parties is either in the public domain or falls within the *Coco v Clark* principle.

Statutory constraints and obligations

Sections 312 and 316 Companies Act 1985
Section 312 Companies Act 1985 renders it unlawful for any payment for compensation for loss of office to be made to a director of a company in connection with the transfer of the whole or any part of the under-taking or property of that company, or as consideration for, or in connection with, the retirement from office, unless particulars of the proposed payment, including its amount, have been disclosed to members of the company and the proposal approved by the company.

Section 316(3) exempts bona fide payments by way of damages for breach of contract or by way of pension in respect of past services from the prohibition in section 312.

Section 317 Companies Act 1985
Section 317 Companies Act 1985, requires disclosure of any contract or proposed contract with the company in which directors are interested. The statutory provision is likely to be mirrored in the articles of association of a private company which, depending upon the nature of the contract, typically give the director the right to vote upon it, provided that full disclosure has been made. The articles of association of a public company, on the other hand, normally restrict the category of contract upon which an interested director may vote.

In the normal course, the relationship between the target company and directors who are members of the buy-out team will be fully and effectively disclosed. Nevertheless, it may be possible in the heat of a complex transaction for a committee of the board to act clandestinely to the extent that the interests of the company and those of the directors may become blurred.

For section 317 to apply, there must be a contract between the company and a third party in which the director members of the buy-out team are interested. In the early stages of a buy-out, any contractual arrangements are likely to be made directly between the company and the buy-out team. Before the making of the offer to acquire the target company or the announcement of the bid, the members of the buy-out team who are also directors of the target company would not normally be interested in any contract within the ambit of section 317.

Section 320 Companies Act 1985

Whereas it may be easy to skirt the provisions of section 317, a continuous eye must be kept upon section 320 Companies Act 1985 since contravention of it may be sanctioned by the avoidance of the particular contract. This section, which subjects substantial property transactions involving directors to the prior approval of shareholders in general meeting, applies to two buy-out mechanisms. The first is the purchase of assets from the target company by a company with which a director is connected, namely Newco. The second is the purchase of the shares in the target company from its parent, again by Newco. For section 320 to apply, however, the requisite relationship between the director and the company which is buying or selling must be established.

Section 320(1)(a) prohibits an arrangement for the acquisition of one or more non-cash assets of the requisite value from the company by a director of that company or its holding company or a person connected with such director, unless the arrangement is first approved by a resolution of the company in general meeting or, if appropriate, by a resolution in general meeting of the holding company. The definition of 'connected persons' in section 346 includes a company in which the director and other persons connected with him are interested in at least one-fifth of the nominal value of the equity share capital or control more than one-fifth of the voting power of the company at any general meeting. The ownership of the share capital of Newco at the time of the acquisition of the target company or its assets will therefore determine whether the transaction is caught by section 320.

Sections 317 and 320 should not cause difficulties in a well planned buy-out because the timing of the transactions to which they relate are within the control of the buy-out team.

As with the common law rules on fiduciary duty of which it is an extension, section 317 requires full and early disclosure. In the context of a friendly buy-out, this should not present a problem.

The application of section 320 will depend upon the relationship between the members of the buy-out team and Newco at the time of the transaction. If this relationship unavoidably causes section 320 to apply, the approval of shareholders in general meeting should not, in the case of a private company buy-out, be difficult to obtain. In the case of a quoted company buy-out, it is probable that shareholders' consent will in any event be required by virtue of the Class 4 provisions in The Stock Exchange 'Yellow Book', Admission of Securities to Listing.

Section 459 Companies Act 1985

The proposed buy-out is always open to attack under section 459 Companies Act 1985 on the ground that the target company's affairs are being or have been conducted in a manner which is unfairly prejudicial to the interests of some part of the members. The decision in *Re Posgate and Denby (Agencies) Ltd* indicates that the Court will be reluctant in the absence of special circumstances to upset a transaction into which the directors had entered in the proper exercise of their powers. In *Re Posgate and Denby (Agencies) Ltd*, breach of fiduciary duty was not alleged. It is to be expected, however, that the Court will look at a proposed buy-out in a different light if the members of the buy-out team have failed to distinguish between and to resolve the inherent conflicts of interest discussed above.

Fair Trading Act 1973
Transactions involving the acquisition of assets whose value exceeds £3 million or more than 25% of the market in particular goods or services are subject to review and prohibition under the Fair Trading Act 1973. Prima facie, a buy-out should not be anti-competitive and therefore is unlikely to be the subject of a reference to the Monopolies and Mergers Commission. The jurisdiction of the Commission, originally established under the Monopolies and Restrictive Practices (Inquiry and Control) Act 1948, is limited to the investigation of structural monopolies rather than monopolies created by agreement. The Commission can act only after a reference to it by the Director General of Fair Trading, the Secretary of State or those responsible for certain other industries.

None of the other major statutes in the area of competition law should be relevant. They are primarily concerned with the competitive effect of certain types of agreement and individual anti-competitive practices. The provisions of Articles 85 and 86 of the Treaty of Rome, dealing respectively with anti-competitive agreements and the abuse of monopoly positions, should not apply to a buy-out.

Financial Services Act 1986
Section 47 of the Financial Services Act 1986 imposes criminal liability for misleading statements and practices. The buy-out team must always be mindful of the ambit of the two sub-sections of the section, discussed later, in the formulation of their plans and the communication of them to third parties.

Regulatory constraints and obligations

If the target company is listed, its conduct and that of Newco and their respective managements will be subject to the rules of The Stock Exchange *Yellow Book*, Admission of Securities to Listing, and those of the City Code on Take-overs and Mergers, which also apply to unlisted public companies. If the shares of the target company are dealt in on the Unlisted Securities Market ('USM'), a separate set of Stock Exchange rules will apply.

The principle which underlies the *Yellow Book* and USM rules is the maintenance of investor confidence by enabling shareholders and the public to assess the position of a company and to avoid the establishment of a false market in its securities. The rules which implement this principle in relation to the preliminary stages of a buy-out are discussed in the section in this chapter on quoted company transactions, as are the rules of the City Code on the timetable of an offer and the communication of relevent information.

The problem of conflict of interest for a member of the buy-out team who is a director both of a listed target company and Newco is addressed in notes 3 and 4 on rule 25.1 of the Code. This rule obliges the board of the target company to circulate its views on the offer, subject to the requirements imposed by note 3 that, first, a director who has a conflict of interest should stand apart from the remainder of the board and that, secondly, the nature of the conflict should be clearly explained to shareholders. Note 4 provides that a director will normally be regarded as having a conflict of interest where it is intended that he should continue to be a director, whether executive or non-executive, of the target company or Newco.

PLANNING THE BUY-OUT

The offer letter

All the parties to the buy-out will spend a prodigious amount of time and effort in putting the transaction together. The management team will therefore wish to have the commitment of the vendor to the sale at the earliest possible opportunity. This is the function of the offer letter.

The offer letter or 'shut-out agreement' is not designed to create legal relationships between the parties except in three areas; disclosure of confidential information; a 'no shop' undertaking (ie that the target company will not be offered to any other prospective purchaser for a given period); and the payment of costs.

The offer letter should not attempt to create legal relationships in other areas, such as price, security and warranties, which should be left to the relevant document, although it should set out an understanding of what is agreed on such matters.

As a result of the High Court decision in *Walford v Miles* (unreported) in July 1989, the parties to the offer letter must be explicit about the creation of legally binding obligations. The case concerned the proposed purchase by W of a business from M. At a time when the negotiations were in danger of breaking down, W agreed with M that M would terminate discussions with any other interested purchaser and would reject any other offer for the business provided that W continued to negotiate and furnished a comfort letter from his bankers confirming the availability of the finance for the purchase, subject to contract. W honoured his commitment within the agreed time frame but M continued to negotiate elsewhere and sold the business to a third party. The judge decided that, on the facts of the case, a legally enforceable agreement had been made despite the fact that the negotiations were otherwise 'subject to contract'. At the date of writing the decision was to be appealed.

The members of the management team who are directors of the target company and more especially of the vendor will be faced with several conflicts of interest which they must resolve. One of these conflicts relates to the disclosure of confidential information to their financiers and their professional advisers. The offer letter from the buy-out team to the vendor must therefore expressly authorise the divulging of the information required by the institutions to determine if the transaction is financeable. In consideration for its agreement to this disclosure, it will be reasonable for the vendor to request that the recipients of the confidential information sign agreements confirming that they will make no use of the information other than for the purpose of evaluating the proposed buy-out.

Of prime importance to the buy-out team is an undertaking from the vendor that the company or the business will not be sold to any other party during a minimum period. The buy-out team will require this comfort in the shape of a legal undertaking both to protect its own position as a suitor and to give it time to obtain commitments from its financiers.

The vendor will have to consider carefully whether it is in a position to agree to such an undertaking. There will be a clear conflict of interest if members of the buy-out team are part of this decision-making process. If they are, the independent directors must be responsible for the decision. If the target company is not listed or is not part of a listed group, the likelihood is that all the shareholders will be accessible and will therefore be in a position to agree to the shut-out clause. Even if there is unanimity amongst the shareholders, the decision in *Re Posgate & Denby (Agencies) Ltd* confirms that, provided the board has complied with due process, an aggrieved shareholder must demonstrate some special circumstances which created a legitimate expectation that the directors would not exercise their power in a way which he alleged was unfair.

The position is more complex where the target company is listed or is part of a listed group because the board will have to have regard to the provisions of the Yellow Book relating to Class 4 transactions and perhaps to major Class 1 transactions.

The third area in which the buy-out team should seek a legal undertaking is the payment of costs. Having decided to dispose of the target company, the vendor will have inured itself to the payment of its own costs. The fees involved in the preparation of the accountants' report and the legal documentation will be substantial and the institutions are unlikely to underwrite them until the transaction has neared the point of no return.

The assumption of risk for fees will therefore be a matter for agreement between the vendor and the buy-out team. From the point of view of the latter, the best position is the agreement of the vendor to underwrite all the costs of the transaction until the transaction is completed, when they can be met out of the funding provided to Newco. If the vendor is agreeable, it will want to limit its exposure to the case where it is directly responsible for the demise of the transaction.

If the buy-out team cannot obtain such a blanket undertaking from the vendor, it should consider negotiating variable fees with its advisers. Accountants, lawyers, and merchant bankers advising the management team might well consider favourably a success related fee which would take into account the risk of the transaction not proceeding. The fees of the advisers to the vendor and of the reporting accountants will not normally be met by the buy-out team. The fees of the latter may be paid by the financiers or passed on to Newco.

The financiers may well ask for commitment fees based on a percentage of monies advanced. Buy-out teams often resist such fees on the ground that financiers will obtain their reward from their participation in the buy-out. If this approach is not successful, the buy-out team might consider negotiating a fee based on a time charge.

The payment of any fees by the target company will fall within the prohibition on financial assistance in section 151 Companies Act 1985. Reliance on the exemption contained in section 153(1) Companies Act 1985 must be viewed against the decision in *Brady v Brady* discussed later in this chapter. If the target company is private, the financial assistance procedures referred to in this chapter can be followed. The disclosure rules set out in section 317 Companies Act 1985 and the articles of association must also be complied with and the members of the buy-out team should ensure that the commitment fees are authorised by a resolution of the board in which they do not participate.

It is better practice to avoid these problems by shifting the responsibility for the payment of fees from the target company to Newco. In this case, the equity participants will be funding the fees.

The buy-out team should be conscious of the risk that a vendor faced with a significantly higher price than that offered by the buy-out team may take the money and run. In this case, however, the vendor may be more likely to honour its undertaking to pay the cost of the abortive transaction. If it does not, it is improbable that the no-shop undertaking will be enforceable by injunction, since damages are likely to be considered an adequate remedy for the loss of opportunity.

The other topics covered by the offer letter will be the parties to the transaction, the purchase price and its calculation and payment, the principle that appropriate warranties and indemnities will be given, pensions and employees. If assets are being purchased, the offer letter should identify them and anticipate any problems posed by the Transfer of Undertakings (Protection of Employment) Regulations 1981. It is in the interest of the management team to encapsulate the principal terms of their offer as comprehensively and concisely as possible in order to avoid wrangling as the transaction proceeds. The offer letter should not aim to create a binding relationship except in the three areas discussed.

In the case of a listed company, the offer letter will trigger an announcement under rule 2.2(a) of the City Code, unless it is subject to pre-conditions. In this case, therefore, the authors of the offer letter must either have their funding in place or make the offer conditional upon its provision.

Issue of a prospectus

The financing of the buy-out may require Newco to offer its securities either to raise funds for its own use or because of the syndication of its securities to a number of investors. The classic example of this exercise is the management-led employee buy-out of the National Freight Company in 1982. The buy-out was effected by an offer for subscription of 'A' ordinary shares to employees, their families and pensioners and 'B' ordinary shares to the banks coupled with a syndicated £51 million loan.

Companies Act 1985

Chapter 1 of Part III Companies Act 1985 governs the issue of prospectuses relating to securities other than those which are listed or the subject of an application for listing in accordance with Part IV Financial Services Act 1986. Since section 81 Companies Act 1985 prohibits a private limited company from offering its shares or debentures to the public, it is critical to establish that any offer made by Newco, if it is a private limited company, falls within the exceptions in section 60 Companies Act 1985. Under section 60(1), the offer will not be treated as made to the public if it can properly be regarded, in all the circumstances, as not being calculated to result, directly or indirectly, in the shares or debentures becoming available for subscription or purchase by persons other than those receiving the offer or invitation, or otherwise as being a domestic concern of the persons making and receiving it. It should be possible for Newco to construct an offer which will fall within this exception.

If the securities on offer are not listed or the subject of an application for listing under Part IV Financial Services Act 1986, the provisions of Part V Financial Services Act 1986, relating to offers of unlisted securities, will apply when that Part comes into force.

Financial Services Act 1986

Besides the provisions relating to issue of prospectuses, the Financial Services Act applies to other areas relevant to buy-outs. The scheme of the Act requires dealing in securities and related activities to be carried on only by authorised or exempted persons. The financiers will fall into one of these two categories. If the financing of the buy-out demands the issue of a prospectus or the syndication of the debt, the relevant document must be issued by an authorised person. The same will apply to any investment advertisement issued in connection with the buy-out. The members of the buy-out team will therefore not be concerned with the technical requirements of the Act relating to offers of securities provided that they have ensured the involvement of a person authorised under the Act in good standing. Of specific relevance to the members of the buy-out team, however, is section 47 of the Act.

Section 47(1) is the successor to section 13 Prevention of Fraud (Investments) Act 1958 as amended by the Banking Act 1979. It imposes criminal liability on any person who (i) knowingly makes a misleading, false or deceptive statement, promise or forecast or (ii) dishonestly conceals any material facts or (iii) recklessly (whether dishonestly or otherwise) makes a misleading, false or deceptive statement for the purpose of inducing, or is reckless as to whether it may induce, another person to enter or offer to enter into, or to refrain from entering or offering to enter into, an investment agreement or to exercise, or refrain from exercising, any rights conferred by an investment.

The test for section 47(1)(a) is dishonesty verging on fraud whereas under section 47(1)(b) the making of a misleading, false or deceptive statement, promise or forecast need only be reckless for an offence to be committed. The courts have held that it is not necessary for the reckless conduct to be fraudulent or dishonest, only seriously negligent.

Section 47(1) is of particular relevance to the preparation of the business plan and forecast on the basis of which the buy-out will be financed and is an added reason for the buy-out team to be conservative in its profit and cash flow projections.

Whereas section 47(1) is concerned with misleading statements, section 47(2) prohibits misleading practices. The section imposes criminal liability on any person who does any act or engages in any course of conduct which creates a false or misleading impression as to the market in or the price or value of any investments, if he does so for the purpose of creating that impression and of thereby inducing another person to acquire, dispose of, subscribe for or underwrite those investments or to refrain from doing so or to exercise, or refrain from exercising, any rights conferred by those investments.

The ambit of this sub-section is wider than that of section 47(1) because deceit or dishonesty or recklessness do not have to be present for the offence to be committed. There are four elements in this section:

i. the 'act' or 'course of conduct'
ii. which must create a false or misleading impression as to the market in or the price or value of investments
iii. the act or course of conduct must be done for the purpose of creating that impression
iv. for the purpose of thereby inducing another person to deal in or refrain from dealing in investments.

It is thought that a mere omission does not necessarily constitute an 'act' or 'course of conduct'. The danger is that a material omission could be an 'act' which gives partial information. The third and fourth elements require positive action and positive purpose. On the face of it, the words of this sub-section are wide enough to include warranties about the target company given by the buy-out team to the financiers if those warranties can be proven to create a false or misleading impression and to have been given to induce the making of the investment.

Although market rigging has been a common law offence for more than 170 years, the sub-section now provides a statutory basis to ban the manipulation of the market in securities. The buy-out team might find the sub-section both a sword and a shield. In a hostile buy-out, the 'ramping' of the target company's shares to create an impression of market interest or to force up the price will be covered. By the same token, the members of the buy-out team must be careful to ensure that their conduct towards the financiers cannot be characterised as deceptive.

Because the ambit of section 47 is so wide and pervasive, the buy-out team must measure their actions and their documentation against its framework. The buy-out team's first line of defence is its own integrity. Its second line of defence is the quality and accuracy of the advice given by its advisers in the negotiations and the preparation of the documentation. Notwithstanding, the members of the buy-out team must be mindful that section 47 imposes criminal liability which reliance on third party advice will not eliminate.

Position of the vendor

There are no particular legal problems associated with a buy-out from an individual or group of individual shareholders who control the company and are members of its board, other than applications for clearance under section 707 ICTA 1988 and section 88 CGTA 1979 which have been discussed in Chapter 4.

If the target is a subsidiary or division of another company, the members of the board of the vendor who are not part of the buy-out team will also be subject to the usual range of fiduciary duties, including consideration of the best interests of the vendor company. Section 312 Companies Act 1985 referred to earlier will also have to be borne in mind, if relevant.

If the vendor is a quoted company, circulars to shareholders could be relevant and the normal rules on circulars and Financial Services Act responsibility will apply. The financial advisers to the vendor are obliged to state in the circular that they consider the transaction to be fair and reasonable so far as the shareholders of the vendor are concerned.

In the case of a bid, the board of a target company will be bound by rule 3.1 of the City Code on Take-overs and Mergers. The vendor will need to ensure that it has the power and authority to sell the target, particularly if it is a member of a group of companies. The vendor must review the negative covenants and cross-collateralisation obligations to which it may be subject in its banking arrangements and take steps to obtain the appropriate releases in good time.

Newco

Newco will usually be an off-the-shelf company. The lawyers acting for the institutions will check that its existence has been fully and accurately documented and the buy-out team's lawyers must therefore be scrupulous in holding the first board meeting, filing the relevant returns with the Registrar of Companies and writing up the statutory books. For the reasons discussed in Chapter 4, the buy-out team will normally subscribe for its shares before the institutions subscribe for theirs. In practice, the completion agenda will ensure that these two subscriptions are separated by a short but decent interval. At the completion meeting, the new articles of association of Newco setting out the agreed share rights will be adopted and the name of Newco changed, if necessary.

The buy-out team should also have regard to the law relating to 'promoters' of a company. Although section 104 Companies Act 1985, relating to the transfer to a public company of non-cash assets, can be avoided if Newco is an off-the-shelf company, the general law on the fiduciary relationship between a promoter and the company created by him will apply.

If the financing of the buy-out calls for Newco to raise funds through a placing or an offer for sale, Newco will be bound to comply with Chapter I Part III Companies Act 1985, Part IV or Part V of the Financial Services Act 1986 and the requirements for listing set out in The Stock Exchange 'Yellow Book' relating to listed companies, or the rules relating to companies whose shares are to be dealt with on the Unlisted Securities Market, where appropriate.

It is likely that the members of the buy-out team will be directors of Newco, as well as directors of the target company and possibly of its holding company. They must therefore be mindful of their obligations relating to the disclosure of information to Newco under rule 19 of the City Code on Take-overs and Mergers in relation to common law rules on confidentiality. Upon completion of the acquisition of the shares or the assets of Newco, the members of the buy-out team will often be minority equity investors and perhaps a minority on the board. If any of the information provided by the members of the buy-out team to Newco proves to be misleading to the extent that the value of the investment of Newco in the target company has depreciated significantly, they would be open to prosecution under section 47(1) and (2) or to an action for damages for misrepresentation. This of course will apply in the event of the non-disclosure of material information.

Status of the target company and its parent: Insolvency Act 1986

As part of the buy-out process, the health of a target company will normally have been rigorously checked by the reporting accountants and insured against through the medium of the warranties and tax indemnity. The worst nightmare for the buy-out team and its financiers is the receivership or liquidation of the target company after completion.

The Insolvency Act 1986 enables an administrator and a liquidator to set aside certain transactions which preceded the administration order or liquidation. All the principals and their advisers will be concerned to ensure that the relevant provisions will not apply. These are section 238 Insolvency Act 1986, which deals with the setting aside of transactions at an undervalue, and section 239, which deals with the preference of creditors.

A transaction can be set aside under section 238 if it is for a considera-tion the value of which in money or money's worth was significantly less than the value in money or money's worth of the consideration pro-vided by the debtor. The company must be unable to pay its debts within the meaning of section 123 of the Act or have become unable to pay its debts in consequence of the transaction at an undervalue. The court will not make an order under section 238, however, if it is satisfied that the company which entered into the transaction did so in good faith and for the purpose of carrying on its business and, at the time it did so, there were reasonable grounds for believing that the transaction would benefit the company. In any event, a transaction at an undervalue can be set aside only if it is entered into within the two years ending with the insolvency.

For a preferential transaction to be set aside under section 239, the recipient of the preference must be a creditor of the company or a guarantor of any of its debts or other liabilities and the company must put the recipient of the preference into a position which is better than the position he would otherwise have had. Again, the company must be insolvent at the time of the preference or become insolvent in con-sequence of it. The preference can be set aside within the two years ending with the insolvency if it has been given to a person connected with the company (otherwise than by reason only of being its employee) and within six months of the insolvency if the recipient of the preference is not connected with the debtor. For the purposes of this provision, a person is connected with a company if he is a director or shadow director of the company or an associate of such a director or shadow director or if he is an associate of the company. 'Associate' is defined in section 435.

The test of an intention to give a preference within the meaning of section 239 was debated in the case of *Re M C Bacon Ltd* ((1989) Times, 1 December). In differentiating between the test under section 44(1) Bankruptcy Act 1914 that there had to be a dominant intention to prefer, Millett J stated, first, that it was sufficient that the decision was influenced by the requisite desire and, secondly, that there must be a desire to produce the effect mentioned in subsection (4)(b) of section 239. Without the second leg of the new test, his Lordship was of the opinion that it would be virtually impossible to uphold the validity of a security taken in exchange for the injection of fresh funds into a company in financial difficulties. A man was taken to intend the neces-sary consequences of his actions, so that an intention to grant a security to a creditor necessarily involved an intention to prefer that creditor in the event of insolvency. According to his Lordship, a transaction would not be set aside as a voidable preference under section 239 unless the company positively wished to improve the creditor's position in the event of its own insolvent liquidation.

If the security package given to the financiers involves the creation of floating charges over the target company's assets, the financiers' lawyers will focus upon section 245 Insolvency Act 1986. This section invalidates floating charges created within 12 months of the insolvency in favour of unconnected persons only if the company was insolvent at the time of the creation of the charge and within two years of the insolvency in the case of the charge created in favour of a person who is connected with the company. 'Connected' has the meaning referred to above. Section 245(1) will not apply, however, to invalidate any floating charge created to secure indebtedness created at the same time as or after the creation of the charge, if it is a continuing security, together with interest on such monies. The insolvency test is the principal reason to require a net assets warranty at completion.

Two threads run through these three sections; the insolvency of the debtor company and the connection of the person who benefits from the transaction, preference or floating charge with the debtor company. In the case of section 238, the company will be presumed to be insolvent, unless the contrary can be proved, where the transaction at an undervalue is entered into with the person connected with the company. Under section 239, the company is presumed to have been influenced by the desire to give the preference to a person connected with the company, otherwise than by reason of being its employee, unless the contrary can be shown. Additionally, a preference given to a connected person is subject to a review for a period of two years before the onset of the insolvency and not for six months. Under section 245, it is not necessary to prove that the company was insolvent where the person in whose favour the charge was created is a connected person. Again, the validity of the floating charge is exposed to avoidance during a two year period if it has been created in favour of a connected person.

The definition of insolvency is important in the context of buy-outs. Under section 240(2), the company must be unable to pay its debts within the meaning of section 123 for sections 238 and 239 to apply. Section 123(2) deems a company unable to pay its debts if it is proved to the satisfaction of the court that the value of the company's assets is less than the amount of its liabilities, taking into account its contingent and prospective liabilities. In a leveraged buy-out, the consolidated balance sheet of Newco and its subsidiaries may well show a deficiency in net assets because of the write-off of goodwill. The balance sheet of the target company should, however, show positive net assets. It is unlikely that the court would construe section 123(2) so narrowly.

If the target company is to give financial assistance in connection with the acquisition of its own shares, its solvency must be rigorously scrutinised. In practice, therefore, sections 238, 239 and 245 should not be problematic.

If the vendor is a company, however, sections 238 and 239 will be in point. The buy-out team should therefore consider enquiring into the solvency of the vendor and should take appropriate warranties.

Two other sections of the Insolvency Act 1986 should be borne in mind, one particularly by lenders and the other by financiers who wish to exercise a management or control function in or over the target company.

The first, section 244, provides for the setting aside of extortionate credit transactions entered into during the period of three years ending with the day on which the administration order was made or the company went into liquidation. A transaction is defined as extortionate if, having regard to the risk accepted by the person providing the credit, either its terms are or were such as to require grossly exorbitant payments to be made in respect of the provision of the credit or it otherwise grossly contravened ordinary principles of fair dealing. The burden of proof that the transaction was not extortionate lies on the provider of the credit. This provision may be of particular relevance to a highly leveraged buy-out in which the interest on the debt is significantly higher than market rate to reflect the additional risk.

The other section is section 214, which is headed 'wrongful trading' in the Act. The Court can order a director of an insolvent company to make a contribution to the company's assets unless, faced with the likelihood of an insolvent liquidation, the director took every step to minimise the potential loss to the company's creditors. *Re Produce Marketing Consortium Ltd (No 2)* [1989] BCLC 520 contains an exposition of the principles governing imposition of liability under section 214.

The section applies to shadow directors and therefore financiers who are able to control the affairs of the target company, not only through board membership but also through the covenants in loan documentation or shareholders agreements.

In the absence of fraud, sections 238 and 239 should not apply to a well managed buy-out. If the vendor is a company, the due diligence process and the knowledge of the buy-out team should be sufficient to eliminate the risk of a transaction at an undervalue or a preference. The technical insolvency of the Newco group on a consolidated basis should not be pertinent, particularly since Newco will, in the absence of total catastrophe, be able to satisfy the solvency test in section 123(1), namely the payment of debts over £750 within three weeks of their demand for payment.

The importance of the due diligence process is more critical if the target company is incorporated or resident in a foreign jurisdiction, or if the vendor or any recent predecessor in title to the vendor is subject to the laws of other jurisdictions.

There are marked variations in insolvency laws, particularly in the United States, which can set traps for the unwary. If the target company is not incorporated or resident in the United Kingdom, the financiers' lawyers should as a matter of course establish that the laws of the applicable jurisdiction do not render it technically insolvent. The diligence process should not end there, however.

If the vendor or any recent predecessor in title is, or has when owning or controlling the target company been, subject to foreign laws, the due diligence process must determine that the vendor can validly transfer title to the target company's issued share capital without fear of a subsequent insolvency procedure overturning or nullifying the transfer. The investigation should include the vendor's predecessors where the vendor has owned the target for a relatively short period.

The need for such extended due diligence is illustrated by the buy-out of a target company ('T') incorporated in England, which was quite clearly solvent. The vendor ('V'), which was a Liechtenstein company, had acquired the shares in T from its predecessor, a US company ('P'). The management team knew of the sale of T by P to V but was not aware of the terms on, or circumstances in which, that transaction had taken place.

The management team also knew that, some months later, P had become the subject of insolvency proceedings akin to UK receivership and so informed the financiers' lawyers. They investigated the constitution and solvency of V to the limited extent possible and supplemented the results with covenants and indemnities from P's former controlling shareholders. Within a year of the successful completion of the buy-out, P had passed into liquidation and its US trustee in bankruptcy issued proceedings in the State of New York, claiming that he was entitled to the shares of T. He alleged, first, that the sale of T to V had been at an 'undervalue'; secondly, that V was a 'connected party' with P as, unbeknown to the management team, its former controlling shareholders beneficially owned or controlled V; and, thirdly, that the management team's buy-out vehicle, a UK company, was not a bona fide purchaser without notice of any defect in the title to T's shares, because the management team had known of the sale by P to V and were thus 'connected'.

The management and the financiers were advised that P's trustee in bankruptcy would almost certainly not succeed in proceedings in England for the rectification of T's share register and that the relevant periods for the application of UK insolvency law had expired. The US law concept of a 'bona fide purchaser without notice' differs materially from English law, however, and US lawyers advised that the management team could not claim to have been 'unconnected' and 'without notice', even though the connection was as tenuous as the mere holding of offices in a subsidiary company. There was also concern that the sale of T by P to V may have been at an undervalue. This was not investigated at the time of the buy-out since, given the lack of information, it was impossible to establish accurately.

However secure title to T's shares was under English law, the management and the financiers were left with no practical alternative other than to settle with P's trustee in order to avoid the likelihood of protracted and expensive litigation and the obtaining of default judgments in the US, rendering subsequent trading in that jurisdiction extremely unsafe.

Quoted company transactions

If the buy-out or buy-in is of a quoted company or a subsidiary or a division of a quoted company, the City Code on Take-overs and Mergers, The Stock Exchange 'Yellow Book', Admission of Securities to Listing and the rules of The Stock Exchange relating to companies on the Unlisted Securities Market, will apply to the transaction as well as the common law rules and statutory provisions.

City Code on Take-overs and Mergers

The City Code on Take-overs and Mergers applies to offers for all listed and unlisted public companies resident in the United Kingdom, the Channel Islands or the Isle of Man. It also applies to offers for private companies which are so resident when:

i.   their equity share capital has been listed on The Stock Exchange at any time during the ten years prior to the relevant date; or
ii. dealings in their equity share capital have been advertised in a newspaper on a regular basis for a continuous period of at least six months in the ten years prior to the relevant date; or
iii. their equity share capital has been subject to a marketing arrangement as described in section 163(2)(b) Companies Act 1985 at any time during the ten years prior to the relevant date (a company whose shares have been dealt on the Unlisted Securities Market or the Third Market); or
iv. they have filed a prospectus for the issue of equity share capital at the Companies Registry at any time during the ten years prior to the relevant date.

In each case, the relevant date is the date on which an announcement is made of a proposed or possible offer or the date on which some other event occurs in relation to the company which has significance under the Code.

The Code will therefore apply to a privatisation of a public company led by the existing management team, or the buy-in to a public company by persons external to the company, whether friendly or hostile.

The planning of any of these transactions must be all the more thorough because of the timetable imposed by the Code. Under rule 2.2(a), an announcement of an offer must be made when a firm intention to make an unconditional offer has been notified to the board of the offeree company. Rule 2.2 requires an announcement to be made in other circumstances, such as the acquisition of shares carrying 30% or more of the voting rights of the company, or where there has been an untoward movement in the share price of the company or in the case of a consortium bid. If the announcement of an offer is premature, the offeror will be more exposed to a counter offer. It is therefore critical that the offeror establishes Newco with the correct shareholding and arranges the funding of the offer before it is obliged to announce its intentions. The buy-out team will have to negotiate the Scylla of

fiduciary and confidentiality duties and the Charybdis of the requirement to make an announcement at the earliest possible stage.

The timetable imposed by the Code, which must be rigorously
adhered to, unless the Panel on Take-overs and Mergers determines
otherwise, is this:

i.   posting of the offer document within 28 days of announcement of
     the offer (rule 30.1)
ii. publication of the views of the board of the target company to its
     shareholders within 14 days (rule 30.2)
iii. minimum offer period of 21 days from the posting of the offer
     document (rule 31.1)
iv. maximum offer period of 60 days from the date of the posting of the
     initial offer document (rule 31.6). The 60 day period will be
     extended in the case of a competing offer
v.   after an offer has become or is declared unconditional as to accept-
     ances, the offer must remain open for acceptances for not less than
     14 days after the date on which it would otherwise have expired
     (rule 31.4)
vi. after 42 days, acceptances may be withdrawn if the offer has not
     become or been declared unconditional as to acceptances (rule 34)
vii. all conditions to which the offer is subject must be fulfilled or the
     offer must lapse not later than 81 days after the despatch of the offer
     document (rule 31.7).

In a public company acquisition, the bidder faces the possibility that it
will not acquire 100% of the share capital of the target company.
Failure to acquire more than 90% of the shares in question may
jeopardise the provision of financial assistance by the target company,
which may be key to the financing package. The financiers may insist
that the offer cannot go unconditional as to acceptances below the 90%
level in order to ensure that section 429 Companies Act 1985 can be
applied and that the provision of financial assistance by the target
company will not be jeopardised by minority objection. The other
critical levels are more than 50%, at which the target company becomes
a subsidiary under the Companies Act 1985 and its board under the
control of Newco, and at 75%, at which special resolutions cannot be
blocked and a tax group between Newco and target is created. The
buy-out team must therefore establish the level at which the financiers
will be prepared to see the offer go unconditional.

Section 429 Companies Act 1985 provides for the expropriation of
the shares of shareholders who have not accepted the offer if the offeror
has, by virtue of acceptances of the offer, acquired or contracted to
acquire not less than 90% in value of each class of shares to which the
offer relates.

If the financiers impose a condition that the offer cannot be declared
unconditional as to acceptances before the attainment of the 90% level,
or if it is anticipated that the offer may not be accepted by a hostile
minority, the offeror may consider a scheme of arrangement under

section 425 Companies Act 1985 rather than a take-over bid under the Code. A scheme of arrangement is attractive because it requires only a 75% majority of the shareholders in the target company to approve it but it does, however, need the sanction of the Court. The scheme of arrangement would provide for the transfer of their shares in the target company against payment of the offer price.

A scheme of arrangement is only suitable, however, to an agreed bid since its success rests upon the recommendation of the board of the target company. If it is an appropriate mechanism, it does present two distinct advantages over a take-over bid. First, the need for only a 75% majority to implement it and, secondly, the absence of stamp duty. Against these advantages must be set the time required to complete the scheme of arrangement, which will depend upon the Court's calendar and may be up to four months, and vulnerability to a competing offer since the transfer of shares will not take place until the Court has approved the scheme.

The effect of rule 16 of the Code on buy-outs should be noted. This rule provides that, except with the consent of the Panel, an offeror or persons acting in concert with it may not make any arrangements with shareholders and may not deal or enter into any arrangements to deal in shares of the offeree company, or enter into arrangements which involve acceptances of an offer, either during an offer or when one is reasonably in contemplation, if there are favourable conditions attached which are not being extended to all shareholders. Note 4 to the rule applies particularly to arrangements for the management of the offeree company to remain financially involved in the business and states 'that the risks as well as the rewards associated with an equity shareholding should apply to the management's retained interest'.

The common law rules on confidentiality are buttressed by rule 2.1 which requires all persons privy to confidential information, and in particular price sensitive information, concerning an offer or proposed offer to treat that information as secret and to transmit it to a third party only if it is necessary and only if the third party is made aware of the need for secrecy. At the same time as maintaining this secrecy, the members of the buy-out or buy-in team must put their finance into place as required by rule 2.5(a). This rule obliges an offeror and its financial adviser to ensure that the funding of an offer is available before the announcement of a firm intention to make that offer. If the buy-out is hostile, the members of the buy-out team will be walking a tight rope between compliance with the Code and their fiduciary duties as directors of the target, including in particular the maintenance of confidentiality.

As noted earlier, rule 3.1 of the Code imposes an obligation on the directors of the target company to obtain competent independent advice on an offer and to inform shareholders of that advice.

Rule 19.4 poses a particular problem if the buy-out team's offer attracts a competing bid. Under this rule, any information supplied by the target company to Newco must on request be furnished equally and as promptly to a less welcome but bona fide offeror or potential offeror. Note 8 on rules 19.1 to 19.4 applies particularly to buy-outs and defines the information which must be furnished under rule 19.4 as that information generated by the target company and its management which is passed on to Newco's financiers. The management team mounting an agreed bid will find itself in the problematic position where, on the one hand, it is desirable and necessary to furnish Newco and its backers with a complete package of information and, on the other hand, that information will thereby become available to a competitor.

Rule 19.6 reinforces the rule 19.4 obligation by requiring Newco, on request, promptly to supply the independent directors of the target company, or their advisers, with all the information which has been made available to the management team's financiers or potential financiers. The application of rule 25.1 has been discussed earlier.

Rule 4 of the Code parallels the restrictions on insider dealing contained in the Companies Securities (Insider Dealing) Act 1985. Rule 4.1(a) prohibits dealings of any kind in securities of the offeree company by any person who is not the offeror and who is privy to confidential price sensitive information concerning an offer or contemplated offer between the time when there is reason to suppose that an approach or an offer is contemplated and the announcement of the approach or offer or of the termination of the discussions.

This Code prohibition and the prohibition contained in the Companies Securities (Insider Dealing) Act 1985 will not apply, however, in the absence of price sensitive information.

Admission of Securities to Listing; the 'Yellow Book'
Chapter 2 of section 5 of the Yellow Book contains the obligations which The Stock Exchange requires listed companies to observe. The raison d'être of these requirements is to secure and maintain the confidence of investors in the conduct of the stock market. To achieve this objective, shareholders and the public in general must have access to the information necessary to enable them to appraise the position of a company and to avoid the creation of a false market in its securities.

It is therefore incumbent upon the target company or its parent not only to maintain strict security but also to release to the market information which might reasonably be expected to have a material effect on market activity in, and prices of, the relevant securities. The guiding principle is that such information should be released immediately if it is the subject of a decision. The Stock Exchange requires in take-over transactions a warning announcement or a temporary suspension of listing when negotiations have reached a point at which the target company is reasonably confident that an offer will be made for its shares or where negotiations or discussions are extended beyond a small group of people. These requirements dovetail with rules 2.1 and 2.2 of the Code.

Section 6 of the Yellow Book lays down the requirements concerning acquisitions and realisations of assets by listed companies and their subsidiaries. Chapter 1 of section 6 divides acquisitions and disposals into five classes, three of which require circulars to be sent to shareholders and two of which require in addition shareholders' consent. A Class 1 transaction requires a circular to be sent to shareholders if any of the four tests comparing net assets, price and profits of the business being sold compared with the equivalent figures for the group as a whole produce a figure of 15% or more, unless The Stock Exchange waives the requirement for a circular. If the comparative tests produce a figure of 25% or more, the acquisition or disposal becomes a major Class 1 transaction and will be conditional on approval by shareholders in general meeting.

The Stock Exchange has proposed, in the light of the European Community Directive on the Mutual Recognition of Listing Particulars, that the obligation to issue a Class 1 circular when the class test falls into the 15% to 25% range should be replaced by a requirement to circulate a copy of a full press announcement to shareholders, which would include a full and detailed explanation of the transaction together with a summary of the trading record and the last audited balance sheet of the business being acquired or disposed of and a statement of significant changes in the financial or trading position of the group. There would therefore no longer be a need for accountants' reports and working capital and indebtedness statements.

Even if shareholders' consent is not required because the disposal to the buy-out team is not categorised as a major Class 1 transaction, it is probable that it will be a Class 4 transaction and will therefore require shareholders' approval. A Class 4 transaction is a transaction between a company and any of its subsidiaries on the one hand and any director, a substantial shareholder or associate of the company or subsidiary on the other hand. Where the target company is a subsidiary of a listed holding company, it is almost inevitable that the buy-out will fall to be treated as a Class 4 transaction unless Stock Exchange dispensation, commonly known as a 'whitewash', is granted. For a Stock Exchange 'whitewash' to be obtained, no member of the buy-out team should sit on the board of the holding company and vice versa.

Rules related to the Unlisted Securities Market
The terms and conditions for entry by a company to the Unlisted Securities Market, the subsequent obligations of a USM company to its shareholders in relation to important transactions and share issues and the provision of regular information to the market are contained in a separate set of rules. The objective of these rules is no different from that of the Yellow Book.

Acquisitions and disposals by USM companies are measured by the same criteria as are applied to listed companies but the percentages differ. When the tests produce a result of 5% or more, the transaction must be announced and notified to the Quotations Department of the Stock Exchange. A transaction will become material at the 25% level, at which a circular must be sent to shareholders. As part of its review of the continuing obligations of listed and USM companies, The Stock Exchange has proposed the raising of the 25% threshold to 35% and the introduction of a new requirement for shareholders approval when the test reaches 75%.

Companies Securities (Insider Dealing) Act 1985
The provisions of the Companies Securities (Insider Dealing) Act 1985 will apply to any individuals involved in the buy-out who acquire price sensitive information about the target company. It should be noted that the Act applies only to individuals and not to companies. Therefore, neither the lending companies nor Newco will be affected by it.

Under section 1(1) of the Act and subject to the defences set out in section 3 of the Act, an individual cannot deal on a recognised stock exchange in securities of a company if he is, or has within the preceding six months been, knowingly connected with that company and if he has inside information. The sub-section defines inside information as information which the individual holds by virtue of being connected with the company, which it would be reasonable for him not to disclose except for the proper performance of his duties and which he knows is unpublished price sensitive information. Section 1(2) extends the offence of primary insider dealing in securities of the company with which the individual is connected to the securities of another company. Subject again to the defences in section 3 of the Act, an individual who is, or at any time in the preceding six months has been, knowingly connected with the company is prohibited from dealing on a recognised stock exchange in securities of any other company if he possesses inside information. For the purpose of this sub-section, inside information is that which relates to any transaction, actual or contemplated, involving his company and that other company, or involving one of them and securities of the other, or to the fact that any such transaction is no longer contemplated. As for section 1(1), the tests of connection, disclosure and possession of unpublished price sensitive information also apply.

Section 1(5) of the Act is of particular application to take-overs. Subject to the defences in section 3, where an individual is contemplating, or has contemplated, making, with or without any other person, a take-over offer for a company in a particular capacity, he is prohibited from dealing on a recognised stock exchange in securities of that company in another capacity if he knows that information that the offer is contemplated, or is no longer contemplated, is unpublished price sensitive information in relation to those securities. Section 14 defines 'take-over offer' as an offer made to all the holders (or all the holders other than the person making the offer and his nominees) of the shares in the company to acquire those shares or a specified proportion of them. Since members of the buy-out team would be caught by sections 1(1) or 1(2), the prohibition in section 1(5) would apply to a buy-in team who had no connection with the target company and would make it an offence for such a member to deal in the securities of the target company except for the purpose of a take-over bid which he is contemplating either alone or with others.

Sections 1(3), (4) and (6) extend the primary prohibitions against insider dealing contained in sections 1(1), (2) and (5) to secondary insider dealing or 'tippee' dealing. For the purposes of the secondary dealing sections, a person must knowingly obtain the price sensitive information. The Court of Appeal Criminal Division decided in the reference made by the Attorney General under No 1/1988 that to 'obtain' means to 'acquire in any way'. The reference concerned information which the respondent had taken no step, directly or indirectly, to secure, procure or acquire. The Court held that it made no difference whether the information on which the 'tippee' dealt was sought out by him or came his way by unsolicited gift. The offence was not one of using information but of dealing in the securities while being in possession of the relevant information.

Primary and secondary insiders cannot evade the prohibition on personal dealing by passing on the inside information to third parties who would then make use of the inside information. Section 1(7) of the Act prevents an individual from counselling and procuring a person to deal or to communicate the information to another person if he knows or has a reasonable cause to believe that the other person will use the information to deal. Section 1(8) deals with the communication of inside information to a third party whom the insider knows or has reasonable cause to believe will make use of the information for the purpose of dealing.

It must therefore be best practice for Newco, the members of the buy-out team and the financiers to refrain from acquiring any shares in the target company.

Friendly and hostile take-overs

The problems of conflict of interest are magnified in the case of a quoted company buy-out, not because the interests of shareholders are different from those of shareholders in a private company, but because institutional shareholders are likely to scrutinise all aspects of the bid, particularly price, more rigorously. Even if the bid is agreed between Newco and the members of the independent board, there is always the risk that a predator will be alerted to the potential of the target company and launch a counter-bid at a premium to the price offered by the buy-out team.

The case of *Dawson International plc v Coates Patons plc* (1988) Times, 25 March illustrates this point. The board of Coates Patons agreed a take-over bid by Dawson International and entered into a 'shut-out' agreement under which the board of Dawson International would not encourage or co-operate with any competing offer. On 27th January 1986, a joint press announcement of the proposed merger was made, including the statement that the board of Coates Patons would recommend acceptance of the offer. On the date that the offer documents were despatched to shareholders, the board of Coates Patons announced an agreed take-over by Vantona Viyella. In an action for breach of contract brought by Dawson International, Coates Patons argued, first, that it was not within the power of a company to bind itself to a recommended particular offer, secondly, that such a contract would conflict with the fiduciary duty of directors and, thirdly, that any such contract would have to be understood to be conditional upon the Dawson International offer remaining the better bid from the point of view of the shareholders of Coates Patons. The case of *Clark v Workman* [1920] 1 IR 107 was cited as authority for the proposition that directors could not fetter their freedom to act in the best interest of shareholders.

In the Court of Session, Lord Cullen said that he did not accept as a general proposition that a company could have no interest in the change of identity of its shareholders upon a take-over or, that by a reason of lack of interest, the company could not enter into a contract of the type in question. Although it was well recognised that directors owed fiduciary duties to a company, his Lordship saw no good reason why it should be supposed that the directors were, in general, under a fiduciary duty to shareholders and, in particular current shareholders, with respect to the disposal of their shares. Directors were not normally agents of the current shareholders and the authorities established no such fiduciary duty. What was in the interests of current shareholders and sellers of their shares might not coincide with the interests of the company.

Lord Cullen restated the view of Brightman J in *Gething v Kilner* (supra) that directors, in supplying information to their shareholders regarding a take-over offer and expressing a view as to whether the offer should be accepted, have 'a duty towards their own shareholders which . . . clearly includes a duty to be honest and a duty not to mislead'. If directors took it upon themselves to give advice to current share-holders, they had a duty to advise in good faith and not fraudulently and not to mislead. The case of *Heron International Limited v Lord Grade and Associated Communications Corpn plc* [1983] BCLC 244 was not authority for the proposition that directors could not agree to recom-mend a bid and not to encourage or co-operate with a rival approach without being in breach of a fiduciary duty to current shareholders.

The management team mounting the take-over will have at the very least a presentational problem if it wishes to raise its bid in the light of a counter-bid. If it does so, it lays itself open to the accusation that the first bid deliberately undervalued the target company.

Until the trial of the action brought by Dawson International, the contractual consequence of breach of a shut-out agreement remains unclear.

Rule 19.1 of the Code permits the supply of information in con-fidence by the target company to a bona fide potential bidder. The board of the target company must always be mindful of its obligation under the Yellow Book to avoid the creation of a false market in its company's shares. Therefore, any information made available to the bidder which might have that effect should be released into the market. Note 7 on rule 19 of the Code circumscribes the bidder's ability to make use of statements derived from information not generally available.

The size of most buy-outs or buy-ins of a listed company dictates that the take-over will be largely debt financed. The problems of obtaining warranties, either in favour of Newco or the financiers, are discussed later. Even if the take-over is friendly, it is improbable that the vendor will give any warranties to Newco which will therefore be obliged to rely on published information.

Buy-ins

'Buy-ins' of listed companies pose special problems additional to the initial purchase of or subscription for shares where the incoming management seeks or is offered equity incentives. These incentives may take the form of options to acquire shares or warrants convertible into ordinary shares or redeemable shares. Options may be grated pursuant to an employee share option scheme or specifically created.

If options are part of the incentive package, the guidelines issued by the Investor Protection Committees, which impose limits on the extent to and conditions on which share options may be granted, must be followed. Equally, the 'Yellow Book', at paragraph 15 of chapter 2 of section 1, restricts a company from issuing options or warrants to subscribe equity capital in excess of 10% of its issued share capital at the time the warrants or options are issued, although shares issued pursuant to employee share option schemes do not count for this purpose.

It should be noted that The Stock Exchange treats convertible shares or other forms of security which can be converted into, or give rise to a right to acquire, equity shares as 'options' or 'warrants' for the purpose of the limitation. Care must therefore be taken to ensure that these restrictions are not infringed, when constructing substantial incentives for an incoming management team. Prior discussion with the Investment Protection Committees may produce a relaxation in their attitude where the circumstances are considered sufficiently exceptional to justify incentives outside the guidelines. The Stock Exchange interprets 'exceptional circumstances' strictly, however, and is therefore less likely to be flexible.

In order to circumvent the 10% rule, it may be possible to structure the rights of any convertible shares, warrants and other forms of security transmutable into equity shares so that they are also redeemable in cash at the option of the company or issuer, if different, irrespective of whether they are also convertible at the option of the management team. The Stock Exchange should accept that such shares or securities do not count towards the 10% limit.

Particular care needs to be taken with regard to the taxation treatment for the individual members of the management team of options and convertible securities. These are discussed in Chapter 4.

Equity finance

The share capital structure of Newco will reflect the allocation of risk and reward among the management team and its backers. Each financier may favour one type of share capital over another but the objective will be the same; to incentivise and reward the management team through ordinary share capital and to provide the financiers with the required balance between current yield and capital appreciation and the ability to realise their investment through a mixture of ordinary, preference and redeemable capital.

Each type of share capital will therefore be issued for a specific purpose. Ordinary share capital carries the most risk, with a low return in the short term but the greatest potential reward in long term capital appreciation. Its right to participate in profits and assets will rank behind the preference and redeemable capital. Even if its holders command more than 50% of the voting power of the target company, its voting power will not be effective in significant issues against the negative covenants contained in the loan documentation, articles of association and shareholders agreements. It will, however, carry the economic value of the company upon a flotation or in a trade sale. For these reasons, the management team is likely to be allotted ordinary share capital. If there is an employee share ownership plan, the employee trust will also hold ordinary shares sometimes leavened with preference shares.

The equity investors will hedge their risk but attempt to maintain their potential for capital gain. They will therefore want a security with the advantages of equity share capital, carrying voting power and the economic value of the company, but which at the same time has the essential characteristics of debt, namely the right to interest and repayment.

These securities may be redeemable ordinary shares, which have all the features of an ordinary share, but are redeemable pursuant to section 159 Companies Act 1985; redeemable preference shares, which carry the right to a fixed dividend and have prior rights in a winding up or convertible redeemable preference shares which also carry conversion rights into ordinary share capital.

The ability to redeem its equity stake enables the financier to realise its investment without a flotation or trade sale. Section 160 Companies Act 1985 requires redeemable shares to be redeemed only out of distributable profits, or out of the proceeds of a fresh issue of shares made for the purposes of the redemption or, in the case of private companies only, out of capital. Given the requirement to service its debt and to pay preference dividends, the target company may find itself unable to effect a redemption out of distributable profits. Distributable profits are defined in section 263(3) Companies Act 1985 as accumulated, realised profits, so far as not previously utilised by distribution or capitalisation, less accumulated, realised losses, so far as not previously written off in a reduction or reorganisation of capital duly made.

The ability to fund a redemption out of capital will be constrained, first, by the provisions of sections 171 to 177 Companies Act 1985, and, secondly, by the likelihood that shareholders will not consent to a redemption out of capital unless it is pari passu.

The power given to a company to purchase its own shares by section 162 Companies Act 1985 will not avail shareholders seeking to recoup their investment for the same reasons. The purchase must be funded out of the company's distributable profits or by the proceeds of a fresh issue of shares made for the purpose.

Debt finance

Share capital in its various guises will fund only part of the buy-out. The balance, and usually the majority, of the finance will be provided in the form of debt. This debt will also have various guises, whose characteristics will depend upon the risk being assumed and the rate of return required by the lender. These have been discussed in Chapter 3.

'Senior debt' is long term finance secured by a first legal charge over the shares in the target company and, subject to compliance with the procedures for the provision of financial assistance, first fixed and floating charges over the assets of the target company. If the senior debt is substantial, it may be syndicated either before or after the completion of the buy-out. From the point of view of the buy-out team, it is preferable to have all the debt finance committed at the earliest possible stage. If the target company is quoted, commitment of the debt finance before the offer is announced is crucial. For this reason, the buy-out team should endeavour to negotiate the debt finance with a prime lender which will syndicate the debt after the buy-out. This is the 'bought deal' and, together with its relative rapidity, has the further advantage that the borrower will be negotiating only with the lead lender in its capacity as agent for the future members of the syndicate.

It is possible that the lead financier providing all or the bulk of the senior debt will participate in the next level of debt (mezzanine finance), as well as the equity.

The providers of mezzanine finance will take into account the fact that redeemable shares can be redeemed only out of profits available for distribution or the proceeds of an issue of shares made for the purpose of redemption. Debt, whether secured or unsecured, does not suffer from this disadvantage. Participation in the equity of the target company can be created via convertible debt or warrants.

If the debt is to be provided from various sources, the question of priority amongst the lenders will arise. It will therefore be a matter for the lenders to agree amongst themselves in a subordination agreement the priority of the application of the proceeds of realisation of assets in a winding up.

Security and financial assistance

The relaxation of the law relating to the provision of financial assistance by companies for the purpose of the acquisition of their own shares in sections 42 to 44 Companies Act 1981 is said to have provided significant stimulus to the growth of management buy-outs. It was a major deterrent for providers of buy-out finance that this finance could not be secured over the assets of the target company, unless the acquisition was of assets alone. In a share acquisition, the only available security was the share capital of the target company.

The law relating to the provision of financial assistance by a company to finance the acquisition of its own shares was first introduced in section 45 Companies Act 1929 which became section 54 Companies Act 1948. The purpose of the law was to protect creditors and shareholders against an unauthorised reduction of capital and to prevent the acquisition of companies with the use of the company's own funds.

The current legislation is found in sections 151 to 158 Companies Act 1985. The basic prohibition is contained in section 151(1) whose opening phrases include the words 'it is not lawful for the company or any of its subsidiaries to give financial assistance directly or indirectly for the purpose of a proposed or actual acquisition'. It should be noted that a prohibited transaction is illegal, not merely void.

The new legislation relaxed the law enshrined in and developed from section 54 Companies Act 1948 in three significant ways. First, it contains a definition of financial assistance, now to be found in section 152 Companies Act 1985. Secondly, the prohibition against financial assistance will not be breached by a transaction undertaken in good faith where the breach is incidental. Section 153(1) contains this general exception to the rule. Thirdly, there is a general relaxation of the prohibition for private companies provided that they comply with sections 155 to 158.

The scheme of the legislation is this:

i.   section 151(1) provides that, subject to the specified exceptions set out in the Chapter, financial assistance given directly or indirectly before or at the same time as the acquisition is unlawful

ii. section 151(2) contains a prohibition against the giving of financial assistance after the acquisition has taken place. This prohibition relates to the reduction or discharge of any liability incurred for the purpose of that acquisition. The reduction or discharge of a liability is defined extensively in section 152(3)

iii. section 152 defines the key phrases used in Chapter VI, sub-section (1) defining 'financial assistance' and 'distributable profits' in relation to the giving of financial assistance, sub-section (2) defining 'net assets' and sub-section (3) explaining the words used in the prohibition contained in section 151(2).

The definition of 'financial assistance' is broad and will catch the viable methods by which the management team might seek to fund or to collateralise the finance required for the buy-out. It is defined as:

i. financial assistance given by way of gift, which includes a transaction with an element of gift, such as a sale at an undervalue
ii. financial assistance given by way of guarantee, security or indemnity or by release or waiver
iii. financial assistance given by way of a loan or any other agreement under which any of the obligations of the person giving the assistance are to be fulfilled at a time when, in accordance with the agreement, any obligation of another party to the agreement remains unfulfilled or by way of the novation of, or the assignment of rights arising under, a loan or any such other agreement. This definition covers payment on deferred terms
iv. any other financial assistance given by the company the net assets of which are reduced to a material extent by the financial assistance or which has no net assets. Sub-section (2) defines 'net assets' as the aggregate of the company's assets, less the aggregate of its liabilities. For this purpose, liabilities include provisions for liabilities or charges considered reasonably necessary for the purpose of providing for any liability or loss which is either likely to be incurred or certain to be incurred, but uncertain as to amount or as to the date on which it will arise. A guarantee given or a loan made by the target company will not fall within this definition of liabilities until such time as the directors of the target company reasonably and prudently believe that the guarantee will be called or that the nominal value of the loan will not be realised.

The prohibitions in section 152(1) and (2) cover not only a loan from the target company to the buy-out team or the giving of security by a target company to collateralise such a loan but also a loan from the target company to repay a loan from an external source, such as a bank, used to purchase the target company's shares, a loan used to pay deferred consideration due to the vendor of the target company or the grant of security over the target company's assets to a third party who had guaranteed the loan to the buy-out team.

The calculation of any reduction in net assets will therefore be based on expectations and projections on which the buy-out itself is founded. Should the projections in the business plan not support the conclusion that there will be no material reduction in net assets, the financial assistance can nevertheless be given by a private company provided it complies with sections 155 to 158. The essential ingredients are that any shortfall in net assets is matched by distributable profits and that the company is otherwise solvent.

The two exceptions to the prohibition in section 153(1) and (2) were enacted to ensure that bona fide transactions which incidentally fall foul of the prohibitions in section 151 are not unlawful. For the exceptions to apply, the principal purpose of the assistance must not be for the acquisition of the shares; it must be an incidental part of some larger purpose of the company and it must be given in good faith in the interest of the company. The phrases 'principal purpose' and 'incidental part of some larger purpose' are not further defined. Given the difficulty of interpreting them and the intangibility of the test of good faith, these exceptions should not be relied upon. It is unlikely that management faced with criminal sanctions for a breach of section 151 or lenders taking security over the target company's assets would wish to do so.

If the costs of the buy-out are met by the target company, there is an argument that, depending on their size, they fall within the exceptions in section 153 but, for the reason set out in the previous paragraph, this is not without risk. The objective must therefore be, however, to insure that such costs are paid by Newco and not by the target company. Even so, the discharge of costs by Newco could fall foul of the prohibition in section 151 (2) since it may be argued that the target company is facilitating the reduction or discharge of a liability incurred for the purpose of the acquisition of its shares. Provided that Newco is put in funds by the payment of a dividend, the mischief of section 151 should be avoided.

The House of Lords in *Brady v Brady* [1989] AC 755, [1988] 2 All ER 617 was able to conclude that financial assistance given to prevent continued management deadlock in, and a probable liquidation of, the company giving the financial assistance was, viewed objectively, in the company's interest. Lord Oliver confessed in his judgment that he had not found the concept of a 'larger purpose' easy to grasp. In the Court of Appeal, O'Connor LJ considered that the larger purpose embraced avoiding the liquidation of a company, preserving its goodwill and the advantages of an established business. Lord Oliver disagreed because, he said, the concept must be narrower than that for which the appellants contended if the exceptions in section 153(1)(a) and (2)(a) were not to provide a blank cheque for avoiding the effective application of section 151.

He therefore concluded that a larger purpose cannot be found in the benefits considered to be likely to flow, or the disadvantages considered to be likely to be avoided, by the acquisition which it was the purpose of the assistance to facilitate. These exceptions must therefore be applied only in the context of *Belmont Finance Corp Ltd v Williams Furniture Ltd (No 2)* [1980] 1 All ER 393. This case raised the question of whether a transaction entered into partly with a genuine view to the commercial interest of the company and partly with a view to putting a purchaser of shares in the company in funds to complete his purchase was in breach of section 54 Companies Act 1948.

Section 154(3) sets out a number of transactions which are specific derogations from the prohibitions in section 151(1) and (2). Those which may be relevant to the funding of the buy-out are:

i.   a distribution of a company's assets by way of dividend lawfully made. The use of the word 'lawful' in the context is confusing; the test might simply be that the distribution must be made in accordance with the provisions of Part VIII of the Companies Act 1985. Section 263(1) prohibits distributions except out of profits available for the purpose, an expression defined in section 263(3) as accumulated, realised profits, so far as not previously utilised by distribution or capitalisation, less accumulated, realised losses, so far as not previously written off in a reduction or reorganisation of capital duly made. Section 264(1) places a further limit on public companies by permitting distributions only if the amount of the company's net assets is not less than the aggregate of its called up share capital and undistributable reserves and if, and to the extent that, the distribution does not reduce the amount of those assets to less than that aggregate. Alternatively, payment of the dividend may need to satisfy the two conditions; compliance with Part VIII and not being prohibited by section 151. The better view is that, since the introduction by the 1980 Companies Act of new legislation relating to dividends, now enshrined in Part VIII of the 1985 Companies Act, the dividend rules protect creditors sufficiently.

In practice, however, it is unlikely that the target company will have sufficient distributable profits available to repay the total purchase price

ii.   a distribution made in the course of the company's winding up. The use of this exemption would be somewhat drastic in the context of a buy-out, given the tax disadvantages inherent in liquidations and the likely damage to trading relationships

iii. a redemption or purchase of shares in accordance with Chapter VII Part V of the Companies Act 1985

iv.   a reduction of capital confirmed by order of the Court under section 137 Companies Act 1985 and a scheme of arrangement under section 425 Companies Act 1985. Again, it is unlikely that either of these routes will be available in the circumstances of a management buy-out

v.   the exceptions in section 153(4)(b), (bb) and (c). The first two sub-sections except respectively the provision of funds used to acquire shares for the purpose of an employees' share scheme and the provision of financial assistance for the purposes of or in connection with anything done by the company to enable or facilitate the acquisition of shares by employees. The former exception has been amended by section 132 Companies Act 1989 which introduces the concept of financial assistance given 'in good faith in the interest of the company' and defines less narrowly the type of financial assistance. This section did not come into force when the Act received the Royal Assent. The latter exception, introduced by the Financial Services Act 1986, considerably widens the definition of an employees' share scheme contained in section 743 Companies Act 1985 so that the use of innovative employee ownership plans falling outside Revenue approved schemes will not be discouraged.

Section 153(4)(c) exempts loans to employees other than directors to enable them to acquire shares in the company. The prohibition against loans to directors is consistent with the general restriction against loans to directors in section 330 Companies Act 1985.

All three exceptions are available to public companies only if the financial assistance does not reduce the net assets of the company or to the extent that it does, the assistance was provided out of distributable profits.

This restriction for public companies is found in section 154(1). Section 154(2) contains the definition of 'net assets'. The determination of net assets for the purposes of this section is more stringent that the calculation required for the purpose of section 152(2), since it is the book values of the assets and liabilities immediately before the giving of the financial assistance which must be used, not their actual values. If net assets are reduced, the shortfall must be made up out of distributable profits. Since the encouragement of an employee participation will find favour with the financiers of the buy-out, the use of distributable profits for the purpose should be permitted by the buy-out documentation.

Public companies can only provide financial assistance if the assistance falls within the exceptions set out in section 153. The mechanism for authorising financial assistance which falls squarely within the prohibitions in section 151 is only available to private companies. An essential feature of the buy-out might therefore be the re-registration of a public target company as a private company following the buy-out. This procedure will pose special problems in the context of a take-over bid.

The procedure for the authorisation of financial assistance given by a private company is found in sections 155 to 158.

(a) The financial assistance must not reduce net assets or, if they are reduced, distributable profits must be available to compensate for the shortfall (Section 155(2)). The more generous definition of net assets set out in section 154(2) applies for the purpose of this section.

(b) The financial assistance can be provided only by private companies and their subsidiaries; public companies can provide financial assistance only as permitted by section 153. Section 155(3) prohibits the giving of financial assistance by a subsidiary where the shares to which the acquisition relates are those of its holding company if there is a public company interposed between the holding company and the subsidiary.

(c) The financial assistance must be approved by special resolution of the shareholders of the company in general meeting, unless the company is a wholly-owned subsidiary (section 155(4)). Where the financial assistance is given by a subsidiary to its holding company, that holding company and any other company which is both the company's holding company and a subsidiary of that other holding company must also approve the financial assistance by special resolution unless the subsidiary is wholly-owned.

(d) A statutory declaration in the prescribed form must be given by all the directors of the company proposing to give the financial assistance. Where the shares to be acquired are shares in a holding company, the statutory declaration must also be made by directors of that company and of any other company which is both the company's holding company and a subsidiary of that other holding company (section 155(6)).

Given the degree of responsibility attached to the making of this declaration, the nomination of directors prepared to make it may be contentious

(e) Section 156(1), (2) and (3) set out the requirements for the statutory declaration. The declaration must state:
  i.   particulars of the financial assistance to be given
  ii. particulars of the business of the company of which the makers of the declaration are directors
  iii. the persons to whom the financial assistance is to be given
  iv. that the directors have formed the opinion, having regard to the state of the company immediately following the provision of the assistance, that there will be no ground on which it could be found unable to pay its debts and that the company will be able to pay its debts as they fall due within the year immediately following the provision of the assistance. If the directors intend to liquidate the company within 12 months of the provision of the assistance, they must also state in the statutory declaration that the company will be able to pay its debts within 12 months of the commencement of the winding up. In forming their opinion about the solvency of the company, the directors must apply the tests laid down in section 123 Insolvency Act 1986 to determine inability to pay debts. The test in section 123(2) is that the value of the company's assets is less than the amount of its liabilities, taking into account its contingent and prospective liabilities, which has been discussed earlier.

(f) Annexed to the statutory declaration must be a report addressed to the directors by the company's auditors stating that they have inquired into the state of affairs of the company and are not aware of anything to indicate that the directors' opinions expressed in the declaration are unreasonable in the circumstances.

It is clear that the directors making the statutory declaration and the auditors reporting on the statutory declaration must be those who are familiar with the affairs of the target company, not only before the buy-out but also after its completion. The logical conclusion is that the members of the buy-out team who have been primarily responsible for the preparation of the business plan are appointed to the board of the target company, perhaps with an undertaking to resign if the transaction aborts, and that the accountants producing the long form report are appointed as auditors. Alternatively, the existing auditors will be in a good position to take responsibility if they have carried out a recent audit. If the existing auditors are not prepared to report on the statutory declaration, they should make known their decision at the earliest possible stage to enable the reporting accountants to focus on this issue.

(g) For the special resolution to be effective, the procedures relating to
its timing and publicity must be followed. The directors' declaration and auditor's report must be made no more than seven days
before the general meeting at which the special resolution is to be
proposed and must be available for inspection at that meeting.
Copies of the declaration, report and special resolution authorising
payment must be delivered to the Registrar of Companies within 15
days from the passing of the resolution. By virtue of sections 157(2)
and 158(2), the holders of 10% of the nominal value of the issued
share capital of the company can apply to the court for cancellation
of the special resolution within 28 days from the date of the meeting
on which the resolution has been passed. It is for this reason that the
acquisition of more than 90% of the company share capital is
critical to the implementation of the financial assistance procedure.

Section 158(4) places a long stop date of eight weeks after the
making of the directors' statutory declaration for the giving of the
financial assistance.

A public company can give financial assistance only within the
limitations of sections 153 and 154. A lender will therefore not be
able to take security over the assets of a quoted target company
unless and until it re-registers as a private company. There are three
levels of shareholding which are critical to this process. The first is
75% to pass the re-registration special resolution under section
53(1) and the financial assistance special resolution under section
155(4). The second is more than 90% to forestall an application for
cancellation of the financial assistance special resolution under
section 157(2). The third is more than 95% to prevent an application under section 54(1) for the cancellation of the resolution to
re-register as a private company.

If financial assistance is key to the financing of the buy-out of a
quoted company, the financiers may be particularly sensitive to the
level of acceptances at which the bid is declared unconditional. The
loan documentation will undoubtedly contain the appropriate conditions. Almost as sensitive is the question of the timing of the
financial assistance since there will be a hiatus between the advance
of the funds to acquire the target and the grant of security over the
assets of the target company. The notice to convene an extraordinary general meeting to re-register the target company as a
private company will be triggered only when the offer becomes
wholly unconditional with at least 90% acceptances. On the same
date, notice will be given to the minority shareholders under
section 428 Companies Act 1985 of the intention to acquire their
shares. Rule 31.8 of the Code requires that the consideration due
under the offer be posted within 21 days of the date on which the
offer becomes or is declared wholly unconditional. The lenders will
therefore advance the requisite funds to enable compliance with
rule 31.8 before the re-registration special resolution has been
passed. After its passing, section 53(1)(c) imposes a 28 day interval

for objections to the re-registration to be heard. During this interval, the compulsory acquisition procedure under section 429 Companies Act 1985 et sequitur can be implemented. It will therefore be some seven weeks after the offer has gone unconditional that the special resolution to authorise the financial assistance can be passed. The financial assistance can be given immediately because the target company will then be wholly-owned.

Capital and stamp duty

Section 141 Finance Act 1988 has abolished the 1% stamp duty on documents relating to transactions of capital companies. Capital duty will therefore no longer be payable on the issue of new shares by Newco. The transfer of the shares in or assets of the target company will be subject to stamp duty at the rate of ½%, unless the acquisition of shares is implemented through a scheme of arrangement.

It is possible in an assets sale to avoid stamp duty on goodwill and on the transfer of debts by executing and keeping the documents of transfer in an appropriate jurisdiction abroad. If the financiers object, a compromise may be negotiated whereby the documents of transfer will be brought into the country on the happening of specified events.

IMPLEMENTING THE BUY-OUT

Acquisition of shares

The acquisition agreement will deal with:

i.   the agreement for sale
ii.   the initial purchase price, adjustments to it and the calculation and payment of any deferred consideration
iii. any conditions relating to the completion of the agreement
iv.   the retention of any part of the purchase price
v.   the completion mechanism
vi.   warranties and indemnities
vii. specific provisions relating to pensions
viii. the protection of the purchaser from unfair competition.

The shape and scope of these provisions, other than relating to warranties and indemnities, will differ little from those found in a classic acquisition agreement. Those relating to the purchase price and its payment will require modification if the vendor has agreed partially to finance the buy-out by accepting debt and/or equity issued by the target company.

It is in the area of warranties and indemnities that the buy-out acquisition agreement will diverge from the classic acquisition agreement.

The maxim *'caveat emptor'* should be rigorously applied to the purchase of shares in or the assets of a limited liability company. In a classic company acquisition, the vendor will therefore expect to give and the purchaser will expect to receive warranties concerning all the significant aspects of the corporate existence of the target company and its accounts, finance, taxation, assets, real property and employees. In addition, the purchaser will attempt to negotiate a tax indemnity.

The warranties serve two functions; primarily to apportion the risk as between the vendor and the purchaser and, secondarily, to act as a checklist for the purpose of identifying historic or prospective problems before a binding contract is signed.

In the classic private company or assets acquisition, it is difficult for the vendor to raise any serious opposition to the principle that, as the proprietor and manager of the target company, it should give the warranties and indemnity.

The conflicts of interest which are inherent in a management buy-out erode this principle. When the buy-out is put together by the management, the vendor will be able to establish a prima facie case to lay the responsibility for the bulk of the warranties and the tax indemnity at the feet of the management team. Management's ability to counter this move will depend on the circumstances, particularly where the target company is a member of a group or where the buy-out team has had limited involvement in areas outside their specific executive portfolios.

Where the buy-out is leveraged, the pressure to give a full set of warranties and indemnities will come from the financiers. The buy-out team may therefore wish to let the lawyers acting for the financiers take the lead in the warranty negotiations. The vendor will be less able to resist giving sensible warranties and tax indemnities if it is aware that they are crucial to the provision of the finance for the buy-out. It may therefore be good tactics to involve each party's lawyers in the warranty negotiations at the earliest possible stage.

A vendor faced by the demand to give a full set of warranties may, in turn, attempt to lay off its liability by requiring the buy-out team to underwrite such warranties. The requirement may take the form of a 'comfort' letter or, at worst, a counter indemnity. The buy-out team should strenuously resist any such demand from the vendor. There is no reason to depart from the principle that the risk should lie with the person being paid to assume it.

If the buy-out is management led and substantially equity financed, it may be that the vendor will be asked to give, and the purchaser and the providers of debt finance will be prepared to accept, fewer warranties.

One of the curiosities with which the acquisitions lawyer is faced is the totally different treatment accorded to the take-over of a quoted company and the acquisition of a private company. It is axiomatic that the purchaser of a listed company will expect no warranty or indemnity cover, except where there are shareholders with substantial stakes who can be persuaded to give limited warranties. Such might be the case in the acquisition of a company whose shares are dealt in on the Unlisted Securities Market and are closely held by a small group of shareholders. The legal rationale for this approach is not evident. The audited financial statements of a quoted company will provide no greater hedge against the purchaser's exposure to the liabilities within the target company than the audited financial statements of a private company, despite the decision in *Caparo Industries plc v Dickman* [1989] 1 All ER 798, [1989] 2 WLR 316. In this case, it was decided that the auditor of a quoted company owed individual shareholders a duty to exercise reasonable care in carrying out his audit and making his audit report but that such duty of care did not extend to any potential investors.

Even if the listed company has published additional information through the medium of circulars sent to its shareholders, a bidder will not have the benefit of the exhaustive analysis of the target company's affairs contained in a full set of well drafted warranties. This convention seems all the more bizarre if the target company is a subsidiary of a listed group, in which case the vendor and the purchaser will treat the sale and purchase as if it were that of a private company.

The paradox is explainable only by the fact that, from a practical point of view, it is usually impossible to obtain warranties from a disparate body of shareholders in a listed company. On the other hand, there is no reason why the purchaser should not seek certain warranties from major shareholders, particularly if they are represented on the board of directors.

The unavailability of warranties to the purchaser of a quoted company in a take-over bid will bedevil the buy-out team and its financiers in the same way. A buy-out of a quoted company will, by definition, be leveraged and consequently there will be pressure from the financiers for significant warranty protection. These financiers will be the same as those who, on another day, will lend substantial sums to a listed company without substantial net worth on the security of a projected strong cashflow and a series of negative covenants. If the private company is floated, the financiers are also likely to resist giving warranties to the sponsor.

The tug of war over warranties is likely to be lost by the side which is most interested in the success of the transaction. If the financiers are particularly keen to participate, they may well take a flexible attitude. Behind every financier, however, there is a credit committee whose inevitable starting position is that there has to be a very good reason for the absence of substantial warranty cover.

The warranty and indemnity discussions will take a different direction if the target company is being sold by an administrative receiver or if the buy-out team is acquiring assets and not shares. In the former circumstance, discussions will be very short. In the latter, the purchaser will not be concerned to get taxation warranties and indemnities nor warranties relating to those liabilities which have been left with the seller of the assets.

Because the level of protection required in an asset purchase is significantly less than that required in an acquisition of shares, the transaction may well be structured around this difference. If it seems at an early stage in the negotiations that the warranty and indemnity issue could be a deal-breaker, some creative structuring by the advisers could satisfy the diverging requirements of the vendor and the purchaser. As an example, it may be possible to hive down the necessary assets to a newly formed company to be acquired by the management team. The vendor will be able to restrict the scope of the warranties and indemnities and the buy-out team will acquire a clean company with selected assets and no liabilities other than those attaching to the transferred assets. The advantages and disadvantages of an asset purchase and the obstacles in its way are discussed more fully in Chapter 4.

Acquisition of assets

The essential difference between acquiring the shares in the target company and acquiring its assets is that, in the former case, the purchaser will acquire a total package of rights and obligations, assets and liabilities, whereas, in the latter case, the purchaser should be able to select the rights and assets which it requires and leave behind the obligations and liabilities which it does not.

It is probable that the taxation problems for the vendor inherent in an asset sale, discussed in detail in Chapter 4, will foreclose this route for the purchaser. Where the vendor is an individual or a group of individuals, the burden of double taxation created, first, when the assets are sold and, secondly, when the proceeds of sale are distributed to the shareholder is likely to stop an asset purchase in its tracks. Only where the vendor is a member of a group or the target business is a division of the vendor is the asset purchase route likely to be a feasible option.

The first task of the parties is to identify the assets being sold and the liabilities being acquired. The selection of these assets and liabilities will influence the nature of the warranties requested by the purchaser. If the buy-out team effectively acquires the balance sheet of the target company with its assets and liabilities, the warranties will be more extensive. The purchaser will not, for example, wish to assume product liability which has arisen before the sale.

The question of which party acquires the benefit of debtors and takes responsibility for paying creditors may be problematic. It is common for the purchaser to seek to acquire the benefit of debtors and not the burden of creditors. The vendor, on the other hand, will not wish to assume the risk of bad debts since they are likely to have been incurred by the management team. The parties are therefore faced by two options; either the purchaser will give value for the debts backed by a bad debt provision or the vendor will retain the benefit of debts and the purchaser will undertake to collect them on its behalf. Whatever is agreed between the parties, the mechanism for dealing with debtors and creditors will require careful drafting.

The buy-out team will want to acquire the benefit of those contracts which are essential to the ongoing business. Because rights, but not obligations, can be assigned, the contracts which are moving across to the new business will require to be novated. In practice, the task of securing all the appropriate third party consents within the time frame allowed is likely to prove impossible. The buy-out team must therefore focus upon those contracts which are critical to the continuation of the business, such as property leases and long term supply contracts. If these contracts are critical to Newco, they may well be significant to the third party in question which will be asked to exchange the covenant of the vendor, with which it is familiar, for the less appealing covenant of Newco.

Whereas this may be less of a problem in dealing with supply contracts, because the trading relationship will continue and the third party will maintain contact with familiar faces, the assignment of a lease of real property may raise difficulties. There is no easy solution to the problem of a landlord which refuses the substitution of the covenant of a company laden with debt for that of the vendor or its group. The members of the buy-out team should resist the giving of personal guarantees and instead procure the giving of appropriate guarantees from the financiers.

The purchaser must analyse carefully finance leases and hire purchase agreements since they normally provide for termination upon assignment or parting of possession with the goods. Premature termination could lead to financial penalty. If the lease or hire purchase company exacts a financial penalty, Newco should ensure that the cost is taken into account in its negotiation of the purchase price.

The transfer of assets is prima facie more expensive than the transfer of shares since the former attracts stamp duty at 1% and the latter at ½%. The burden can be mitigated by ensuring that the appropriate assets are transferred by delivery. Stamp duty cannot be avoided on a transfer of real property.

The avoidance of stamp duty on the assignment of debts by the appointment of Newco as the vendor's agent to collect them may find no favour with the financiers since it will mean a reduction in the critical funding requirement. The financiers may not be too keen on the simple stamp duty avoidance route of executing and retaining the agreements abroad. On the other hand, a sympathetic banker may agree to an undertaking in the documentation that the transfer documents will be brought into the jurisdiction and stamped if required. This also applies to the transfer of goodwill.

The purchase of assets does not give rise to a problem under the financial assistance provisions of section 151 Companies Act 1985 so that the assets purchased by the buy-out team can be used to secure the finance.

The application of section 320 Companies Act 1985 to the acquisition of shares has been discussed earlier. On its face, the section is likely to be more pertinent to an asset sale and therefore the timing of the management team's investment in Newco for the purpose of the definition of 'connected persons' will be critical.

It is customary for the purchaser to seek an indemnity against any liabilities relating to the business transferred and incurred before the transfer date and for the vendor to seek an equivalent indemnity in respect of liabilities incurred after the transfer date. The indemnity requested by Newco may well be resisted by the vendor on the ground, common in buy-outs, that Newco had been running the business before the transfer date and therefore has the pertinent knowledge. When it comes to the allocation of risk, the vendor will always find it difficult to refute the proposition that it is effectively being paid to assume it.

The Transfer of Undertakings (Protection of Employment) Regulations 1981 apply to the transfer of all or part of a business as a going concern and protect the accrued rights of the employees of the target business by their automatic transfer to Newco. Because all liabilities, except in respect of occupational pensions, pass to the purchaser, it is important for Newco to compute them and to obtain appropriate warranty and indemnity protection.

The Regulations provide that an employee is automatically unfairly dismissed if the reason or principal reason for the dismissal, either before or after the transfer, is the transfer or a reason connected with it. The exception to this general rule is a change in work force owing to economic, technical or organisational reasons. An employee dismissed for these reasons will generally be entitled to a redundancy payment, provided that he has been employed by the business for at least two years.

Unless the vendor and the relevant employees have concluded an agreement before the transfer relating to any dismissal which takes place as a result of the impending transfer, the obligation to pay compensation for unfair dismissal to the dismissed employee will pass from the vendor to Newco upon transfer. From the point of view of both the vendor and Newco, a planned dismissal programme in advance of plans for any transfer may reduce their exposure to claims for unfair dismissal and redundancy payments. If it is not commercially feasible to implement dismissals before the transfer, Newco should consider adjusting the purchase price to take account of the cost of redundancy and unfair dismissal payments. In addition, any employee receiving compensation for a dismissal should be asked to sign ACAS Form COT 3 by virtue of which he accepts the compensation payment in full and final settlement of all claims against the vendor and Newco.

The vendor is also obliged by the Regulations to inform an independent 'recognised' union of the proposed transfer. Both the vendor and Newco are under a duty to consult with recognised unions whose members in their employ may be affected by the transfer. The penalty for a breach of this obligation is a maximum of two weeks pay for each affected employee. Although it is not clear from the Regulations, the obligation to meet this liability could pass from the vendor to Newco; Newco should therefore ensure that it has the appropriate protection in the assets sale agreement.

Given the obligation on the vendor to inform trade union representatives in sufficient time to allow consultations to take place if any employees in either company will be affected by the transfer, it is important for both the vendor and Newco to ensure that employees do not learn about the proposed transfer of business second hand. A formal announcement to employees should therefore be made if possible before, or if not, at the same time as any public announcement.

Warranties

The instinctive reaction of the purchaser of a company to wring from the vendor a full set of warranties and indemnities will be unsympathetically received by the vendor in a buy-out. By definition, the promoters of the purchase of the target company will be the very executives who have detailed knowledge of its affairs. Yet the vendor is being paid its price for the target company and that price must include the assumption of risk if the bargain between the vendor and the buy-out team is deficient.

The warranties and indemnities in a buy-out take on a different dimension and are not just concerned with the eliciting of information and the allocation of risk. The financiers will be just as concerned as the buy-out team to underpin their knowledge of the target company. The financiers will not regard the transaction as 'bankable' unless reasonable warranties are available.

The definition of 'reasonable' may be decided by the internal credit committees of the financiers. If the target company is private and the buy-out is management driven without significant debt, the warranties may be limited to those with which both the vendor and the buy-out team feel comfortable and which satisfy the providers of external debt finance.

If the same transaction is highly leveraged, the risk for the financiers will be significantly greater and they will therefore demand warranty protection commensurate with that risk. The most highly leveraged buy-out is likely to be that of a quoted company. Yet the financiers will be obliged to rely on the information available in the public domain to limit their exposure. This is the paradox discussed earlier.

The negotiations between the vendor and the buy-out team and their respective advisers on the scope and the extent of the warranties should be conducted with an eye to the financiers which will be looking over the shoulder of the buy-out team. These negotiations are likely to begin by the vendor refusing to give extensive warranties on the ground that the buy-out team already possesses the requisite information. The buy-out team will counter by demonstrating that shares in a private company are unsaleable without some warranty cover.

In the case of a management buy-out where management injects a significant proportion of the buy-out price, the warranties may be less extensive because of less institutional pressure. The greater the institutional involvement, the more extensive will be the warranty and indemnity protection required. If the buy-out team is unable to obtain from the vendor those warranties which it considers to be reasonable, it may nevertheless find itself faced with the requirement to give the missing warranties to the institutions. It is therefore very much in the interest of the buy-out team to ensure that there is no mismatch between the warranties which it is receiving from the vendor and those which are being asked for by the institutions. For this reason, the buy-out team may be well advised to involve the lawyers acting for the institutions in the warranty negotiations.

The buy-out team can adopt two other approaches. First, the warranties can be given directly by the vendor to the institutions, the buy-out team supplementing them as required with a provision to ensure that there is no duplication or overlap. Secondly, the vendor may agree to the assignment to the financiers of its warranties given to the buy-out team. The vendor will naturally oppose any demand which increases its exposure. In practice, it is unlikely that the creation of a direct warranty link between the vendor and the financiers will have this effect. From the point of view of the financiers, it is preferable to have recourse under a warranty claim against the person who has received the purchase consideration. For the members of the buy-out team, the advantage of not being in the liability loop for a significant number of the warranties is obvious.

Institutions are notoriously voracious in their desire to be the beneficiaries of warranties and just as renitent to give warranties in the appropriate circumstances.

The management team should focus on those areas of the business of which its knowledge is more theoretical than practical. If the target company is a member of a group, it is likely that its tax affairs will have been dealt with at group level and that therefore members of the buy-out team will have little or no knowledge of them. The same will apply if the responsibility for funding, pensions, insurance and ownership of certain assets has been taken at group level. The buy-out team may feel that it requires less protection when it comes to the day to day trade of the company. On the other hand, the institutions will scrutinise this area of warranty protection carefully since they will have to be satisfied that the trade will generate the cashflow required to repay the indebtedness.

Typically, warranties will be divided into eight groups, covering the corporate life of the target company, its accounts, finance, taxation, trading and contracts, real property, employees and assets.

The first group is concerned with the authority and capacity of the vendor to sell the shares in the target company, the ownership of the shares, details of the target company and its subsidiaries, if any, its capital, articles of association and statutory books and compliance with statutory and regulatory requirements. These facts should be easily verifiable and therefore the relative warranties should not be problematic. For both the buy-out team and the financiers, they are important.

Warranties of the latest audited accounts and management accounts, stock, work-in-progress and bad debts are normally needed since the buy-out will not be fundable if the financial position of the target company cannot be easily and accurately ascertained.

When it comes to warranties on other financial matters, such as capital commitments, distributions, borrowings and loans, and on taxation, the vendor, if a member of a group of companies, is likely to have more knowledge than the members of the buy-out team. Warranties in the financial area may well be capable of relaxation since it is probable that, as part of the buy-out, the target company will be refinanced. Basic warranties on tax are essential, however, to ensure that the net worth of the target company is not reduced by unknown tax liabilities.

It is in the area of trading and employees that the management team will be most under pressure to accept responsibility for warranties. The judgment of the financiers will in large measure be based upon their assessment of the management team, its knowledge of the business of the target company, its ability to manage it profitably and the loyalty and commitment of key employees. They will therefore want reassurance on all these points.

If the buy-out is debt financed and involves the giving of financial assistance by the target company, the financiers will require extensive warranties on the real property and other assets owned by the target company.

If the vendor is a member of a group of companies, the warranties relating to group taxation will need to be more carefully crafted.

The warranties particularly appropriate to a buy-out cover the following areas:

i.   the target company will have net assets at completion within the meaning of sections 154 and 155(2) Companies Act 1985. The target company will not be in a position to give financial assistance unless it can satisfy section 155(2), which authorises the financial assistance only if net assets are not reduced by its provision or, to the extent that they are, if the assistance is provided out of distributable profits. As discussed earlier, the net assets are calculated by reference to book values immediately before the financial assistance is given. It may be necessary, therefore, to supplement a net assets warranty by a completion balance sheet to ensure that the financial assistance can be given

ii. group taxation. If the target company is a member of a group, Newco will wish to protect itself against any liability arising out of termination of the group structure. Section 278 ICTA 1970 imposes a liability to corporation tax on capital gains where a company, which has acquired a capital asset from another group company, ceases to be a member of that group while owning the asset. The target company will be deemed to have sold and immediately re-acquired the asset at market value. Newco must therefore identify the assets to which the charge to taxation will apply and provide for the tax payable, as well as obtaining appropriate warranty and indemnity protection

iii. the future trading relationship between the vendor, if it is a member of a group of companies, and the target company. If the relationship has been informal, it will be necessary to formalise it in the standard trading terms of one or other of the parties

iv. intellectual property. The value of 'brands' has been recognised by the enormous prices paid for companies with well known and reputable brand names. It is essential for the purchaser to have complete assurances on the validity of the marks and brands owned by the target company and the continued use of any trademarks and brands within the vendor group.

The vendor may insist upon qualifying certain warranties by its 'awareness' in those areas in which the buy-out team is more likely to have day-to-day knowledge. Typically, these areas will include the financial, trading and contractual position of the target company as well as its payroll. The extent to which the buy-out team accepts any such qualification will depend on the sort of control which the vendor has exercised over the strategic and day-to-day activities of the target company. Alternatively, the vendor may require the management team to write a comfort letter or a letter of representation in which the members of the management team will be asked to confirm that they know of no reason why the vendor cannot give the specified warranties. The acceptance or rejection of the vendor's requests will depend upon the tenor of the negotiations. The management team should always remember, first, that it is accepting the multiple risk of buying the target company, giving warranties to third parties about that company and incurring significant personal indebtedness to pay the purchase price to the vendor. It is therefore entirely reasonable for the buy-out team to take the position that the vendor should put its mouth where the money is. If the vendor proves recalcitrant, the management team will do better to acquiesce in the specific qualification of specific warranties or a comfort letter rather than to find itself without the comfort of any warranties in the disputed areas and an absolute requirement by the institutions that they be given to them.

The vendor is likely to make another demand on the buy-out team as part of the give and take of the warranty negotiation. The vendor's argument that the management team will have actual knowledge of many of the areas on which it is seeking warranty protection may be extended to the preparation of the disclosure letter with the result that the letter may be qualified by such knowledge.

Indemnities

Whereas the purpose of the warranties is to compensate the purchaser for loss of bargain, the indemnities will act as an insurance policy, entitling their beneficiary to pound for pound recompense upon the occurrence of the relevant event.

If the purchaser can prove that it has suffered loss because of a breach of warranty, the purchase price will be reduced as a result. Section 41

Capital Gains Taxes Act 1979 gives effect to this by providing for a retroactive adjustment to the taxation liability.

In contra distinction, the essence of the indemnity is to restore the person who has suffered the damage to the status quo ante. In its origin, the taxation indemnity in a company acquisition agreement was based on the principle that the target company should be indemnified if it suffered a liability to taxation which arose through the act of a third party without the benefit of a corresponding right of recovery or reimbursement.

It is now standard practice for the purchaser to extend the taxation indemnity to any fiscal liability of the target company and for the vendor to seek to restrict the ambit of that indemnity. Whatever the merits of the respective positions of vendor and purchaser, the natural and proper beneficiary of the taxation indemnity is the target company and it is therefore prima facie unreasonable for it to extend to the purchaser. The insistence by a purchaser that it should have the benefit of the taxation indemnity will give rise to the anomaly that a liability to taxation could give rise to a claim under three different heads. Under the first head, a claim by the purchaser will lie for breach of warranty. Under the second head, the loss will give rise to an indemnity in favour of the company. Under the third head, the purchaser will be able to claim under its indemnity by virtue of a depletion in its assets caused by the taxation liability. The possibility of a triple claim must therefore be excluded by the vendor.

The case of *Zim Properties Ltd v Procter* (1984) 58 TC 371 and the Inland Revenue concession of 19 December 1988 generated by it have served to reinforce the practice of extending the benefit of the indemnity to the purchaser. The case established that the contingent right to receive an indemnity payment is an asset of the target company which is disposed of upon payment under the indemnity. The payment is taxable because the right was acquired for no consideration and without a corresponding disposal so that there is no allowable expenditure to reduce the chargeable gain.

The Inland Revenue concession states that the principle in *Zim* will not apply to payments made by the vendor to the purchaser, whether under warranty or indemnity, so that section 41 CGTA 1979 will operate to adjust the purchase price. Payment to the target company is not exempted from the *Zim* principle and will generally be subject to corporation tax. The purchaser may therefore insist that payments to the target company are grossed up to compensate for the tax charge.

It is clearly in the interest of the vendor to meet a warranty claim rather than to pay under an indemnity since the vendor will require the purchaser to mitigate its loss and the taxation treatment of a payment under a warranty is more favourable. The purchaser should remember that, under section 41 CGTA 1979, no allowance is made in computing capital gains for any contingent liability in respect of a warranty or representation made on a sale of property other than land until the contingent liability crystallises. Since this section refers specifically to a warranty or representation, it is considered that it does not permit any adjustment for a payment under an indemnity.

The blanket indemnity against taxation liabilities, which is now standard practice in acquisition agreements, is frequently extended to cover any breach of warranty. It is desirable from the point of view of the purchaser because it will not have to prove loss of bargain and it will not be required to mitigate its loss. The vendor is therefore well advised to resist such an indemnity and to require the purchaser to rely on its common law rights arising from breach of warranty.

An attempt by the buy-out team to extend the tax indemnity in this way is likely to upset the delicate balance of the warranty negotiations. The buy-out team should therefore resist the temptation to seek a 'kitchen sink' indemnity and should instead identify those liabilities which are likely to crystallise, which may have not been taken into account in the calculation of the purchase price and are therefore more amenable to a limited indemnity. Besides group taxation, obvious areas are liability for defective goods, litigation above a specified ceiling, dilapidations and unfunded pensions liabilities.

The purchaser is bound to be faced by a request for the same provisions limiting the liability of the vendor as are found in an arm's-length transaction. These will include limitations in amount and in time. The buy-out team should argue for a ceiling on the vendor's liability extending to the full amount of the purchase price, a threshold below which claims will not be brought of not more than, say, ½% of the price, a period during which claims can be made for breach of tax warranties and under the tax indemnity of six years from the end of the current accounting reference period and on the other warranties and indemnities of at least two accounting reference periods and the time to absorb the audited financial statements for the second accounting reference period.

The starting point and the outcome of the discussions on the limit of liability will be influenced by several factors, including the nature of the business being acquired, the proximity of the most recent audit, problems highlighted in the accountants' report, the completeness of the warranties and indemnities and the general atmosphere of the transaction. To reduce its own exposure, the vendor may ask for a 'swings and roundabouts' clause under which it will get the benefit of any over-provision or over-statement in the last accounts as a cushion against warranty claims.

Disclosure letter

The disclosure letter is the first line of defence to a claim under the warranties given by the vendor to Newco and by Newco to the financiers. For this reason, it is likely to be as hotly negotiated as the warranties themselves. It is quintessential for the buy-out team, faced as it will be by a plethora of agreements, not to lose sight of the importance of this document.

The function of the disclosure letter from the purchaser's side is to supplement the information gathered by the warranties and, from the vendor's side, to derogate from or to qualify specific warranties so as to render them toothless. The buy-out team should consider two issues; first, to respond to the vendor's request for assistance in the preparation of the disclosure letter and, secondly, to decide which of the disclosures to accept and therefore how much of the risk to run. The buy-out team's attitude will be shaped by its knowledge of the business, by its calculation of the financial consequences of accepting the disclosures and by its ability to qualify the warranties given to the institutions by the same disclosures.

The production of the disclosure letter will be complicated by the accountants' report. The institutions will commission the report as part of their due diligence but it is likely to be made available to the buy-out team to enable it to assess the areas in which warranty and indemnity protection cannot be foregone. The vendor may seize upon the opportunity to disclose the contents of the accountants' report to the purchaser. If the pertinent provisions in the acquisition agreement are well drafted, the vendor will be hoist by his own petard because it will be warranting the truth, accuracy and completeness of the accountants' report. It is a better solution for the vendor, with the institution's consent, to disclose specific and uncontentious portions of the accountants' report.

The vendor may also attempt to obtain a warranty of the accountants' report from the buy-out teams, particularly if it has been responsible for the provision of the information on which the report has been based. The buy-out team should view such an attempt in the overall context of the warranties required of it.

Hive down

Most of the problems associated with an asset purchase can be avoided by the simple expedient of a transfer of the trade and the relevant assets to a newly formed subsidiary. The sale price will be left outstanding on inter-company loan account and it will be repaid on completion of the purchase of the company. This is standard practice when the vendor is an administrative receiver.

The practice can be extended, however, so as to provide the purchaser with the ability to select the assets which it requires but to discard the attendant liabilities.

Pensions

The smooth progress of an asset sale is likely to be impeded by two of its component parts, both involving third parties and therefore less susceptible to control by the vendor and the purchaser. These are the assignment of contracts and leases and the transfer of pension entitlements of employees from the vendor to the purchaser. Although the Transfer of Undertakings (Protection of Employment) Regulations do not require that contracts relating to occupational pension schemes are transferred to the new business, Newco will undoubtedly wish to provide similar pension benefits to its workforce. The options available to it are discussed in the next chapter.

Newco must obtain full details of the vendor's scheme at the earliest possible opportunity and either obtain an up-to-date actuarial report on it or commission such a report from its own actuary. The costs of such an exercise should not be overlooked. With an up-to-date report available before completion of the assets purchase, Newco should be able to rely on a warranty from the vendor that the scheme is fully funded and the transfer value is sufficient to cover all accrued obligations in respect of the employees being transferred. These warranties should be backed by an indemnity.

If the report is not available before completion, Newco should take more extensive warranties and indemnities and consider retaining part of the purchase price against the issue of a satisfactory actuarial report. Since the liability attaching to a substantially under-funded scheme could wreck the buy-out, all the parties to it should keep their eyes on the pensions ball from the earliest moment. The pension implications are dealt with in more detail in Chapter 6.

Conditions and rescission

Given the pressure on all parties to sign a binding agreement at the earliest possible stage, it is likely that they will exchange contracts before certain pieces of the complex jigsaw are put into place. In this event, the agreement will be conditional upon the completion of the jigsaw.

Depending upon the timescale and complexity of the transaction, the following issues may be dealt with in the hiatus between exchange and completion:

i.   Revenue clearance under section 707 ICTA 1988
ii.   Revenue clearance under section 89 CGTA 1979
iii.   shareholders' resolution or Stock Exchange whitewash
iv.   the release and refinancing of intra-group guarantees, accounts and indemnities
v.   the accountants' report
vi.   payment of a dividend
vii.   finalisation of a completion balance sheet
viii. keyman insurance.

Taking each in turn:

i.   despite the elimination of the difference between the higher rates of income tax and the capital gains tax rate, a clearance under section 707 ICTA 1988 should still be sought. The characterisation of the purchase price as a gain will defer payment of the tax, particularly when roll-over relief can be obtained, and will often give rise to a reduced liability. This is discussed in more detail in the tax chapter

ii.   if the vendor has agreed to accept securities of Newco in satisfaction or partial satisfaction of the purchase price, it will want to
obtain the protection of section 88 CGTA 1979

iii.   if the target company is part of a quoted group, the disposal of the
shares or assets is likely to constitute a Class 4 transaction for the
purpose of the Yellow Book. Either the shareholders must
approve the disposal in a general meeting or The Stock Exchange
must grant dispensation from the requirement to obtain shareholders' consent.

    If the transaction satisfies the test for a major Class 1 trans-
action, shareholders' consent will be required in any event.

    If the vendor is not a listed company, the shareholders may
nevertheless be required to approve the disposal by virtue of
section 320 Companies Act 1985. The notice convening the meeting will be despatched on the date of signature of the binding
agreement so that there will be a delay of at least 17 days unless
consent to short notice can be obtained

iv.   if the target company is a member of a group or the business has
been run as a division, the vendor and the purchaser will need, at
an early stage, to determine the method by which the intra-group
indebtedness, guarantees and indemnities will be refinanced and
replaced. This process must be carefully monitored in order to
ensure that the arrangements do not constitute financial assistance
under section 151 Companies Act 1985.

    The replacement of guarantees and indemnities can pose par-
ticular problems for the buy-out team which will also be assuming
responsibility for the repayment of the loan finance and may
therefore find it difficult to persuade the beneficiaries of guarantees
and indemnities to exchange the solidity of the vendor group for the
likely frailty of Newco. A partial, but short term solution, is for the
vendor to agree to keep the guarantees and indemnities in place
against the counter indemnity from Newco. Alternatively and more
usually, the lending banks may agree to substituting their guarantees as part of the package. The guarantee will have a cost, however

v.   it is quintessential for the buy-out team to have the finance in place
at the earliest possible stage. This will be achieved by an offer
letter from the financiers which will be open for a specific period
and subject to conditions precedent, one of which will almost
certainly be a satisfactory accountants' report. A further condition
precedent imposed by the financiers might be a minimum net
tangible asset value of the target company on the date of exchange.

    Unless the time frame is unusually leisurely, it is not always
possible for the accountants to be able to finish their report by the
date for exchange of contracts, particularly where the transaction
is complex by reason of its size or its overseas aspects. By this
stage, however, the financiers should be able to take an informed
view of the transaction.

    The negotiation of the offer letter is most important for the members of the buy-out team. They should make every attempt to reduce the number of conditions precedent and to ensure that their meaning and scope are precise

vi.   where the vendor is an individual and not a company, the equalisation of higher rate income tax with the personal capital gains tax rate gives the buy-out team an opportunity to reduce the purchase price by the payment of a dividend from the target company to its shareholders. They will pay income tax at an effective rate of 20% on the dividend received, equivalent to 15% higher rate tax on the dividend plus the associated tax credit. This is explained in more detail in Chapter 4.

If there is a group election in place between the vendor and the target company, this route is also available

vii. if the lenders are looking to a satisfactory net tangible asset position because the buy-out is highly leveraged, a balance sheet as at exchange of contracts will have to be drawn up. Since the most recent audited financial statements are likely to be out of date, the work involved in producing this balance sheet might require some considerable time

viii. the financiers are likely to insist that the target company take out insurance cover on the lives of the key members of the buy-out team in order to give some measure of protection to their investment. It is not uncommon for the financiers to insist that the keyman insurance is in place as a condition to completion. If the premium is paid by the target company, as opposed to Newco, the question of financial assistance under section 151 Companies Act 1985 may arise. The payment should, however, fall within the 'incidental' exemption in section 153(1), provided that it satisfies the test in *Brady v Brady* (above).

Completion

The completion agenda for the acquisition of the target company will not look very different from that in a classic company acquisition. It will be more complex, however, because of the number of parties involved.

The timing of the resignation of directors and auditors must be carefully orchestrated, however. Where a company is being purchased on deferred terms related to future profits, or where part of the consideration is being calculated by reference to a completion balance sheet, the completion agenda will not always provide for the auditors of the target company to resign at completion. If there is an earn-out, they may well stay on as joint auditors and if there is a completion balance sheet, their resignation will be effective only after they have certified it. In the context of a buy-out, the auditors may be called upon to play their role in the financial assistance process.

Protection of the purchaser

Just as in any arm's length acquisition agreement, Newco will want to take steps to protect the goodwill it has acquired. The enforceability of agreements to protect confidential information is not in doubt. Care must be taken in drafting the restrictions relating to non-competition since the courts have the power to strike down any agreement reached between the parties if they consider them to be against the public interest. It is not uncommon for one party to a non-competition covenant to contend after the event that it is unenforceable if it acquires a commercial interest in the field in which it has undertaken not to compete.

Given the nature of a buy-out, it should not be difficult to reach a sensible accommodation between the parties. The problem area is likely to be a future acquisition by the vendor which includes the prescribed business. The purchaser can protect itself by permitting the carrying on of the prescribed business provided it is incidental to the other businesses of the vendor or by obliging the vendor to offer to sell the prescribed business to it.

The restrictions against the vendor poaching the customers or employees of the target company should also be sought by the purchaser.

The Restrictive Trade Practices Act 1956 applies to agreements between two or more persons carrying on business within the United Kingdom in the production or supply of goods or in the supply of services under which restrictions are accepted by two or more parties relating to the supply or receipt of those goods or services. Agreements to which the Act applies are registrable with the Office of Fair Trading. They may also be brought before the Restrictive Practices Court to determine whether the restrictions are contrary to the public interest.

The Restrictive Trade Practices (Sale and Purchase and Share Subscription Agreements) (Goods) Order 1989 and the Restrictive Trade Practices (Services) (Amendment) Order 1989, SIs 89/1081 and 89/1082, exempt agreements for the sale and purchase of shares in a company or of a business and agreements for the subscription of shares in a company, which satisfy certain conditions, from the provisions of the Restrictive Trade Practices Act 1976 requiring the registration of restrictive trade agreements for the supply of goods and the supply and acquisition of services. For the exemption to apply to sale and purchase agreements, 50% in nominal value of the issued share capital of the target company must be transferred or agreed to be transferred to one purchaser or to more than one purchaser, each of which is a member of the same group; the registrable restrictions must be of the type described in section 6(1)(c) to (f) of the 1976 Act; such restrictions can only be accepted by any vendor, any member of the same group as any vendor or any individual; the restrictions to be disregarded must only limit the extent to which the persons accepting them may compete with the company or business which is the subject of the sale or be involved in any business which so competes; and the restrictions to be disregarded can be operative for no longer than the permitted period. This is either five years from the date of the agreement, or where there are restrictions accepted by an individual who is to have a contract of employment with, or a contract for the supply of services to, the target company, the purchaser or its group, they must last no longer than a period from the date of such agreement ending two years after the date of the expiry or termination of the contract of employment or supply of services, if it is longer than five years.

Even if the agreement is registrable, section 21(2) of the Act will operate to dispense it from an investigation by the Restrictive Practices Court provided that the restrictions are not obviously against the public interest.

The penalty for failure to register a registrable agreement is that the restrictions are void and no party to the agreement may give effect to the restrictions. In order to avoid this draconian consequence, it has been common practice to provide in the agreement that any restrictions which require registration will not be effective until registration. The two 1989 statutory instruments will remove the necessity for this practice in most circumstances.

As well as protecting the newly acquired goodwill against the activities of the vendor, the buy-out team should consider requesting similar protection from the financiers. Such protection might take the form of an undertaking from the financiers not to invest in a competing business in a given geographical area for a specified time.

Warranty and indemnity insurance

The second line of defence to a warranty claim is warranty and indemnity insurance. If the warrantors are confident that the warranties and indemnities have been tightly drafted, that their exposure is suitably limited in time and amount and that any skeletons appear in the disclosure letter, recourse to such insurance should not be necessary. If it is available, it is likely to be both expensive and subject to exclusions which may render it nugatory. Nevertheless, it may be prudent to obtain quotations as soon as the draft accountants' report is available.

Subscription agreement

The subscription agreement contains the mechanism for the investment by the institutions in Newco and the warranties given by the buy-out team which will buttress that investment decision.

The subscription agreement will deal with the allotment and issue of the equity and debt in Newco to the institutions and, if appropriate, to the vendor of the target company, any conditions precedent to the subscription, the arrangements for completion of the subscription, the warranties given to the institutions and the limits on liability under these warranties, the disclosure letter relating to the warranties and the restrictive covenants given to the institutions to protect their investment.

Frequently, the subscription agreement is combined with a shareholders agreement, which will be treated separately in the next section.

Given that the buy-out team will have already subscribed for all its shares in Newco, the subscription agreement will be made among those members of the buy-out team who are in a position to give warranties to the institutions, the institutions themselves and Newco.

The buy-out team must consider which of its members are appropriate parties to the agreement. This decision will be influenced by the institutions' preference that all the buy-out team gives the requisite warranties. If the buy-out team is small, this preference will be difficult to resist. If the buy-out team is large, or if it is evident that a limited number of its members have the knowledge to give the warranties, the buy-out team should insist that only the appropriate members become parties to the subscription agreement. In any event, all the buy-out team members should ensure that their liability is several, and not joint. If this proves unacceptable to the lenders, they should settle amongst themselves a contribution agreement under which each member will bear only his pro rata share of any liability.

Newco will be a party to the subscription agreement since it will be issuing the new shares to the institutions.

If the institutions are numerous or if the loan is being syndicated, the lead institution will become party to the subscription agreement as agent for the other institutions or members of the syndicate.

The vendor of the target company should not be a party to the subscription agreement even if it is to receive debt or equity issued by Newco.

At completion, the following will happen:

i. the shares will be issued to the investors against payment of the subscription monies, the investors will be entered in the register of members of Newco and share certificates will be sealed and issued
ii. the financial assistance procedure will be implemented, if the target company is private
iii. the loan documentation will be entered into and the appropriate charges executed
iv. the directors nominated by the institutions will be appointed
v. the service agreements between Newco and the key members of the buy-out team will be signed and exchanged
vi. the keyman insurance on these key members will be put in place.

The relationship between the buy-out team and the financiers, which will have been collaborative in the planning of the buy-out, will turn adversarial when it comes to the warranties and indemnities required by the institutions. The relative positions of each group may be anomalous. It is common for the financiers to involve themselves with each phase of the acquisition of the target, first to lend their experience to the buy-out team, secondly to protect their future investment and thirdly to ensure that the agreement for the acquisition of the target company contains nothing prejudicial to their interests. As part of this last process, it is likely that the financiers will involve themselves in the negotiation of the warranties and indemnities required of the vendor to the extent of actively supporting the buy-out team's own advisers. Such intervention can have two purposes; it enables the buy-out team to bring pressure on a third party in a negotiation which may often prove difficult because of the employee/employer relationship of the vendor and the management team and, secondly, to cast the financiers in the role of the requisitionist of extensive warranties.

Although their decision to make the investment will be based on their own assessment of the investment opportunity, the financiers will want as many warranties from the management team, as well as from the vendors, as they consider are appropriate to the circumstances of the transaction. These will include the corporate status of target, its most recent audited and management accounts, its borrowings and other liabilities, its tax position, real property and intellectual and industrial property and its commercial position.

In addition, the financiers are likely to ask for warranties of the business plan as well as the notorious 'sweeper up' warranty. This warranty requires the disclosure of any facts or circumstances relating to the assets, business or financial condition of the target which, if disclosed, might be expected to effect the investment decision of the institutions or the documents. It is invariably hotly contested and should be displaced by the argument that the institutions have the benefit of specific warranties.

A warranty of the business plan should be limited to its careful preparation and the reasonableness of opinions and forecasts.

If the agreement for the acquisition of the target company is not deficient in its warranty and indemnity cover, the management team should have no difficulty in giving the same warranties to the institutions or assigning their benefit to them. Similarly, the management team should be able to warrant matters within its specific knowledge or for which it has taken express responsibility, such as the business plan or aspects of the accountants' report.

Nevertheless, it is axiomatic that the members of the management team who are giving the warranties to the institutions will feel uneasy about an extension of their exposure to financial risk. In a management led buy-out without significant debt, it is likely that a large proportion of the equity finance will be provided by members of the management team. In this circumstance, they can fairly argue that they are already taking the risk of injecting their own cash into the buy-out and that therefore the double jeopardy of extensive warranties is inappropriate. If this line of argument is rejected, the negotiations on the limits on their liability will be all the more keen.

There is an alternative approach which might commend itself to a management team unable to cope with contingent liability under the warranties. This involves an adjustment to the ratchet mechanism discussed in Chapter 3 which will have the effect of increasing the shareholdings of the institutions in the event of a warranty claim which cannot be met by the management team. The management team's advisers will inform it that material warranty claims are rare in a transaction which has been competently and efficiently handled and recommend that it should not dilute its hard won equity stake.

If only selected members of the management team give the warranties, they should hedge their exposure by a contribution agreement with the other members of the team, even if the institutions accept that the warranties are several and not joint.

The buy-out team should also bear in mind that, upon a future disposal or flotation of the shares of Newco, warranties will have to be given to the purchaser or to the issuing house. The buy-out team may find that the institutions and their representatives on the board of Newco will be reluctant to accept any such responsibility or liability. In their warranty negotiations with the institutions, the buy-out team could do well to require, as a quid pro quo, sensible warranties from the institutions at the time of disposal or flotation. This requirement should be formalised in an undertaking in the shareholders agreement.

The buy-out team should also bear in mind that the institutions will think carefully before demoralising the management team by extravagant warranty claims, thus reducing the value of their investment.

The management team should fiercely resist the giving of any indemnities. The taxation position of the target will be more than adequately covered by the warranties and tax indemnity given by the vendor. The management team are unlikely to have entered into any transaction which might impose a secondary liability to taxation on Newco or the target and against which, therefore, these companies will be entitled to be indemnified. The institutions may well require the key members of the management team to give restrictive covenants in the subscription agreement on the ground that they are more easily enforceable when given in support of the investment. Such restrictions will typically include agreements:

i.   not to carry on or be concerned in any business which competes with the business of the target
ii. not to assist any person engaged in any competitive business
iii. not to poach customers or employees
iv. not to interfere with any trading arrangements of the target company or use any similar trading name.

The key managers will be confronted with a similar set of restrictions in their respective service agreements. The termination of a manager's service agreement will normally be linked to an obligation to sell his shares in Newco. In such circumstances, it should not be difficult for the management team to reject the restrictive covenants in the subscription agreement as excessive.

The subscription agreement should also cover the responsibility for the payment of the costs of the transaction.

Shareholders agreement

The purpose of the shareholders agreement is to govern the management of Newco and target and to regulate the relationship between the shareholders of Newco to the extent that these issues are not covered in the articles of association of Newco. It will therefore deal with:

i.   the proceedings of the board
ii.   conduct of the affairs of Newco and target
iii. restricted transactions
iv.   transfers of shares
v.   the disposal or flotation of Newco.

The constitution of the board of Newco will determine the way in which the agreement deals with the conduct of the company's affairs and transactions which are restricted and subject to a superimposed decision-making process.

In the nature of the larger buy-out, the management team is unlikely to control the board either at completion or in the short term after it. The buy-out team should therefore seek the protection appropriate to minority shareholders. If, on the other hand, the buy-out team initially has board control or can acquire it in the short term, the institutions will want the same protection. Members of the buy-out team on the board of Newco should consider entrenching their position on the board by the division of the ordinary share capital into two classes, each carrying the right to appoint and dismiss its own directors. A management team with a minority of the ordinary share capital will thus have voting rights at board level disproportionate to its shareholding. If the institutions are sympathetic to this structure, they may nevertheless insist that the entrenched positions fall away in the event that there is a profit haemor-rhage over a defined period or that the management team commits a material breach of the shareholders agreement.

The balance between the protection of each class of shareholder at board level and the operation of the company untrammelled by a bureaucratic management structure may be difficult to achieve. Having committed to the buy-out team morally and financially, the institutions will be loath to interfere in the management of Newco and its sub-sidiaries. By the same token, the buy-out team will not wish to sub-stitute a new set of masters for those whose replacement has been the object of the exercise. Recognising that the demotivation of the management team is likely to reduce the value of their investment, the institutions should be persuaded to adopt a 'hands off' policy which will be capable of reversal only in carefully drawn circumstances based on failure to repay debt or to meet turnover or profit targets.

The composition of the board is therefore of particular importance. In its initial discussions with the financiers, the buy-out team should have carefully evaluated the financiers' approach to the issue of control and the shareholders agreement should therefore contain no surprises.

That part of the agreement dealing with the conduct of the affairs of Newco and the target will contain positive obligations. These will include:

i.   the business of the group will consist exclusively of the business which is the subject of the buy-out. The institutions may wish to have the right to veto any diversification
ii.   the management of the company will be determined at duly

convened meetings of the board. All shareholders will recognise the value of institutionalising the decision-making process and instilling at an early stage the disciplines required of a company grooming itself for a flotation

iii. the board will determine the general policy of the group on the basis of the business plan. It constitutes a useful control mechanism to establish the parameters within which the management can work and should, at least in the early stages of the company's new life, prevent any divergencies between management and the institutions on the commercial direction of the company

iv. the business plan will be updated annually. Any material departure from the previous plan is likely to be the first area in which the members of the buy-out team will find themselves in conflict with the board representatives of the institutions

v. the production of regular management accounts and cashflows

vi. during the initial period following the buy-out, the communication of the cash position to the institutions

vii. approval of capital expenditure outside the business plan

viii. production of audited accounts and the holding of the annual general meeting within respectively three and four months of the accounting reference date

ix. the appointment of auditors. The institutions will often insist on a reasonably sized firm able to cope with the growth of the business and the demands of a flotation

x. appointment of bankers

xi. the agreement for the acquisition of the target company, the subscription agreement, the shareholders agreement, the articles of association, the service agreements and the banking documents will not be varied without the consent of the institutions

xii. the relevant parties, including in particular Newco and the target company, will comply with and enforce all the terms and conditions of the transaction documents

xiii. dividend policy. It is unlikely that the structure of the finance will permit the payment of dividends on the ordinary shares until the preference shares have been redeemed or converted and any debt has been fully repaid

xiv. cheque signing authority.

In addition, the shareholders agreement may provide for the frequency of which meetings of the board are to be held and the circulation of the agenda, if these matters are not dealt with in the articles of association.

It is the practice of some venture capitalists to superimpose a control organ whose function is similar to that of a supervisory board in the two-tier management structure of continental public companies. This organ, sometimes called an audit committee, will be a duly established committee of the board consisting, typically, of the finance director of Newco, a representative of the buy-out team and a representative of the institutions. Its function will be the general management control of the financial and fiscal affairs of the group with a selective power of veto.

Depending upon the composition of the board, the minority share-holders will demand that major decisions affecting their investment cannot be taken without their consent. The extent of the minority protection and the nature of the approval-giving process are sensitive areas whose handling at the stage of drafting the shareholders agreement may well set the tone of the future relationships between the parties. It is not uncommon to find a list of up to forty restricted transactions covering changes to the capital structure of Newco, transfers of shares, acquisitions or disposals of businesses and companies, establishment of partnerships and profit sharing arrangements, issue of debentures and other debt securities, making of loans, taking or grant of interests in land, change of accounting reference date, delegation of the powers of the board to a committee, amendments to service agreements, engagement of employees with a remuneration package above a certain level, change of auditors and bankers, initiation of litigation or arbitration other than to collect trade debts, any claim or election for taxation purposes, changes in accounting or reporting practices, research and development expenditure outside the business plan.

The construction of the approval-giving process may reflect the composition of the board. Alternatively, each category of decision may be subject to a different process. As examples, the consent of the majority of the board may be required; or the consent of the majority of the board together with a separate majority of the directors nominated by the institutions; or an increased threshold such as three-quarters of all directors; or unanimity. The permutations are numerous.

To the extent that the transfer of shares in Newco is not entirely regulated by the articles of association of Newco, the shareholders agreement will contain complementary or supplementary provisions. Such provisions would include an absolute prohibition on any transfer of shares for an initial period, say two years, in order to emphasise the commitment of each party to the others. If there is such a prohibition, it may be lifted in the cases of bona fide transfers to trustees created for the benefit of spouses and issue and to companies controlled by the transferring shareholder provided that this is coupled with an obligation to re-transfer the shares in question in the event that control is lost. This derogation would be backed by an obligation on the transferor to ensure that the transferee entered into obligations identical to those undertaken by the transferor.

Both the buy-out team and the institutions will have the flotation of Newco or its disposal in contemplation. The shareholders agreement should therefore attempt to plan for the future.

The timing of the flotation will depend on a number of factors outside the control of the shareholders. Nevertheless, the institutions may attempt to impose their will on the buy-out team by providing in the shareholders agreement that they have the right to procure flotation at any time after a given date unless Newco has received advice from a reputable stockbroker or merchant banker properly instructed for the purpose that the flotation is not appropriate. From the point of view of the members of the buy-out team, it would be appropriate only when the ratchet has produced the greatest benefit for them. Given the limits of the art of crystal ball gazing, it is sensible that the shareholders agreement be silent on the question of the timing of a flotation.

It should, however, address the key issue of share disposal in the flotation. Flotation will mean that the buy-out has been successful. If the financiers are long-term investors, they will want to sell the minimum number of shares to the public. For the same reason, the managers will wish to retain the maximum number of shares. Given that a flotation on the unlisted securities market requires at least 10% of the shares of Newco to be offered to the public and that full listing requires at least 25%, it is as well to settle the matter at a time when the parties are capable of greater objectivity. The shareholders agreement should therefore set out clearly the obligations to sell shares to the public, restrictions on disposals of shares after the flotation to safeguard the after-market, the giving of warranties and indemnities to the issuing house and the reorganisation of the share capital of Newco, if required.

The shareholders agreement should also cover the issues which will be faced upon an offer for all the share capital of Newco. In addition, it is in the interest of both the management and the investors to insert a 'piggy-back' clause which requires a shareholder in receipt of a bona fide offer for its shares from a third party to procure the same offer for the other shareholders as a condition precedent to any disposal.

Articles of association

Of all the documents generated in a management buy-out, the articles of association of Newco are likely to be the most complex. The articles will contain not only the provisions normally found in private company articles (but writ considerably larger) but also the basis upon which the future wealth of the buy-out team will be calculated. The articles will deal with the capital structure of Newco, the variation of class rights, new issues of shares, the ratchet mechanism and transfers of shares, borrowing powers, including in particular provisions for the reward of successful managers and the penalisation of failures.

The articles setting out the capital structure will reflect the basis on which the finance is being provided. For example, the management team may be allotted ordinary shares with limited special rights, such as the right to appoint a separate class of directors and the payment of a nominal dividend until the redemption or conversion of the institutions' shares.

The institutions may be allotted a mixture of redeemable preference shares, which may be convertible, with extensive class rights. Ordinary shares of a class the same as or similar to that allotted to the managers will also be issued to the institutions.

New issues of shares will not normally be permitted, given the inability of the buy-out team to finance them and their dilutionary effect. An issue of shares made to redeem preference shares in order to move the ratchet may also have such an effect unless it is carefully planned.

The purpose of the ratchet and the effect on it of Chapter II of Part III of the Finance Act 1988 have been discussed. The events which trigger the ratchet require careful and detailed drafting. They will include:

i.   the maximum and minimum number of ordinary shares to which the managers will be entitled as a result of the operation of the ratchet
ii.   the period over which the ratchet will operate
iii. the events which will trigger the operation of the ratchet.

These may be:

i.   the achievement of a specified level of profits over a specified period
ii.   value on flotation
iii. value on disposal.

A profit-related ratchet is the most complex. Advisers familiar with earn-out mechanisms will be aware of the similarities between them and ratchets. The problems are:

i.   a carefully drawn definition of profits. If the profits are to be post-tax, it is suggested that they are defined as 'profits or loss on ordinary activities after taxation' in accordance with lines 14 or 16 of formats 1 or 2 respectively in section B Schedule 4 of the Companies Act 1985 or the equivalent if formats 3 or 4 of that schedule are used.
      The effect of carry foward tax losses on the ratchet should also be considered since, in the absence of a specific provision to the contrary, they will not be deducted in computing the profits measured by the profit and loss account of a particular accounting reference period
ii.   the effect of extraordinary and exceptional items. To avoid controversy, it is suggested that profits are calculated after charging or crediting exceptional items but before charging or crediting extraordinary items or tax on extraordinary items
iii. the effect of acquisitions made by Newco or target. Since the achievement of maximum benefits under the ratchet will be welcomed by all shareholders, the institutions should be able to afford a relaxed attitude to the effect of acquisitions on the ratchet, unless a new issue of shares is required to pay for the acquisition.

The provisions in the shareholders agreement dealing with the conduct of the company's affairs and restricted transactions will be stronger if they are included in the articles of association since their contractual effect will extend to any incoming shareholder and they are a matter of public record. The latter point is only of cosmetic importance given the protection afforded by section 35 Companies Act 1985 (as amended by section 108 Companies act 1989) to persons dealing with a company in good faith. It is therefore common for institutions to insist that the restrictions are part of the class rights of their redeemable preference shares. The consent of 75 per cent of the holders of a particular class is required to vary such rights.

The limit on the borrowing powers of Newco will be largely academic in the light of the covenants in the banking documents. Careful attention should be paid, nonetheless, to the drafting of the borrowing powers so as to include items which are generally in the nature of borrowing and to exclude those which are not. An example of the latter is loan notes or debentures issued by a purchaser to a vendor in order to preserve the right of the vendor to roll-over relief under section 85 CGTA 1979 in an earn-out acquisition.

Next to the construction of the ratchet mechanism, the most vexed issue will be the pre-emption provisions governing the transfer of shares. The problems posed in a long form private company pre-emption article will be present with some added convolutions.

The first issue is the valuation of the shares to be transferred. The variations on the theme include a fair price determined by the auditors as a going concern, willing buyer/seller basis, the price offered by a bona fide third party purchaser, a price calculated by reference to the price earnings ratio for the sector based on the latest audited financial statements and American poker or Russian roulette. These gambling games are shorthand for a mechanism whose object is to ensure that the seller asks and receives a sensible price for its shares by giving the proposed purchaser the right to buy the shares on offer or to sell its own holding of shares to the seller at the price placed on them by the seller.

Since the capital structure is likely to include at least two classes of shares whose economic effect and voting rights will have been carefully balanced in structuring the buy-out, any upsetting of this balance must be managed in the pre-emption provisions. The most practical solution is for pre-emption to apply within each class of shares before they are offered outside the class. Thus, the shares held by the institutions would first be offered to other institutional shareholders pro rata to their holdings, then to the managers, then to the nominated buyer. In the case of the shares held by the management team, the considerations are different. It would be appropriate for the shares held by the management to be offered to other employees selected by the board or to an employee share trust, then to the other manager shareholders pro rata to their holdings, next to the institutions and finally to the nominated buyer.

The pre-emption provisions would not normally apply to transfers to family trusts and associated companies.

The transfer of a controlling interest can be dealt with by a 'piggyback' mechanism. For this purpose, a controlling interest must be carefully defined. Ignoring the definitions of control in sections 416 and 840 Income and Corporation Taxes Act 1988, the three obvious bench marks are more than 25% to block a special resolution, 30% or more as contemplated by rule 9.1 of the City Code on Take-overs and Mergers and more than 50% to block an ordinary resolution.

As an alternative to the 'piggy-back' clause, the articles might contain a 'shot gun' provision requiring the minority shareholders to sell to a third party at the price offered by it in the event that the majority shareholders have so elected.

The institutions will be keen to ensure that management shareholders do not alienate their shares for some time after the completion of the buy-out. Such a provision may be in the shareholders agreement or in the articles, which will not recognise the service of a transfer notice within a specified period. As a corollary, both institutions and managers are unlikely to countenance the retention of any shares by a manager who ceases to be employed by a member of the Newco group. Section 78 Finance Act 1988 will not operate so as to prevent a restriction contained in the articles of association which obliges an employee shareholder whose employment has terminated to transfer his shares. In such circumstances, it is both logical and practical for shares which thus become available to be offered to employees who are not shareholders within the ambit of section 78. Shares sold by a departing employee may be valued differently, depending upon the length of time that they have been held. It is clearly not appropriate for the departing shareholder to receive full value if he voluntarily terminates his employment within a period of, say, two years of completion of the buy-out. The same must apply if his employment is terminated for cause. It becomes more difficult to calculate a price with the lengthening of service or if the employee has been wrongfully or constructively dismissed. One solution is to provide for a ratchet whose factors will be based on length of service and reasons for termination of the employment. Another is to adopt rules similar to those of an executive share option scheme approved under section 185 and Schedule 9 Income and Corporation Taxes Act 1988 with a lengthy qualifying period subject to a limited number of exemptions.

If the employee shareholder dies or is seriously incapacitated, it would not be equitable for the value of his shareholding to be discounted.

Service agreements

The transfer provisions in the articles of association affecting employee shareholders will be linked to the termination provisions of the key employees' service agreements. The investors will insist upon service agreements for the same reasons as an issuing house in a flotation: protection of the investment. In the negotiation of their service agreements, the members of the buy-out team are faced with a dilemma, that of balancing the total cost of their remuneration package against its effect on the bottom line of the profit and loss account and therefore on the operation of the ratchet.

Investors will want the service agreement to run for a period of at least three years. The manager will view such a period against the perspective of the growth in value of his shareholding, the forced disposal of that shareholding if he leaves voluntarily within the minimum period or involuntarily for cause and the obligations to repay any personal loans he may have taken out to fund his acquisition of shares in Newco.

The manager will therefore focus on the drafting of the termination clause. He will wish to ensure that the events permitting the company to terminate his employment are tightly drawn and that prolonged ill-health will not trigger the expropriation provisions under the articles.

POST ACQUISITION

A critical problem faced by the purchaser of a company is the motivation of those key employees who have not benefited financially from the acquisition. The purchaser must ensure that these employees are provided with sufficient incentive to produce profits after the departure of the proprietors of the company. Investors in a buy-out are faced with the same problem. If the employees have not participated in the buy-out through the medium of an employee share option scheme, a solution is for Newco to put into place a share option scheme approved under section 185 and Schedule 9 Income and Corporation Taxes Act 1988 or, if appropriate, an unapproved share option scheme.

CHAPTER 6

Pensions – the forgotten element

INTRODUCTION

Pensions are frequently not considered, or not considered in sufficient detail, when the terms of a buy-out are negotiated. Yet, pensions can be critical to the success of the venture in two important areas: first, the financial implications and second, the stability of employee relations.

From a financial point of view, a pension scheme can either be an asset or a liability. In the former case a surplus in the pension scheme can provide a useful form of short term finance whereas a deficit could be a severe drain on financial resources. It is worth noting that, over the long term, the cost of a good pension scheme could be as much as 25% of payroll overall with most of this being met by the employer; and it is not uncommon to find that the value of the assets in a pension scheme is as great if not greater than the total value of the business.

This situation is accentuated by the introduction of the Statement of Standard Accounting Practice No 24 (SSAP 24) which has removed much of the flexibility which existed previously in charging pension contributions to the profit and loss account.

At the time of the buy-out there is bound to be a feeling of uncertainty amongst employees, and it is essential that their confidence is restored as soon as possible. The proper treatment of pension rights and expectations will be an important element in this process. The provision of competitive pension arrangements will, if properly communicated, help to foster good employee relations and aid in the recruitment, motivation and retention of staff.

Despite their importance, pensions are frequently overlooked, often as a result of a perceived lack of information to assess the position. Often detailed discussions on pensions are deferred until after the buy-out has been completed, the deal going ahead based on an assurance of 'full-funding' or 'sufficient coverage of the liabilities'.

Later in this chapter it will be shown that there is now a great deal of information available and that there are significant risks associated with accepting the vendor's valuation of the pension scheme.

It is assumed in this chapter that prior to the buy-out a pension scheme is in existence covering some or all of the employees. If this is not the case much of what follows will not of course be relevant. However consideration should in any event be given to the desirability of a pension scheme following the buy-out and whether some allowance should be made for pension scheme contributions in Newco's calculations. It is also assumed that, in the interests of good employee relations, Newco will wish to continue with some form of pension scheme (but not necessarily at the same level as the current arrangements). If this is not the case, the employees would normally be entitled to their normal leaving service benefits from the vendor's pension scheme and possible redundancy payments if employment were not continuous. It is worth noting that to discontinue or to cut back significantly the pension scheme may be construed as altering the employees' terms and conditions adversely and lead to claims of constructive dismissal.

In practice, a number of situations can arise. One of the principal points of difference will be concerned with the availability of and access to information relating to the pension scheme(s). In most cases, the purchaser will have direct access to most of the relevant information, particularly if a member of the buy-out team is also a member of the pension scheme; it is possible that a member of the buy-out team has been involved in the management of the pension scheme but care is required in using privileged information obtained as a trustee. Since buy-outs are generally friendly, access to information is not normally a problem.

In other situations, access to information may be restricted, eg if the buy-out is contested or in the case of a management buy-in. In the latter case, particularly if the buy-in is hostile, the purchaser may have to rely entirely on information contained in the company's accounts and other published sources giving details of company pension schemes and their advisers.

Accordingly, this chapter deals with situations where there is both unlimited access and also where only published information is available. The financial implications are considered separately for:

i.   a buy-out involving the acquisition of a whole pension scheme(s)
ii. a buy-out involving part of the membership of a pension scheme(s) either due to the purchase of a subsidiary company or the transfer of employees spread across a company or group of companies

TYPES OF PENSION SCHEME

Pension schemes in the UK can be divided into the following main categories:

i.   personal pension schemes, ie individual arrangements introduced from 1 July 1988 or prior to that date, self employed annuities for the self employed and persons in non-pensionable employment
ii. occupational pension schemes, ie pension schemes sponsored by an employer and normally established on either a 'money purchase' or 'defined benefits' basis.

Personal pension schemes

There is no requirement for an employer to contribute to a personal pension scheme; but the full rate of National Insurance contributions (as opposed to the reduced rate which would apply for an employee who was contracted-out of the state earnings related pension scheme, SERPS) would be payable for an employee with a personal pension scheme.

Personal pension schemes continue irrespective of a change of employment and are independent of the employer. An employer may, however, agree to make contributions to a personal pension scheme whilst the individual concerned remains in employment with that employer.

Occupational pension schemes

Occupational pension schemes are sponsored by an employer and the employee's membership ceases on the termination of employment. They fall into two main categories:

i. money purchase schemes which usually provide for contributions to be paid into the scheme from the employee and employer at defined rates; the benefits emerging from the scheme are dependent on the accumulated value of these contributions at the time of the employee's retirement, or earlier death or withdrawal
ii. defined benefit schemes which provide for, as the name suggests, a defined level of benefits, typically one sixtieth of final salary for each year of pensionable service from normal retirement date (65 for males and 60 for females). Thus the employee is assured that his income in retirement will be at a known level in relation to that preceding retirement. However, from the employer's point of view there is an open-ended commitment to provide whatever contributions are necessary to provide the benefits.

In recent times hybrid schemes have been developed involving a combination of money purchase and defined benefits, eg a benefit of one sixtieth for each year of service may be provided with a guarantee that benefits will not be less than the accumulated value of contributions at a given rate.

There are clear differences between money purchase and defined benefit schemes and each has certain characteristics which are particularly relevant for a buy-out.

It is useful to consider these separately both in the context of the vendor's scheme, before the buy-out, and in establishing a new pension scheme after the buy-out.

Before the buy-out

Money purchase schemes should prove to be fairly straightforward. The principal points to note are the levels at which the employer is required to contribute and whether there are any outstanding contributions which are due but have not been paid. The calculation of a transfer value payable from a money purchase scheme is also straight-forward being the sum of the amounts in each member's account at the date of transfer.

By contrast defined benefit schemes are much more complicated and an actuary will need to be appointed to assess the financial position and/or advise on the transfer value which could be payable to another pension scheme.

After the buy-out

Money purchase schemes are simple to administer, easily understood by the employees and involve a fixed level of contributions by the employer. The employer loses control over the level of benefits emerging under the scheme which could be a disadvantage if the employees are long serving since attention then tends to be focussed on benefit levels. The whole of the transfer value from the vendor's scheme will normally pass to the benefit of the members including any surplus under a previous defined benefits scheme.

Defined benefit schemes are complicated to administer and the employer takes on an open-ended liability albeit that a scheme can be terminated at any point in time with limited liability falling on the employer. Whilst benefits can be tailored to suit the particular circumstances, defined benefit schemes tend to operate to the advantage of long serving employees compared to short serving employees. Any gains from investment performance on the scheme's assets can be used to offset the employer's costs as opposed to those automatically falling to the benefit of the members of the scheme. The employer has flexibility over the level of contributions paid into the scheme to fund the benefits which can be advantageous if there are constraints on cash flow in the short term.

The remainder of this chapter is principally concerned with defined benefit schemes but mention will be made of money purchase schemes where relevant.

SOURCES OF INFORMATION AND INITIAL APPRAISAL

As a result of the Social Security Act 1986 and subsequent regulations on disclosure of information, a great deal of information is now available to members of pension schemes and recognised trade unions either automatically or upon request. These together with the main points of interest in the context of buy-outs are as follows:

Explanatory booklet

A booklet must be issued automatically to all members of the pension scheme containing a description of the main benefits provided under the scheme and the basis for contribution payments. In addition, senior employees may have their benefits varied in accordance with special letters or service agreements. Details of benefits such as permanent health insurance, accident or private medical insurance may be contained in other documents. The booklet may contain references to benefits provided on a discretionary basis such as increases to pensions in payment and augmentations on early retirement or redundancy. However, these references should be checked against other sources including the trustees annual report and accounts, the actuarial valuation report and, if possible, with the vendor directly.

Trust deed and rules

A copy of the trust deed and rules is available to members on request. This is the governing document of the pension scheme and will set out in detail the terms and provisions of the scheme, powers of the trustees and basis for Inland Revenue approval. Of particular interest are the clauses concerning the payment of transfer values out of the scheme. For a defined benefits scheme, an individual member leaving the pension scheme would be entitled to a transfer value reflecting the actuarial value of his leaving service benefits (ie deferred pension) based on salary and service at date of leaving. However many schemes provide for an enhanced transfer value related to the members' expectations including allowances for future salary increases and discretionary benefits, and possibly to a share of any surplus (subject to there being sufficient funds and often at the discretion of the trustees with the approval of the company) in the event of a large number of members leaving the scheme as a result of a company sale (often called a 'block' or 'bulk' transfer). The provisions for refunds of surplus to the employer and on winding-up the scheme will also be important particularly if a whole scheme is being acquired. In these days of predator protection some trust deed and rules contain clauses which are aimed against a predator using the pension scheme's funds to his advantage – so called 'poison pills' – eg, there may be restrictions on powers to change the trustees or amend the benefits following a change of ownership.

Trustees' annual report and accounts

This is available on request but a large number of schemes provide a shortened version automatically. Amongst other items the trustees' annual report and accounts should contain:

i.   names of trustees and their advisers
ii.   scheme membership
iii.   size of fund and financial prospects
iv.   policy with regard to post-retirement pension increases
v.   investment arrangements
vi.   revenue account and balance sheet
vii.   statement by the actuary giving level of security on wind-up
viii. recommended contribution rates and brief description of actuarial funding methods and assumptions.

Announcements to members

From time to time the trustees may issue announcements to members relative to changes which have not at the time been reflected in scheme documents.

Actuarial valuation report

The main purpose of an actuarial valuation report is to determine the contributions the employer must pay in addition to those payable by the members in order to ensure the solvency of the scheme. The report contains a description of the actuarial funding method and assumptions adopted for calculating the contribution rate and an assessment of the solvency level on both a winding-up and an on-going basis. Whilst this is perhaps the most important document, it may be out of date (by 3 years or more) and could have been overtaken by events. Announcements to members, number of employees as shown in company accounts, and the trustees' annual report and accounts may give some clues as to possible changes.

Company accounts

Company accounts will show pension contributions, ex-gratia or unfunded pensions paid from revenue and number of employees. Prior to the publication by the UK Accounting Standards Committee of SSAP 24 pension scheme contributions in company accounts could bear no relationship to the long term cost of the pension scheme and thus profitability of the company. SSAP 24 will require a significant increase in the disclosures made in company accounts about pension schemes for company accounting years beginning on or after 1 July 1988. This information will enable a reasonable financial assessment of the pension scheme to be made by a purchaser with access to expert advice. Details of the requirements of SSAP 24 are contained in Appendix 3.

If there is a wide discrepancy between the number of employees and members of the pension scheme the rights or otherwise of non-members to join the pension scheme should be investigated.

Other published information

Membership handbooks produced by, for example the National Association of Pension Funds, and Pension Funds and their Advisers contain summary information which can be useful in some situations.

It should be noted that the whole of the above information should be available in circumstances where the buy-out is conducted on a friendly basis. The vendor's actuarial advisers would also normally be instructed to provide additional clarification on the financial position of the pension scheme, if required. In hostile situations, however, the buy-out team may have to rely solely on information contained in company accounts and other published information.

Much of the above information should be straightforward and self-explanatory. It is now a matter of interpretation. Before considering this, however, it is necessary to unravel some of the mysteries of an actuarial valuation.

UNDERSTANDING AN ACTUARIAL VALUATION

The main purpose of an actuarial valuation of a defined benefits pension scheme is to determine the rate at which the employer must contribute to the scheme in order to provide the benefits payable from the scheme.

It is important to note that the contribution rate can only be estimated and is a function of the funding method adopted and the actuarial assumptions. These govern the pace of funding or the rate at which assets are built-up to meet the future liabilities: not the long term cost. The actual contributions are a function of the actual experience and can only be quantified precisely after the termination of the scheme. The principal funding methods which are normally encountered in the UK are explained below. Under each method the process involves discounting the expected future benefit outgo (allowing for assumed rates of salary growth, mortality, withdrawal, retirement and increases to pensions in payment) at the assumed future rate of investment return in order to determine the capital value of the liabilities at the valuation date. Similarly the expected future income from existing investments can be discounted to determine the capital value of the assets. Alternatively the assets may be valued at market value or at average market value.

Funding methods

Aggregate Method
The purpose of the Aggregate Method is to determine a stable rate of contribution, expressed as a percentage of salaries, for the present members. The capital value of all prospective benefits payable to the present members allowing for service before (past service) and after (future service) the valuation date is compared with the value of the existing assets. The balance of liabilities, ie not already covered by existing assets, determines the amount to be met by future contributions. The capital value of the required future contributions is normally expressed as a level percentage of the future salaries of the existing members.

AGGREGATE METHOD

ASSETS	LIABILITIES
FUTURE CONTRIBUTIONS	PROSPECTIVE BENEFITS
EXISTING ASSETS	

As stated above, the contribution rate should remain stable for the existing membership, provided the assumptions are borne out in practice. However, as new entrants to the scheme are normally younger than the existing membership they will cause the contribution rate to fall due to the longer period over which to discount their benefits. The method also leads to over-funding, ie the ratio of existing assets to liabilities attributable to past service but based on projected salaries will normally exceed 100%. This stems from the fact that contributions paid for an individual member in the early years are more than sufficient to meet the cost of benefits accruing, whilst the reverse is true in later years so the level of funding for an individual member first increases to above 100% and then reduces to 100% immediately preceding retirement.

Attained Age Method

The purpose of the Attained Age Method is similar to that of the Aggregate Method, ie to produce a stable rate of contributions. However the liabilities are divided between past and future service which permits greater flexibility in the funding of a surplus or deficiency by varying the period over which it is amortised.

Future service benefits

The capital value of benefits arising for future service (ie service after the valuation date) is calculated for present active members. This is then equated to a level percentage of future salaries to determine the contribution rate for future service benefits or the 'normal' contribution as it is sometimes referred to. As in the case of the Aggregate Method, this leads to over-funding all other things being equal.

Past service benefits

The liabilities for service accrued to the valuation date but allowing for projected salaries to retirement are calculated for active members. The liabilities for pensioners and deferred pensioners are added to this sum to give the total past service liability. This is then compared with the value of the existing assets.

In the event of a shortfall (ie the past service liability exceeds the value of existing assets) special contributions are required in addition to the normal contributions; and in the event of a surplus (ie the existing assets exceed the past service liabilities) special contributions are in effect negative and are offset against the normal contributions. Under the Attained Age Method there is a wide choice of methods available for determining the level of special contributions (positive or negative) which essentially vary the pace at which a surplus or deficiency is amortised. Special contributions can be determined as fixed instalments or as a level percentage of salaries spread over the existing members' working lifetime. In the latter case the Attained Age Method is equivalent to the Aggregate Method.

It is worth noting that for a pension scheme in surplus the level of special contributions can be geared to offset the entire cost of future service benefits for a limited period – the so called 'contribution holiday'.

ATTAINED AGE METHOD

ASSETS	LIABILITIES
NORMAL CONTRIBUTIONS	FUTURE SERVICE BENEFITS
SPECIAL CONTRIBUTIONS	PAST SERVICE BENEFITS
EXISTING ASSETS	

Projected Unit Method (sometimes also referred to as Projected Unit Credit Method or PUC for short)

The purpose of the method is to obtain a level of funding of 100%, ie for the existing assets to equal the value of past service benefits allowing for projected salaries at retirement. Thus if the assumptions are borne out the method should not lead to over-funding as is the case with the Aggregate and Attained Age Methods. Liabilities are calculated separately for past and future service benefits and special contributions are payable in respect of past service benefits as explained for the Attained Age Method. The normal contribution rate is determined as the cost of benefits accruing in the year following the valuation date allowing for projected salaries at retirement.

PROJECTED UNIT METHOD

ASSETS	LIABILITIES
NORMAL CONTRIBUTIONS	ONE YEAR'S BENEFIT ACCRUAL
SPECIAL CONTRIBUTIONS	PAST SERVICE BENEFITS
EXISTING ASSETS	

Since the cost of one year's benefit accrual is dependent on age, the normal contributions will increase with the age of the membership (due to the reducing period over which to discount their benefits) unless there are sufficient new entrants to maintain a stable age distribution. The method may be unsuitable, therefore, for pension schemes with declining memberships.

Other funding methods

The above cover the majority of funding methods encountered in the UK. Other methods include the Entry Age Method (which is similar to the Attained Age) and Discontinuance Funding Method. The latter is akin to the Projected Unit Method but without an allowance for projected salaries at retirement. Instead, an allowance is only made for current salary at the valuation date plus any statutory revaluation on leaving service. Thus caution is required if Discontinuance Funding has been applied since the resulting contribution rates are likely to understate the long term cost on an on-going basis and the funding level is likely to be much lower than those which would apply for other funding methods. Nevertheless, benefits are sometimes projected over periods of greater than one year, perhaps up to 20 years (called a control period) in which case the Discontinuance Method tends to the Projected Unit Method. Similarly, the Projected Unit Method tends to the Attained Age Method if a control period is adopted, approximating to the average remaining service lives of the existing membership.

Actuarial assumptions

Whilst the funding method has a significant impact on the results of an actuarial valuation, the choice of assumptions can have an even greater impact.

Actuarial Assumptions can be summarised as follows:

Demographic Assumptions – Mortality rates
Withdrawal rates
Retirement rates
(normal, early and ill health)

Financial Assumptions   – Interest rate
Salary escalation
(promotional and general increases)
Post retirement pension increases
Dividend growth
(for valuation of assets)

The demographic elements of the basis should aim to reflect the experience as closely as possible. However there is a tendency for certain demographic elements to err on the side of caution, particularly in the case of withdrawal rates which normally understate the experience. However, caution is required in the case of retirement rates particularly if generous benefits apply on early retirement (eg unreduced benefits), including retirement on medical grounds, since on some occasions the actual liabilities may be significantly understated.

Turning to the financial assumptions there is much greater room for variation. It is normally desirable to describe the assumptions in real terms (ie relative to the rate of price inflation) as follows:

Normal Range

Real rate of interest 3% to 5%

Real salary escalation 1% to 3%

Real pension increases –5% to 0%

Real dividend increases –2% to 0%

The assumed long term rate of price inflation is added to the above to obtain the absolute level of the assumptions. For example, for price

inflation of 5% pa, the above real rates of interest convert to absolute
rates of 8% to 10% and the real pension increases convert to absolute
rates of 0% to 5%.

Example

In order to illustrate the impact of both the actuarial funding method
and the assumptions on the contribution rate, consider a typical
member as follows:

Sex:	Male
Age:	45 years
Joined Scheme:	age 35 years ie 10 years' past service
Salary:	£10,000 pa
Pension:	one sixtieth of final salary for each year of service
Normal Retirement Date:	Age 65.

The contribution rates required for this typical member as he
approaches retirement vary according to the funding method as
illustrated in Figure 1 on the next page (the same actuarial assumptions
have been used in each case, principally a rate of interest of 9% and
salary escalation of 7%). The first point to note is that the contribution
rates required at age 45 according to the funding method vary as
follows:-

	Contribution Rate *% pa*
Aggregate	13
Projected Unit	12
Discontinuance	11

Whilst the Projected Unit and Discontinuance Methods produce lower
rates initially, the contribution rates rise to 18% and 28% respectively
as the member approaches age 65 whereas the rate for the Aggregate
Method remains at 13%.

In practice, for an on-going pension scheme new entrants will replace
leavers and it is likely that the age (and sex) distribution for the pension
scheme as a whole will remain stable. In this event, the Projected Unit
Method will lead to a stable contribution rate, whereas stability under
the Discontinuance Method will also depend upon the past service
distribution remaining constant.

Turning to the level of funding produced by the above methods, the
results for our typical member, expressed in terms of the amount of
assets are illustrated by Figure 2 on p 169. Compared to the Projected Unit Method, for which assets match liabilities, Aggregate produces over-funding and Discontinuance under-funding.

At age 45, the funding level expressed both in terms of the amount of
assets and as a percentage (ie ratio of assets to liabilities allowing for
projected salaries to retirement) is:

Figure 1: Contribution Rates under different methods

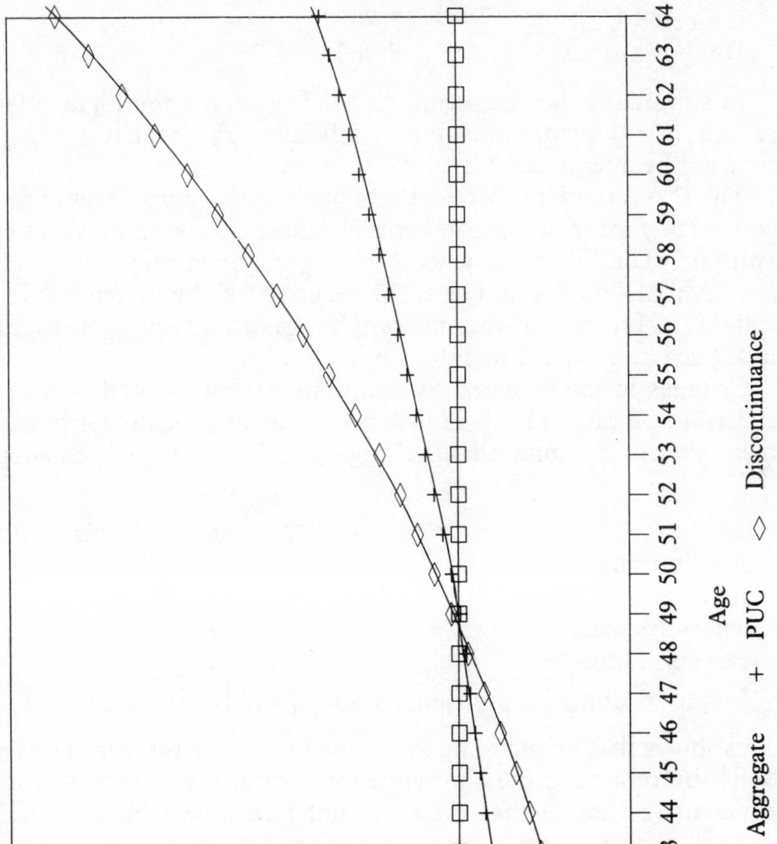

	Funding Level	
	£000	%
Aggregate	14,100	120
Projected Unit	11,800	100
Discontinuance	8,900	75

In summary, the Aggregate Method produces the highest level of security for the employees but at a funding rate which the employer ·may not be able to afford.

The Projected Unit Method achieves a satisfactory level of funding and a stable contribution rate provided there is a continuous flow of new entrants. The Discontinuance Method can be expected to produce a low level of funding and thus the security for the employees and the stability of future contributions will be especially vulnerable to changes in the make-up of the membership.

Changes in the actuarial assumptions have a marked effect on the contribution rate. This is illustrated in the table below for our typical member and assuming that the Aggregate Method has been adopted.

	% pa	% pa	% pa
Assumptions:			
Investment Return	9	9	10
Salary Increases	7.5	7.5	7
Pension Increases	5	0	0
Required Contribution Rate	18	12	10

This shows that by reducing the level of salary increase in the assumptions, by removing the allowance for future increases to pensions in payment (assuming that these are not guaranteed in the rules) and increasing the assumed level of future investment returns both in absolute terms and in relation to future salary increases, the contribution rate falls from 18% pa to 10% pa.

Whilst both the actuarial funding method and assumptions have a significant impact on the level of contributions payable to the pension scheme from time to time it should be stressed that these merely control the incidence of payment. The actual cost will be governed entirely by the benefits provided under the scheme and the actual experience.

IMPLICATIONS FOR BUY-OUT

Having carried out an initial assessment, and having understood in general terms the basics of an actuarial valuation, the reader should now be in a position to assess the financial implications of the pension scheme.

At this stage we are concerned with two main issues:

i.   adjustment to the purchase price if a complete pension scheme is being taken over

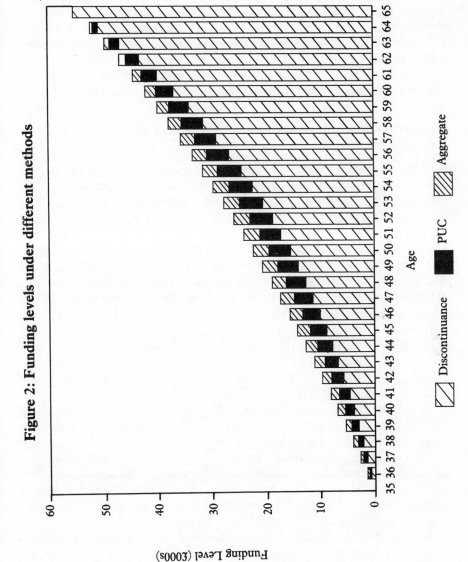

Figure 2: Funding levels under different methods

ii. bulk transfer payment if only part of the membership of a pension scheme is involved in the buy-out; and an adjustment to the purchase price if appropriate.

In each situation, the aim is to negotiate terms which are to the advantage of the purchaser. Subsequent to the buy-out, consideration will need to be given to the on-going contribution requirements. As this involves other considerations as to benefit design and funding strategy, it is dealt with in a later section. It should be noted, however, that the more advantageous the terms are the greater the flexibility there will be following the buy-out.

In this section, it will be assumed that the purchaser has access to all relevant information including the latest actuarial valuation report.

Acquisition of whole pension scheme: adjustment to purchase price

As a general rule if the purchase price is based on the value of net assets being acquired, as in an asset transfer, the purchase price should be adjusted for any difference between the value of the assets of the pension scheme and the liability in respect of benefits arising from service completed prior to the buy-out but allowing for projected salaries. If the difference is positive, ie there are surplus assets, the purchase price could in theory be increased and if the difference is negative, ie there is a deficiency, the purchase price should be reduced. It is therefore in the interests of the purchaser to place a minimum value on the assets and a maximum value on the liabilities. Alternatively, if the purchase price is based on a multiple of current earnings, it is relevant to compare the rate of contributions being paid to the pension scheme, and charged to the profit and loss account, with the contribution rate which will be required if the pension scheme is to be maintained in its current form following the buy-out.

In this case, it is in the interests of Newco to place as high a level as possible on the on-going contribution rate to reduce the level of earnings and hence the purchase price.

In practice, matters may not be so clear cut and a combination of the above approaches may be appropriate. Moreover, the position of the purchaser and the size of the numbers involved relative to other aspects of the deal will determine whether and to what extent an adjustment to the purchase price can be successfully negotiated.

In order to illustrate the principles involved, consider the acquisition of a pension scheme as follows:

Example

Defined benefits plan

- pension of one sixtieth of final salary at normal retirement date (NRD) 65 (males) 60 (females).

- male members can retire early at any time between age 60 and 65 with their full accrued pension (prior to age 60 pensions are actuarially reduced for both males and females).
- post retirement pension increases are not guaranteed but increases of around 3% per annum have been awarded previously on a discretionary basis.
- members are required to contribute 4% of salary

Membership

- 100 current pensioners with annual pensions in payment of £250,000
- 50 deferred pensioners with annual pensions from NRD of £100,000
- 500 active members with annual salaries of £5,000,000

Latest Actuarial Valuation

Funding Method – Aggregate
Assumptions   – Rate of interest: 9%
                 Rate of salary growth –
                    General increases: 7%
                    Promotional: no allowance
                 Pension increases after retirement: no allowance

                 Mortality: Standard tables
                 Withdrawals (other than early retirement): about 10% pa
                 Early retirement:no allowance
                 Assets: valued at market value

Valuation balance sheet

Capital value of liabilities		£ million
Current Pensioners		2.0
Deferred Pensioners		0.2
Active members*		
– for past service	5.8	
– for future service	7.4	
Total actives		13.2
Total Liabilities		15.4
Capital value of assets		
Existing assets	7.2	
Members' contribution @ 4%	2.0	
Company's contributions @ 16%	8.0	
Total Assets		17.2
Surplus (ie excess of assets over liabilities)		1.8
Company's balancing rate at which surplus is eliminated		12.4%
Funding level		90%

*If the actives' liabilities are not apportioned between past and future service liabilities it can be derived from the funding level (ie ratio of past service liabilities to value of existing assets) as follows:

Past service liabilities = $\dfrac{\text{Value of assets}}{\text{funding level}}$

$= \dfrac{7.2}{.9} = 8.0$

Past service liabilities for active members
= total past service liabilities − liabilities for current pensioners and deferred pensioners
= 8.0 − 2.0 − 0.2 = 5.8

Future service liabilities for active members
= total liabilities for active members − past service liabilities for active members
= 13.2 − 5.8 = 7.4

The theoretical adjustment to the purchase price, prior to adjustments for tax and changes to the funding method and/or assumptions, is shown below. This depends on whether the valuation of the company is based on assets or earnings.

Assets based

	£ million
Value of past service liabilities	
Current Pensioners	2.0
Deferred Pensioners	0.2
Active members	5.8
	8.0
Value of existing assets	7.2
Deficiency	0.8

This shows that the purchase price should be reduced by £0.8 million, being the amount of the deficiency. This is despite the valuation disclosing a surplus! The surplus as will be seen below is a function of the assumed rate of future contributions and is not relevant in the context of an asset sale.

Earnings based
It is assumed for the purposes of this example that the company's contribution to the pension scheme is taken at the rate of 16% in the determination of current earnings. Following the buy-out it is possible to eliminate the on-going surplus of £1.8 million by reducing the company's contribution rate from 16% to 12.4%. Hence earnings can be increased by 3.6% of salaries or £180,000 per annum. Assuming that a multiple of 10 is used to value future earnings the purchase price could be increased by £1.8 million. It should be noted that due to the

introduction of SSAP 24, this complication may not now arise in practice; in the future, pension contributions will be charged to the profit and loss account at the rate of 12.4% even though actual contributions may have been 16%.

The above amounts have been determined using the vendor's actuarial valuation funding method and assumptions. The purchaser will normally wish to adopt a method and assumptions which maximise his position from a negotiating point of view. This might proceed on the following lines.

Funding method
The funding method impacts on the required contribution rate on an on-going basis and is relevant if the purchase price is earnings based. As shown earlier the Aggregate Method normally produces the highest level of contributions compared to other funding methods and therefore it is in the purchaser's interest to retain this method for negotiation purposes.

Assumptions
Several of the actuarial assumptions may be considered to be reasonable namely:

  rate of interest of 9%
  general salary increases of 7%
  rates of mortality and withdrawal.

However, the liabilities may be understated due to no allowance being made for:

i. promotional salary increases
ii. discretionary pension increases
iii. early retirement.

Following discussions with the purchaser, the purchaser's actuary determines that the following amendments to the actuarial assumptions are reasonable in order to allow for prior practice and experience:

i. allowance for promotional increases of 1% in addition to the general increases of 7% pa making 8% pa in total – adjustment A
ii. allowance for discretionary pension increases of 3% pa – adjustment B
iii. males assumed to retire early on average at age 62 with an unreduced pension – adjustment C.

The approximate effect of the above adjustments on the items in the valuation balance sheet are as follows:

Capital value of liabilities for:	Adjustment			Compounded Effect
	A	B	C	
	%	%	%	%
Current pensioners	–	15	–	15
Deferred pensioners	–	20	–	20
Active members				
– past service	5	20	10	40
– future service	10	20	15	50
Members' contributions	5	–	–5	–
Company's contributions	5	–	–5	–

The other item which needs consideration is the value placed on the existing assets. The starting point is market value. This can be taken as read provided that the figure has been taken from audited accounts. However, care is required if certain of the assets are unmarketable or include investments in the vendor's shares (ie self investment). Care is also required if the assets consist of insurance policies as the value shown may not necessarily reflect the surrender value of such policies.

In addition to determining the market value of the assets, actuaries quite often use other valuation methods and in particular the 'discounted cash flow method'. Essentially these methods are designed to smooth out fluctuations in the market value of the assets since distortions could otherwise arise when the market value of assets, which is subject to short term fluctuations, is compared with the value of the liabilities determined on a long term basis. In this example, it is assumed that the purchaser's actuary decides to use the discounted cash flow method which produces a reduction in the value of the existing assets of 10%.

The revised valuation balance sheet now appears as follows (previous figures are in brackets):

Revised Valuation Balance Sheet

Capital value of liabilities	£ million	
Current pensioners	2.3	(2.0)
Deferred pensioners	0.2	(0.2)
Active members	2.5	2.2
– for past service	8.1	(5.8)
– for future service	11.1	(7.4)
Total actives	19.2	(13.2)
Total Liabilities	21.7	(15.4)

Capital value of assets	£ million	
Existing assets	6.5	(7.2)
Members' contributions at 4%	2.0	(2.0)
Company's contributions at 16%	8.0	(8.0)
Total Assets	16.5	(17.2)
Surplus	–	(1.8)
Deficiency	5.2	–
Company's balancing rate at which surplus/deficiency is eliminated	26.4% pa	12.4% pa

The revised adjustments to the purchase price before tax considerations are now calculated as follows.

Assets based

Total past service liabilities		*£ million*
Current pensioners	2.3	
Deferred pensioners	0.2	
Past service for actives	8.1	
		10.6
Value of existing assets		6.5
Deficiency		4.1

There is now a deficiency of £4.1 million compared to £0.8 million prior to adjustments. In theory, therefore, the purchase price should be reduced by £4.1 million.

Earnings based
In order to eliminate the revised on-going deficiency of £4.1 million, the contribution rate must be increased from 16% to 26.4%. The reduction in future earnings will be 10.4% of salaries or £520,000 pa compared to an increase of £180,000 pa prior to adjustments. The reduction in purchase price is therefore £5.2 million on a pre tax multiple of 10.

Failure to obtain an appropriate adjustment to the purchase price will mean reduced profitability for Newco. If this is to be avoided, a number of steps may be considered, all of which have industrial relations implications:

i.   cut back or discontinue the practice of granting discretionary pension increases
ii.   restrict the use of the early retirement option (this may be counter productive for other reasons)
iii. close the scheme for future new entrants
iv.   directly reduce the level of future service benefits
v.   wind-up the scheme.

The existing trustees, including the level of employee representation, and the company's powers of appointment and removal of trustees will have some bearing on how easily some of the above changes may be carried out in practice.

Surplus Regulations
Surplus Regulations introduced under the Finance Act 1986 place a limit on the amount by which the assets of a pension scheme can exceed the liabilities in order for the scheme to be fully approved for tax purposes.

The Surplus Regulations provide for the assets and liabilities of a pension scheme to be determined on a prescribed basis. A surplus exists if the assets exceed 105% of the liabilities. Such surplus might be eliminated by one or more of the following methods; otherwise certain tax reliefs may be lost:

i.   a reduction in or suspension of contributions for a period of not more than 5 years
ii.   improvement in the level of members' benefits
iii. a refund of surplus to the company subject to a free standing tax charge of 40%.

If the acquired scheme is in surplus, as determined by the Surplus Regulations, one or more of the following adjustments to the previous calculations may be appropriate:

i.   a deduction for a free standing tax charge of 40% of surplus which may be refunded to the company
ii.   loss of tax relief on investment income (and hence the use of a net rate rather than a gross rate of interest for discounting liabilities) on that part of the fund which is deemed to be in surplus
iii. possible utilisation of surplus for the benefit of members rather than the company.

It should be noted that if the trust deed and rules do not permit a refund of surplus to the company, some allowance should be made for loss of tax relief and/or benefit improvements thereby reducing the level of surplus which is available for the benefit of the shareholders. There may also be some pressure for benefit improvements from the standpoint of maintaining good employee relations. Tax on a refund should of course should be taken into account in the purchaser's calculations.

Other considerations
i.   the latest valuation may be out-of-date by up to 3 years. Have any significant events such as changes in membership or benefit structure occurred since the last valuation which may have either improved or worsened the financial position of the scheme? Some clue may be obtained from the trustees' annual report and accounts which should refer to any significant changes
ii.   are there any other benefit provisions in addition to those contained under the pension scheme? These might be provided on an ex-gratia basis (out of company revenue) or may be expected either as a result of previous practice or by agreement eg augmentations on early retirement or redundancy
iii. could other employees not recently included under the pension scheme apply to join following the transfer? Provided that there are no benefits accruing for service prior to the scheme this would not affect the past service position. Increased past service liabilities may arise, however, for new entrants joining senior executive schemes which frequently provide for an uprating of prior service benefits.
      The contribution rate for new entrants is likely to be lower than for the existing membership particularly if the current contribution rate includes an element for funding a prior service deficit. Contributions would however be levied on an increased payroll

iv. any adjustment to the purchase price may be net of tax. However, if the purchaser makes special funding payments to the pension scheme, tax relief may be spread forward over several years. Moreover the rate of tax payable by the purchaser may be lower than that payable by the vendor. To avoid some of these complications it may be preferable to persuade the vendor to make special funding payments prior to the buy-out.

Bulk transfer

The previous section covered the situation of a buy-out which involved the acquisition of a whole pension scheme. Many of the considerations which were relevant in those circumstances also apply to the situation of a buy-out involving employees who represent only part of the membership of a pension scheme. In this case, consideration must be given to the method of calculating the transfer value from the vendor's scheme or 'bulk transfer payment' as it is commonly known.

The situation described above may arise if the purchaser is acquiring a subsidiary which may be defined as a 'participating company' under the rules of the pension scheme or a cross-section of employees across the group. From the point of view of the purchaser, the principles involved are much the same. However, in the former case there may be greater protection offered under the trust deed and rules of the scheme – bulk transfers in respect of participating companies are sometimes based on a 'share of fund principle'. Whether this is worth anything in practice, depends upon the degree of discretion given to the actuary, the trustees and the company in paying a transfer of up to this level; as will be seen below, there is also considerable scope for placing different interpretations on 'share of fund' which in turn can have a dramatic impact on the level of the transfer payment.

For the purposes of the illustrations below it is assumed that the employees involved in the buy-out are fairly typical of the membership as a whole and represent 50% of the total active membership of the pension scheme. It is also assumed that no current pensioners and former members with entitlement to deferred pensions are to be transferred.

The Projected Unit Funding Method has been adopted and the valuation balance sheet appears as follows:

Capital value of past service liabilities	Total Membership £ Million	Transferring Membership £ Million
Pensioners	50	–
Deferred Pensions	10	–
Active members	40	20
Total Liabilities	100	20

Capital value of assets

Existing Assets	120	?
Surplus	20	?
Normal contribution rate	10% pa	10% pa
Less amortisation of past service surplus	4% pa	?
Net contribution rate	6% pa	?

There is a number of methods for the calculation of the transfer value in respect of the transferring members:

(i) *Value of leaving service benefits*

The total of the members' individual transfer values, based on completed service and current salary, could be paid. This figure may not be derived from the valuation balance sheet above but, for the purposes of illustration, is assumed to be £12 million.

(ii) *Past service reserve*

The value of the benefits arising from completed service but on projected final salaries = £20 million.

(iii) *Share of fund*

(a) $\dfrac{\text{Total value of existing assets}}{\text{Total value of past service liabilities}} \times$ past service liabilities for transferring members

$= \dfrac{120}{100} \times 20 = \text{£24 millions}$

(b) $\dfrac{\text{Value of existing assets} - \text{liabilities for pensioners}}{\text{Total value of past service liabilities for pensioners}} \times$ past service liabilities for transferring members

$= \dfrac{120 - 50}{100 - 50} \times 20 = \text{£28 million}$

(c) $\dfrac{\text{Value of existing assets} - \text{liabilities for pensioners and deferred pensioners}}{\text{Value of past service liabilities for active members}} \times$ past service liabilities for transferring members

$= \dfrac{120 - 50 - 10}{40} \times 20 = \text{£30 million}$

To summarise, depending on the method which is adopted for the calculation the bulk transfer value, the level of the payment varies as follows:

Method	Transfer Payment £ million
(i)	12
(ii)	20
(iii)(a)	24
(b)	28
(c)	30

It should be noted that the transfer payment can vary quite considerably depending upon the method of calculation and even if based on a share of fund. The reader will appreciate that the variations arise from differences in the amounts retained in the vendor's pension scheme to cover liabilities for pensioners and deferred pensioners. As in the case of the acquisition of a whole pension scheme, it is for the purchaser's actuary to place his own assessment on the liabilities.

Calculation of transfer value: assets based

If the buy-out is asset based it is normal for the bulk transfer to be calculated as the value of the members' accrued benefits including allowance for projected salaries at retirement. It is also desirable to include a provision for discretionary benefits (particularly increases to pensions in payment) if the members have an expectation to such benefits as a result of the vendor's previous practice.

The purchaser's actuary will need to agree the assumptions with the vendor's actuary. Provided that the transfer payment is within the transferring members' share of the fund (£30 million in this case) it should in theory be met from the vendor's pension scheme subject to the trust deed and rules.

If on the other hand the expected transfer payment from the vendor's scheme is lower than the required amount as advised by the purchaser's actuary the amount of the shortfall should be deducted from the purchase price or the vendor should make a special payment to make good the shortfall.

Calculation of transfer value: earnings based

In these circumstances, it is appropriate for the transfer value to be calculated as the transferring members' share of the fund since, in theory, this will leave the contribution rate unchanged and, hence, earnings after the buy-out. Again it will be for the purchaser's and the vendor's actuaries to agree the basis for the calculations. The purchaser's actuary will also need to assess the on-going contribution rate following the buy-out, taking account of the agreed basis for the transfer value. If this rate is higher than the current rate of contributions included in the level of earnings used for valuing the company, the purchaser should seek to obtain a reduction in the purchase price or alternatively a shortfall payment.

As is the case in the acquisition of a whole pension scheme, failure to obtain a satisfactory transfer value and/or adjustment to the purchase price will place a financial strain on Newco following the buy-out.

Members' consent

As a matter of good practice, members should be asked to give their consent to the transfer in writing. Indeed, arising from the Occupational Pensions Board's (the 'OPB') Report on Protecting Pensions –

Safeguarding Benefits in a Changing Environment, Government regulations are expected shortly which will prohibit transfers without consent unless the purchaser's actuary can certify that the members' rights and expectations to prior service benefits will not be worsened by the transfer. It is unlikely that such a certificate can be given in practice, in view of the broad definition of rights and expectations. These may, for example, include discretionary pension increases to the extent that a previous practice has been established.

Transfers from insurance companies

If the vendor's scheme is insured either through a deferred annuity or managed fund contract, certain special features may arise as follows:

i.   a cash surrender value may not be available under a deferred annuity contract or, if it is, the level could be penal or the insurance company may only permit a transfer to its own managed fund
ii. there may be a delay in obtaining an up-to-date cash surrender value
iii. there may be restrictions or penalties on realising managed fund units.

Transitional period

Immediately following the completion date, the employees concerned can either be treated as having left service with no further benefits accruing under the vendor's scheme or they may continue their membership for a limited period whilst the purchaser establishes a new scheme.

Although, in either case, entitlement to benefits can be fully protected there are advantages to the purchaser if a transitional period can be negotiated:

(a) A transitional period provides breathing space during which time the various arrangements for establishing a pension scheme can be made:
   i.   Legal documentation and Inland Revenue approval.
   ii. Review of benefit structure including actuarial costings.
   iii. Investment management.
   iv. Administrative arrangements.
   v.   Insurance of risk benefits (eg death, ill-health).
   vi. Communications with employees.

(b) If a transitional period does not apply, and the employees are treated as having left service at the completion date, past service can of course be granted on joining the new scheme (ie service between completion and joining date). However, complications arise in the case of employees who die, leave the service of the new employer or retire prior to the establishment of the scheme. It will also be necessary to arrange for the insurance of risk benefits during the interim period.

(c) With a transitional period, the complications under (b) do not arise as these are automatically catered for under the vendor's scheme. It is also likely that the employees will feel more comfortable with the arrangement whereas there could be uncertainty and an element of suspicion in the event of a break in their membership of a pension scheme.

Adjustment to the calculations of the transfer value

There are a number of possible approaches to the calculation of the transfer value between the completion date and the payment date. These are basically designed to be broadly neutral (within the limits of practicability) but can sometimes have different effects depending on experience.

The normal approach is to determine the transfer value at completion and to make adjustments for the following:

i.   Investment return to the date of payment
ii. Contributions paid by the purchaser and the employees (if any) less insurance premiums paid by the vendor (if any) to cover risk benefits
iii. Exits ie deaths, withdrawals and retirements during the transitional period.

An alternative approach which is sometimes adopted is to determine the transfer payment at the transfer date. Whilst this does away with some of the adjustments indicated above it is not recommended as there are risks to both the purchaser and the vendor. In particular, the purchaser may not get value for any contributions paid between completion and the payment date; and the vendor is at risk from the purchaser increasing salaries unduly and thus increasing benefits. However, safeguards can be obtained through the introduction of suitable wording in the acquisition agreement.

THE NEGOTIATIONS – SUMMARY

At some stage in the negotiations, it is essential that an actuary is brought in who can be expected to act independently from the vendor's actuary. The actual stage in the proceedings will depend upon the likelihood of the buy-out proceeding and the likely financial significance of pensions in relation to other aspects of the deal.

The aim of the negotiations is to ensure that any surplus/deficiency in the pension scheme is properly reflected in the purchase price and in the case of a partial transfer of employees the aim should be to maximise the transfer payment from the vendor's scheme. This is both in the interests of the employees concerned (in protecting their future security) and the new employer to give the maximum room for manoeuvre when it comes to financing the new pension scheme. As a minimum, it is essential that any potential deficiencies are identified prior to the sale so that an appropriate allowance can be made in the purchaser's calculations if the vendor is unable or unprepared to make good the shortfall. The steps in the negotiations are as follows:

i.   the purchaser's actuary should carry out an approximate actuarial valuation for the employees involved in the buy-out. Ideally, this should be based on actual membership data but if this is not available then approximations can be made. The actuarial assumptions and funding method adopted would be chosen by the purchaser's actuary (possibly after discussions with the purchaser) and would not necessarily be the same as those used for the latest actuarial valuation of the scheme. In particular they should include an allowance for any discretionary benefits where there is an established practice and hence expectation on the part of the employees. The purposes of this actuarial valuation are to determine the amount required to cover the past service benefits and the contribution rate required to cover future service benefits assuming for the moment that these will be on the same formula as the current scheme

ii. an assessment should be made of the financial position of the vendor's pension scheme. Ideally, this should be based on the latest actuarial valuation report but if it would be inconvenient to obtain a copy more approximate calculations may be obtained from information contained in the Trustees Annual Report and Accounts, and from the UK statutory accounts. The main purposes of this assessment are to determine the assets available to cover the liabilities under the pension scheme and the possible range of transfer values from the vendor's scheme in the event of a partial transfer of employees

iii. by making a comparison between the results of the investigations under i. and ii., it is possible to see which direction the negotiations will take, eg if there are insufficient assets in the pension scheme it will be a case of negotiating an additional payment from the vendor to make good the shortfall or alternatively negotiating a reduction in the purchase price. In the event of there being more than sufficient assets to meet the required transfer value, it will be a case of attempting to negotiate a share of the surplus, whilst minimising any addition to the purchase price

iv. the purchaser's and vendor's actuaries will need to agree the assumptions for determining the surplus/deficiency under the pension scheme and the basis for any transfer payment. This unfortunately is not always straightforward. It is a well known fact that if two actuaries are asked the same question there are bound to be at least three different answers. Various methods have been employed to hasten this part of the proceedings including the 'locked room technique' – as the name implies the actuaries concerned are simply locked in a room until they have reached agreement and this has not yet been known to fail

v. as with all negotiations it is hoped that a compromise, acceptable to all parties, can be reached. Failing this however it is for the purchaser's actuary to advise the purchaser of the financial implications of the proposed basis. As described earlier this will depend to a large extent on whether the purchase is assets or earnings based

vi. if the purchaser is unable to negotiate a satisfactory adjustment to the purchase price it will be a matter for him to take a view on the size of the discrepancy in relation to other aspects of the deal. In extreme cases a transfer value may be declined or the purchaser may discontinue with the proceedings.

ACQUISITION AGREEMENT

The fact that a pension scheme exists will need to be documented in the acquisition agreement together with warranties that full particulars have been disclosed in writing to the purchaser and that the assets of the scheme are sufficient to meet the liabilities if all members were to leave service at completion or, alternatively, a deficiency were to be disclosed.

In the event of a partial transfer of employees it is essential that the basis for the calculation of the bulk transfer payment is documented in as clear a way as possible with nothing (of any significance) left for interpretation after completion. In this respect the acquisition agreement should contain the following clauses.

(a) *Calculation of the transfer value*
Often wording is encountered such as, 'The transfer value (from the vendor's pension scheme) shall be determined in accordance with the trust deed and rules of the vendor's scheme'. Put another way this quite simply means 'name a figure'. Wording referring to 'share of fund' is equally vague and could mean almost anything as will have been seen earlier.

To describe the calculation of the transfer value in detail is quite complicated and the preferred approach is to set this out in a letter from the vendor's actuary to the purchaser's actuary which can be appended to the agreement. This should contain a description of the benefits upon which the transfer value is based, the actuarial assumptions and the method of adjustment between the completion date and the payment date. Even then, disagreements can occur as to the interpretation of the actuary's letter following the buy-out.

(b) *Shortfall provision*
It should be recognised that the trustees would not normally be a party to the acquisition agreement. Therefore it is desirable to require the vendor to make good any shortfall if the transfer value paid by the trustees is lower than the agreed amount.

This would certainly be required if the pension fund were known to be in a deficiency, subject, of course, to what had been negotiated.

As a further protection, the trustees of the vendor's scheme may be asked to endorse the basis of the transfer payment. However, this may be impractical in the time available.

(c) *Guarantees*

Essentially the buy-out team should avoid giving too many guarantees as these could prove to be onerous. Examples of guarantees which sometimes appear in agreements are as follows:

i. the transfer value or pension scheme assets will only be used for the benefit of the transferring members or similar wording. Vendors quite often ask for this sort of guarantee since it shows that they are considering the interests of their employees and putting an obstacle in the way of the purchaser if an attempt to 'asset strip' the pension scheme is made following the buy-out. If this is to be complied with precisely it means that the purchaser would have to run the scheme as a 'closed fund' with any surplus being used to augment members' benefits or the members would have to be given a 'money purchase' guarantee, ie that their benefits would not be less than their share of the transfer value accumulated in line with investment returns. This is unreasonable for a defined benefits scheme under which the employer is liable to make good any deficiencies in the future and who should therefore be able to take advantage of any profit (through reductions in contributions). A more reasonable approach is for the purchaser to agree to provide benefits under his scheme which are of 'equivalent value' or 'no less favourable' overall to those which applied under the vendor's scheme for past service. This gives flexibility as to the format of the benefits but will ensure that the members receive fair value for money.

ii. the purchaser will establish a pension scheme for both service before and after the completion date which is no less favourable than the vendor's scheme. Whilst as stated above, it is reasonable to provide this type of undertaking for service prior to the completion date (provided sufficient assets are transferred), it is unreasonable to place restrictions on the level of future service benefits.

ESTABLISHMENT OF NEW SCHEME

In this section the considerations involved in establishing a new scheme are discussed briefly. A new scheme will need to be established if there is a partial transfer of employees and a bulk transfer payment. The issues covered will also apply in general to the management of an existing scheme if a whole scheme is acquired as a result of the buy-out.

In order to establish Newco's scheme, consideration will need to be given to:

i.   benefit design
ii.   funding strategy (defined benefits scheme)
iii. investment arrangements
iv.   legal documentation
v.   administrative arrangements
vi.   appointment of trustees
vii. communications with employees.

The aspects which are significant financially are considered briefly below.

Benefit design

Provided that no restrictions have been imposed on the buy-out team under the purchase and sale agreement in respect of benefits which accrue from future service there will be freedom to select the type of pension scheme which best fits in with the purchaser's objectives.

Whichever option the purchaser adopts, in the interests of good employee relations, it will be desirable to be able to show that the new arrangements are broadly comparable (even if in a different format) to the vendor's scheme. For ease of communications the most straight-forward option would be to establish a scheme on similar lines to the vendor's pension scheme.

The level of the employees' awareness and appreciation of the existing scheme and trades union involvement will obviously be important factors in deciding upon this issue.

As the logical starting point, the purchaser should ask the following questions about the existing scheme:

i.   is it affordable?
ii.   does the scheme provide benefits where they are most needed eg to the stayer, early leaver or early retirement?
iii. how does it compare with competitors' pension arrangements?
iv.   will it help to recruit, retain and motivate employees?
v.   can the necessary administration be accommodated?

In the event of there being a major shift in the future arrangements, including loss of pension rights, compensation can be achieved through the provision of alternative benefits to pensions eg insurance cover, medical and long term disability benefits, or additional salary.

Funding strategy

The ultimate cost of a defined benefits pension scheme is determined by the level of benefits and the actual experience particularly with regard to investment return and salary growth if benefits are linked to final salary. However, there is a wide range of actuarial funding methods and assumptions which can be adopted in the funding of a defined benefits scheme. By changing the funding method and/or assumptions it is possible to alter the pace at which the benefits are funded eg to pay less now and more later.

Whilst there is a fair degree of freedom to employ different funding strategies in the management of cash flow, as a consequence of SSAP 24, the determination of pension costs in the profit and loss account is now subject to regulation.

In the case of a money purchase scheme, the company's contribution rate will be determined as part of the benefit design.

Investment arrangements

For a defined benefits scheme, the rate of investment return achieved on the assets of the scheme is the principal determinant of future cost. This may be illustrated by the actual cost of providing the benefits for a typical pension scheme according to the level of future investment return as follows:

Rate of contribution for male aged 45 according to actual rate of investment return

Investment Return % pa	Contribution Rate % pa
9	12.0
10	9.3
11	7.3
12	5.8

In each case allowance is made for salaries to increase at 7% pa.

It is therefore important to give careful consideration to the selection of investment arrangements. For a scheme which provides benefits linked to final salary at retirement and increases to pensions in payments linked in some way with price inflation (either partially or in whole) it is necessary to achieve a real rate of return.

This in effect means that a substantial part of the assets should be invested in equities as the following table shows.

Rates of increase (% pa) for given periods ending on 31 December 1988

	5 years	10 years	20 years
UK Equities	19.2	21.1	14.2
UK Gilts	11.1	14.6	10.8
Cash	10.9	12.5	11.0
Price Inflation	4.9	7.9	9.8
National Average Earnings	7.6	10.5	11.8

It should be noted that whilst equities have outperformed both the rate of price and earnings inflation, the return from equities is volatile. However, this would not normally be of concern since the pension scheme will have a strong positive case flow for many years ahead and there will be no foreseeable risk of a forced sale of investments at depreciated prices. Benefit outgo, principally by way of pensions, will build up only gradually with the retirement of active employees.

APPENDIX 1

Glossary of buy-out terms

BES

The Business Expansion Scheme was introduced by the Government to allow private investors to offset the cost of buying shares in unquoted companies against their top marginal rate of tax. Individuals may fund small management buy-outs, gaining BES relief, as long as they are not involved in managing the business and their shareholding is no more than 30%. For larger buy-outs, money from BES funds or schemes may be used to back buy-outs.

Bought deal

Sometimes, in order to be able to move quickly, the provider of finance will buy the target company and hold it temporarily before restructuring it as a buy-out and syndicating the finance. This is known as a 'bought deal'.

Business plan

A business plan is a prerequisite to attempting to raise finance for an MBO. It will typically include: Background of company; Market information; CV's of key management; Financial history; Financial projections; and Funding required and structure.

Buy-back

One possible exit route, where the company buys back the shares held by its investors.

Chinese walls

Barriers put up inside financial organisations to segregate functions that could lead to conflicts of interest.

Corporate venturing

This is where a large industrial or commercial company buys shares in a small company either directly or through a venture capital fund. This often allows the large company to gain access to 'high-tech' research, whilst controlling the level of its investment.

Cumulative participating preferred ordinary shares (CPPOs)

This class of share is often subscribed by investing institutions. It allows the investors to benefit from preferential rights as to dividend and capital, and to share to some extent in the profits of the company.

Debentures
A debenture is a document containing an acknowledgement of indebtedness by a company. It is usually secured by a charge on the assets of the company. Debentures are often taken by bankers as part of the buy-out finance.

Development capital
Finance for growing companies which already have a track record. Finance for buy-outs is normally classed as development capital.

Dividend cover
The amount by which dividends are covered by after-tax earnings. If a company pays a dividend of 8p per share out of earnings of 8p per share, the cover is one. If earnings rise to 16p and the dividend remains at 8p, the cover is two.

Due diligence
Detailed analysis and appraisal of the background of the company, its management and the business plan. This will be carried out by investors before reaching a decision as to whether or not to back a buy-out. The investors often use accountants to perform part of this work.

Earn-out
A formula by which the final price to be paid to the vendor for the acquisition is set as a multiple of actual future earnings. A proportion of this is normally paid 'up-front'.

Equity kicker
Holders of unsecured debt or inadequately secured debt are in a relatively high risk position. To compensate for this, they are sometimes given an equity kicker, which gives them the option of subscribing for shares at a price which, if the company is successful, will give the option holder a profit at the time of exercise.

Exit route
Investors exit when they sell their shareholding in Newco, often several years after the buy-out. This may be by a stock market flotation, a buy-back of shares or a trade sale.

Factoring
This is one way of increasing cashflow after a buy-out. A factor provides finance to the company based on an agreed percentage of its trade debtors and then collects the cash when this is received from the debtor.

Feasibility study
This is similar to a business plan but is usually prepared by the investors or accountants acting on behalf of the investors as opposed to by the management team itself.

Fixed charge
Security provided to a lender on a fixed asset, such as land and buildings. The debt element of the funding for a buy-out may be secured by a fixed and/or floating charge.

Floating charge
A floating charge is a charge over all the assets of a business, including stock. The terms of a floating charge will determine when such a charge will 'crystallise' or become enforceable. Typically a lender is able to enforce his charge if the company defaults on its loan agreement, for example by not meeting certain agreed covenants.

Gearing
Borrowings, as a percentage of shareholders' funds. If £4 million has been borrowed, and equity is £1m, the gearing is 400%.

Goodwill
The difference between the purchase price paid for Newco and the fair value of its separable assets.

Hands-off
A hands-off investor takes little active involvement in the management of Newco, leaving the managers to manage their own affairs.

Hands-on
A hands-on investor participates in the management of Newco, often taking a non-executive post on the board.

Hive across
Similar to hive up or hive down (see below).

Hive down
A hive down is normally used where only part of an existing company is being purchased. The vendor transfers the trade and assets of that particular business to Target, a newly created subsidiary. Target is then purchased by Newco.

Hive up
The trade and assets of newly acquired Target are hived up into Newco following the buy-out. This is often carried out for tax and legal reasons.

Indemnities
The vendor will often be required to indemnify the purchaser against any potential liabilities, such as tax or litigation, which have arisen prior to the buy-out, but which are not known or are not disclosed to the purchaser by the vendor.

Internal rate of return
The average annual rate of return to an investor over a given period. Calculation of this will include dividend distributions and exit proceeds. The anticipated internal rate of return is used by the investor in determining an appropriate deal structure.

Junior debt
Debt where secured (or 'senior') debt holds superior security. Also known as 'subordinated' debt.

Junk bonds
High yielding, high risk unsecured paper pioneered by US banks for use in leveraged buy-outs. Junk bond investors normally hold a wide portfolio of bonds so that the inevitable failures are more than offset by the successes.

Key man insurance
Life insurance held by Newco in respect of key management personnel.

Lead investor
The investor who originates and structures the financing of a buy-out, and who normally takes the largest share in a syndicated investment. The lead investor is likely to take a hands-on role on behalf of other investors in the syndicate.

Majority shareholding
Where a management team holds more than 50% of Newco. This is the usual situation for small and medium sized MBOs.

Mezzanine finance
An intermediate form of funding, between debt and equity. This is a relatively high risk investment, and the provider of it is often rewarded with a high return, often by way of an equity kicker.

Minority holding
Where the management team holds less than 50% of Newco. This may be the case in larger buy-outs.

Newco
The buy-out is usually carried out through a new company into which the management team invests. This company is normally referred to as Newco.

Non-executive director
A director who has no role in the day-to-day operations of the company, but usually attends board and other meetings and becomes involved in projects as and when deemed appropriate.

Participating shares
A preference share which has a right to receive a share of profits over and above any fixed preference dividend rights.

Preference shares
These rank ahead of ordinary shares if the company is wound up, and usually receive a dividend (either fixed or participating) before ordinary shareholders.

Price earnings ('P/E') ratio

The valuation of a share based upon a multiple of post-tax earnings per share. If post tax earnings per share are 8p, and the company has a P/E ratio of 10, each share will be valued at 80p. P/E ratios are the most usual method of valuing companies.

Ratchet

An incentive arrangement where the management team receives a bigger share of the equity if the company performs well and less if it does badly.

Rate of return

The percentage rate which the investor receives on his investment.

Redeemable shares

Shares which may be re-purchased or redeemed by the company on terms which are determined at the time the shares are issued.

Sale and leaseback

One way of improving cash flow after a buy-out. The company sells assets (such as buildings) to a financier (often a pension fund) and then leases them back.

Second round financing

Financing that may be required by Newco at some point after the initial buy-out, either for expansion or because Newco is experiencing difficulties.

Secondary purchases

Where one investor sells part or all of his stake to another. This is often done to spread the risk of a large investment.

Section 151

Section 151 of the Companies Act 1985. This prohibits (except for specified exceptions) a company from providing financial assistance for the purchase of its own shares. This can cause problems in buy-outs, and particularly in a public company buy-outs. However, specified exceptions in Section 151 allow financial assistance to be provided if certain conditions are met.

Senior debt

Debt, provided by the financial backers of the buy-out, which is secured and which ranks ahead of junior debt.

Sensitivity analysis

An analysis of how sensitive the financial projections contained in the business plan are to changes in key assumptions.

Service agreements

An agreement signed between an employee and employer in which the employee contracts with the employer to provide services for a specified period on defined terms. This is mainly to provide financial security to both investors and management.

Shareholders agreement

An agreement signed between the company's shareholders, often at the time of the buy-out. The purpose is usually to prevent majority shareholders carrying out specified actions which may be against the interests of the minority.

Subordinated debt

Loans which in terms of security are repayable after other loans provided to the company. Often referred to as junior debt.

Syndicated investment

An investment which is too large and risky to be carried by one investor and which is therefore shared among several providers of finance.

Target company

The company to be bought out.

Track record

The background of both the company and its management. Both are key factors in an investor's decision as to whether it will back a buy-out.

Trade sale

Where Newco or the investor's stake in Newco is sold to a commercial or industrial company. It is a possible exit route. A less welcome trade sale is where the management team is beaten by a third party in its attempt to purchase Target.

Vendor

The entity selling the Target company.

Vendor finance

Finance provided by the vendor, either indirectly through deferred payment terms, or directly by the vendor retaining a shareholding in Target, or taking a minority shareholding in Newco.

Yield

The annual (or regular) return from an investment. The yield will normally be either interest or a dividend.

Accounting for the buy-out

The typical structure for a buy-out is for the management team together with the outside investors to form a new company 'Newco' and for Newco to purchase the company or business. The accounting for this transaction at the date of acquisition and the impact on future profitability can be very important and can be an element affecting the deal structure itself. There are two key issues. Firstly, quantification of the goodwill arising from the transaction. Secondly, the treatment of the goodwill through the accounts.

Accounting standards on goodwill and acquisition accounting are still evolving but are currently dealt with in standard statements of accounting practice (SSAP) Nos 14, 22 and 23. For a fuller understanding of this area the relevant SSAPs and the discussion paper on fair value in the context of acquisition accounting should be read. It should be noted that there are likely to be revisions made to SSAP 22 during 1990.

In simple terms goodwill is the difference between the fair value of the separable net assets acquired and the fair value of the consideration. This is illustrated by way of an example.

Example

Newco raises finance (£3m equity and £7m debt) and buys for £10m MBO Limited which has separable net assets valued at £8m ie goodwill of £2m.

Newco-Company only balance sheet at acquisition

Share Capital	£3m	Investment in MBO Limited	£10m
		Debt	(£ 7m)
			£ 3m

Newco-Consolidated balance sheet at acquisition

Share Capital	£3m	Goodwill	£ 2m
		Net Assets	£ 8m
		Debt	(£ 7m)
			£ 3m

Under SSAP 22 goodwill cannot be carried indefinitely in the balance sheet. It has either to be amortised to the profit and loss over a reasonable period or written off directly to reserves in the year of acquisition, the latter being the preferred accounting treatment. In the above example the directors of Newco decide to amortise the goodwill. There is no maximum time limit for the amortisation stipulated by the SSAP although the period has to be supportable by commercial substance. In the United States the equivalent accounting standard stipulates the maximum amortisation period to be forty years and as a result this has been used in the UK. In this example the amortisation period is chosen as ten years. This would give a charge to the consolidated profit before tax each year of £200,000.

If Newco intends to float or sell for any period up to ten years from the buy-out date the exit value may be reduced by the price earnings ratio times the after tax profit impact of the goodwill amortisation. Before showing the numerical impact of the example, consideration needs to be given as to whether there should be a tax effect on the amortisation. Certainly, goodwill amortisation attracts no tax relief from the Inland Revenue in the UK. However, where a decision is made to amortise goodwill it may be appropriate to set up a related deferred tax credit which will be written back to profit and loss over the amortisation period, to offset the impact of the additional tax charge. In the above example, when the goodwill of £2m is set up a deferred tax credit of £0.7m (being £2m times the current tax rate of 35%) could also be set up. Each year over the 10 year amortisation period goodwill amortisation of £200,000 and a tax credit of £70,000 would be booked in the consolidated profit and loss account. In this way the post tax profit impact each year would be £130,000.

Where goodwill is written off directly to reserves in the year of acquisition the profit and loss account is protected but net assets in the balance sheet are depleted as shown below.

Newco – consolidated balance sheet after writing off goodwill

Share Capital	£3m	Net assets before debt	£8m
Reserves	(£2m)	Debt	(£7m)
	£1m	Net assets	£1m

Where the goodwill is greater than the tangible net assets (for example for service companies) or where the buy-out is more highly geared, it is not unusual to see negative net assets in the consolidated balance sheet once goodwill has been written off.

Dividends

Where goodwill is written off immediately, and negative reserves are shown in the consolidated balance sheet the question as to whether dividends can be paid arises. The company balance sheet will show positive reserves since the investment in the buy-out company will be carried at cost (unless there is a permanent diminution in value). This is important because the concept of distributable reserves is only relevant in company terms not in consolidated terms. Accordingly Newco will not necessarily be prohibited from paying dividends to its investors even though the consolidated balance sheet shows negative reserves. It should be noted however that if the buy-out company earns profits Newco will only be able to pay dividends to its shareholders if the buy-out company passes up those profits to Newco by way of dividend or charge.

In the above example Newco purchased the shares in the buy-out company and recorded the investment at cost in the company balance sheet. A potential problem arises where the assets, liabilities and business of the buy-out company are purchased rather than its shares. In such a situation the goodwill arising is known as 'purchased goodwill' as opposed to 'consolidated goodwill' and Newco will only have a company balance sheet. As a result the goodwill which is written off will have an immediate impact on reserves. However it is acceptable for the write-off to be debited initially to non distributable with an annual transfer to distributable reserves. The same amortisation period would be used for the transfer from non distributable to distributable reserves as would have been the case had the goodwill been consolidated goodwill and the board of directors of Newco chose to amortise the goodwill through the profit and loss account. It does mean however that over a period the amount of distributable reserves will be reduced and where the goodwill is substantial this could have a significant impact on Newco's ability to pay dividends.

It is important therefore, where there is significant goodwill involved, to consider very carefully whether an asset deal should be agreed. Where the business that is being bought out is not contained within a separate company one way to overcome this problem is for the vendor to hive down the business and assets to a newly formed subsidiary which can then be purchased by the management team. There are obviously tax consequences and these are dealt with in Chapter 4.

Quantification of goodwill

One of the main reasons for the discussion on how to account for the buy-out is the importance of achieving profit projections following the buy-out. Management teams should be given every chance to achieve these and the quantification of goodwill can have a significant impact on future profitability.

SSAP 22 gives guidance on quantification of goodwill and there is currently a discussion paper, issued by the Accounting Standards Committee, on fair value in the context of acquisition accounting.

The discussion which follows is limited to just a few potentially important assets and liabilities which may have an immediate impact on post buy-out profitability and which need to be considered before the buy-out goes ahead to determine whether acquisition or merger accounting is appropriate and how the deal should be structured in order to achieve the desired objective.

1. *Pension plans*

   These are dealt with in Chapter 6 and are extremely important from a commercial view point in pricing and structuring the deal. However from an accounting view point, under acquisition accounting any over or under funding should be set up in the acquisition balance sheet and written back/off to profit and loss over a reasonable period.

2. *Rationalisation costs*

   Any costs to be incurred in closing or increasing the efficiency of the company's operations or part of the company's operations should be provided for in the acquisition balance sheet in determining fair value under acquisition accounting. Often, following a buy-out, management decisions can be taken which prior to the buy-out may not have been acceptable since the impact on the profitability of the company may have been severe.

3. *Future losses, where appropriate*

   If one of the buy-out company's operations is generating losses and that operation is to be closed it may be appropriate to provide for future losses up to closure. Once again this will increase goodwill arising on acquisition but will protect the future profit and loss account to the extent that the goodwill is written off directly to reserves.

4. *Properties*

   Under acquisition accounting these should be revalued to market value. Accordingly, where property has a value greater than its book value the depreciation charge will increase and have an impact on profitability in periods after buy-out.

APPENDIX 3

Accounting for Pension Costs

The Institute of Chartered Accountants in England and Wales published in May 1988, SSAP 24, Accounting for Pension Costs. Company accounts, for financial years beginning on or after 1 July 1988, which are compiled on the basis of a 'true and fair view', must conform with the basis of determining pension accounting cost and disclosure in accordance with SSAP 24.

The objective is that the cost of pensions should be charged against profits on a systematic basis over the expected future working lifetime of the employees.

For defined contribution schemes, the charge against profits should normally be the actual contributions paid to the scheme in that accounting period.

Defined benefit schemes are more complicated and the same example as used previously has been used for illustration below. For simplicity it has been assumed that the actuarial valuation was carried out at the start of the first accounting period for which SSAP 24 was adopted. SSAP 24 requires that the pension cost should be divided between regular cost and variations from regular cost:

i. *Regular cost*
   The regular cost should be calculated by the actuary as a substantially level percentage of the current and expected future pensionable payroll and should represent his best estimate of the cost of providing the pension benefits promised. The actuarial method used must include full allowance for future salary increases for in-service members. Assuming that the results of the actuarial valuation are appropriate for SSAP 24 purposes, the regular cost in the example given in Chapter 6 would be the contribution required to meet the future service benefits for active members of 10.8% of salaries, giving a regular cost of £540,000.

ii. *Variations from regular cost*
    Variations from regular cost should be allocated over the expected future working lifetime of scheme members. Examples of variations are deficiencies or surpluses arising from differences between the scheme's actual experience and the assumptions made, changes in assumptions, and benefit improvements. However, there are some exceptions to this rule where cost variations are

permitted (in some cases required) to be spread over a shorter period.

When implementing SSAP 24 for the first time, there is a choice available between allocating the cumulative deficit or surplus over the expected future working lifetime of scheme members, or capitalising the deficit/surplus as a balance sheet provision/ prepayment. If the first option were adopted the variation cost in the example would therefore be the contribution of 1.6% of salaries required to meet the deficiency of assets over the past service liabilities for all members, giving a variation cost of £80,000. The total pension cost is the sum of the regular cost and variation cost and would be 12.4% of salaries or £620,000. This is also the balancing contribution rate disclosed in the actuarial valuation. If the balance sheet option were adopted, then the past service deficiency of £800,000 would be taken as a balance sheet provision and the variation cost would be zero. However interest could be charged/credited on balance sheet provisions/prepayments, in which case there would be an additional charge of 9% on £800,000, or £72,000. The total pensions cost would then be £612,000, being the sum of the regular cost and the interest charge. It is important to note that the interest charge will be a reducing item as the balance sheet provision is written down over time.

In both these cases the pensions cost is a better guide to the long term cost of the scheme than the 16% of salaries which the company is currently paying, and which would have been shown as the pensions cost before SSAP 24 was adopted. It is therefore likely that reported profits will show a better picture of the profitability of the company.

A refund obtained under the Finance Act 1986 by the employer, net of tax at 40%, may be recognised in the accounts in the year in which it is received, subject to appropriate disclosure.

Increases to pensions in payment and deferred pensions

Increases to pensions in payment and to deferred pensions which are specified in a scheme's rules must be taken into account in the actuarial assumptions.

In the case of discretionary pension increases, where these are likely to be granted on a regular basis, the preferred treatment is that they should be allowed for in the actuarial assumptions. If no part of such increases have been anticipated in the actuarial assumptions, the capitalised value should be taken into account in the year in which the increases are granted, to the extent that they are not covered by a surplus. In the case of the illustration it would be preferable to change the regular cost and variation cost to reflect the expectation that discretionary pension increases will be given in the future. If this is not done, the capitalised value of future increases would be taken into account in the year of award due to the deficiency position of the pension scheme.

Balance sheet

To the extent that there is a difference between the pension cost charged and the pension cost actually paid into the pension scheme, the balance sheet will contain a net pension provision or prepayment according to whether the accumulated pension cost is greater or less than the actual contributions paid.

In the example, the company contributes 16% of salaries, or £800,000. The year end balance sheet will therefore be:

	'allocation' option	'balance sheet' option
(Provision) prepayment at start of year	0	(800,000)
Company payment for year	800,000	800,000
(Total accounting cost for year)	(620,000)	(612,000)
(Provision) prepayment at end of year	180,000	(612,000)

It will be seen that a balance sheet provision or prepayment can provide useful additional information in interpreting the SSAP 24 figures. However, care needs to be exercised. A common case will be where the fund has a substantial surplus so that the company is taking a 'contribution holiday', but where the sum of the regular and variation costs is still positive. In this case a balance sheet provision will be created, and it is easy to assume that the fund is in a poor state as the company is apparently under-contributing. When considering an asset based buyout, it would therefore be wrong to take into account in the purchase price any balance sheet creditors or debtors due to the pension scheme, without considering why they have occurred.

Disclosures

For defined contribution schemes, the pension cost will normally equal the contributions payable but any outstanding or prepaid contributions should also be disclosed.

For defined benefit schemes, a large number of disclosures will be required. These include details of the latest formal actuarial valuation or review indicating the actuarial method used and the main actuarial assumptions; the market value of the scheme's assets; the level of funding (ie the actuarial value of existing assets divided by the actuarial value of accrued liabilities allowing for future salary increases); and comments on any material surplus or deficiency indicated by the level of funding. In addition, details of any significant changes expected in the company's future pension costs should be given.

In the example, it would be disclosed that a rate of interest of 9% was used, coupled with an allowance of 7% for future salary increases. The market value of assets of the scheme was £7,200,000 and the level of funding was 90%.

All the company's schemes may be combined for disclosure purposes unless this would prevent a proper understanding of the accounts.

Prior to SSAP 24, existing disclosure requirements were minimal – recognition that a pension scheme existed was all that was required. The pensions cost reflected in the profit and loss account was equal to the actual contribution to the pension scheme which could be distorted by contribution holidays or special payments. The actuarial basis for determining the contribution rate could also vary widely as explained in previous sections.

SSAP 24 will undoubtedly increase the information available to a prospective purchaser who does not have access to actuarial valuation reports and scheme documents. In theory, a purchaser should be able to derive the on-going contribution rate expressed as a level percentage of salaries and hence determine the company's earnings, free from distortions due to special contributions or contribution holidays. It is also possible to determine the surplus or deficiency in the pension scheme from the funding level which will be relevant if the purchase is asset based. Any deficiency on discontinuance (ie wind-up) must also be quantified.

The disclosure of the actuarial assumptions and funding method would also enable approximate adjustments to be made to both the on-going contribution rate and funding level on alternative bases if appropriate.

Of further benefit to the purchaser, is the requirement that the capitalised value of unfunded or ex-gratia benefits, met out of company revenue, must be reflected in the accounts.

However there are a number of qualifications to the usefulness of SSAP 24 disclosures:

(a) SSAP 24 is not specific on the allowance to be made for discretionary pension increases in the determination of pension cost and funding level, and accordingly treatment will vary.

(b) Implicit actuarial assumptions are permitted (ie the basis overall should be a best estimate but not necessarily each individual assumption); this will make an objective assessment of the basis by an outsider a difficult task.

(c) Although the funding level will be disclosed, the basis for valuing the assets may not be disclosed thus preventing a surplus or deficiency to be quantified in absolute terms: the market value of the assets of the pension scheme will be disclosed; but this does not necessarily represent the value placed on the assets for the purposes of determining the funding level, a useful measure of the value of the pension scheme relative to the capital value of the company.

(d) If several pension schemes and possibly several actuaries are involved there may be a major lack of detail eg the basis may be disclosed as 'interest rates from 9% to 7% and rates of salary increases from 8% to 5%'.

(e) Disclosures may be distributed throughout the accounts eg the pension effects of extraordinary events (such as a company sale) may be disclosed along with other extraordinary items. Exceptional variations in the experience, such as significant reductions in scheme membership from redundancies/early retirements, could lead to distortions in pensions cost as SSAP 24 allows their effects to be amortised over a short time span.

(f) Multinational companies are not required to determine pensions cost for their overseas pension schemes if it would be 'impractical'.

(g) Information on subsidiaries is not given separately; no information is available on the provisions of the trust deed and rules, suitability of the assets or self-investment.

In summary, SSAP 24 disclosures are a poor substitute for the actuarial valuation report, trustees' report and scheme documentation unless the pension arrangements are straightforward and no attempts are being made by the company concerned to conceal sensitive information from predators. Nevertheless, SSAP 24 will undoubtedly reduce the worst distortions of pension schemes on the profit and loss account.

Index